Careers and Corporate Cultures

Careers and Corporate Cultures

Managerial mobility in large corporations

Hugh Gunz

Basil Blackwell

British Library Cataloguing in Publication Data

A CIP catalogue record for this book is available from the British Library

Library of Congress Cataloging in Publication Data
Gunz. Hugh.
Careers and corporate cultures: managerial mobility in large corporations/Hugh Gunz.
p. cm.
Bibliography: p.
Includes index.

ISBN 0−631−15859−6

1. Corporate culture. 2. Career changes.
3. Career development. 4. Executives. I. Title.
HD58.7.G86 1989
658.4′09−dc19 88−28787 CIP

Typeset in 10 on 11½pt Times
by Setrite Typesetters Limited
Printed and bound in Great Britain at
The Camelot Press Ltd, Southampton

Contents

Acknowledgements

Many people have helped me with this book, not least the managers I interviewed who gave so generously of their time. Richard Whitley has been a constant source of ideas, constructive criticism and encouragement. I should also like to single out for particular thanks Dan Gowler, Karen Legge, Tom Lupton, John Morris and Alan Pearson as early and valued mentors who helped me into the strange world of organizational behaviour, and the UK Social Science Research Council (as it then was) which, in the mid-seventies, was still able to encourage people into the social sciences and chose to do so in my case. My family, too, has put up with a lot, most particularly my wife, Liza Badley, whose help with ideas, data analysis and reworking earlier drafts of the book has been invaluable. Dan Burg, Sally Gunz and John McCutcheon were also most helpful with their comments on the text. Finally, I would like to express my gratitude to the Dean and Faculty of the Faculty of Business at McMaster University, who generously provided me with the facilities I needed to finish writing the book while on sabbatical leave there.

Part I
Introduction

1
Introduction

The impulse that started me on the study which led to this book was an observation I made during my shortish career with a multinational petrochemicals company. This concerned what it seemed to take to get ahead in the firm. From the perspective of the technologist I found it puzzling that, so far as I could tell, the more I got to know about the detail of whatever it was that I was responsible for, the less likely it was that I would be selected to join the elite group headed for top jobs.

When I got the chance to study this apparent paradox some years later I discovered that it was well known. It was almost as if there were two groups of managers: the ones who understood their operations, often called 'specialists', and the so-called 'generalists' who could turn their hands to manage anything. The world seemed to be split broadly into two camps, each supporting one type of manager. Specialists were seen by some as overly narrow in their outlook and hopelessly un-businesslike and by others as the only ones who really knew how to run their business. The generalists were variously attacked as glib, superficial and short-term in their outlook or lauded as the rising generation of true 'professional managers'.

I also found that there had been surprisingly little research on the question of who is right. Managers' careers have certainly been studied, but only in fairly general terms. Although we know quite a lot about managers' education, their social class background, how often typically they change employer and how many business functions they tend to have worked in, we know very little in detail about their work experience. So even the first step — establishing the relative proportions of specialists and generalists — does not seem to have been taken.

As I became drawn into the study of managers' careers I grew increasingly aware that the specialist—generalist distinction was not the only one. But what I read in the literature did not adequately describe what I saw happening in practice. Is, for instance, someone who had made a career in IBM, whizzing between one assignment and the next within its vast and very complex marketing organization, a specialist or a generalist? There is talk in the literature about 'functional' and 'general' management careers, but how does one describe the careers of the sort of successful managers I had seen, who had started in one function, been given a head office special assignment (usually to do with business development), then moved to another function, and so on? I even had difficulty with the apparently simple question of what constituted a 'function'. For example, is the job of running an engineering organization employing thousands of professionals and craftsmen a functional or a general management job?

This book sprang from my attempts to get to grips with problems like these. I set out to try to learn more about the kinds of careers managers had in large corporations. I interviewed managers from four large manufacturing companies about their careers, to find out what they had done during their working lives in as much detail as I reasonably could. The companies, the names of which are fictitious, are introduced briefly in table 1.1. Two (Norchem and Prestex) were divisions of much larger groups, while the remaining two (International Systems Engineering, or ISE, and Cemco) were groups of companies. Only a few of the divisions of ISE and Cemco were included in the study. I shall give more detail on each company later in the book when it becomes relevant. The 115 managers I interviewed were evenly spread across the four firms.

Table 1.1 Summary details of business units in study

Organization	Form	Total numbers employed[a]	Industries[a]	Technologies[a]
Norchem	Division of company	11 000	Performance chemicals	Batch
Prestex	Division of company	10 000	Textiles	Process
International Systems Engineering	Group of companies	7 300	Computing, electronics, engineering	Small batch, large batch
Cemco	Group of companies	8 300	Engineering and construction materials	Process

[a] In the cases of Cemco and ISE the information in the table applies to the parts of the organizations in the study.

I found, looking at the biographies I obtained, that the variety was bewildering and the patterns complex. Even the least exciting career had had its twists and its unique features which made it hard to fit into one of the career types which I had read about. This is evidently why so much of the literature effectively stops at the level of simple statistics. To make progress one has to find a way of describing careers in order to analyse them. Careers, however, are in a sense complex paths through a kind of space−time continuum where the nature of the space is hard to define. Is the space the place in the organization the person occupies, and if so, how does one represent that? Or is it the person's own state of development − where, so to speak, they are at at the time? These, I discovered, are just a few of the problems that beset the career researcher.

As I became more deeply immersed in the biographical data I found that certain ways of depicting the managers' careers seemed to be causing particular shapes to start emerging in the mist of complexity and confusion. In each of the corporations I studied there seems to be an underlying logic to the careers of its managers. It is not that everyone has exactly the same kind of career in each firm, but that there are themes which keep recurring. Managers from each firm have a characteristic way of talking about their careers, a characteristic set of concerns about where they are going and a characteristic way of measuring the progress that they and their colleagues are making.

These career cultures, as I came to think of them, are usually quite distinctive of each firm, and the reasons became evident as I reviewed what else I knew about the companies. It is as if one can look at each organization as a kind of child's climbing-frame or jungle gym (depending on which side of the Atlantic one sits) over which its managers scramble to make their careers. The 'shapes' of the climbing-frames, as I shall call them from now on, play a large part in determining the patterns of the managers' careers, and the distinctiveness of the career cultures come about because the shapes of the climbing-frames vary from firm to firm.

Of course, the shape of the climbing-frame does not completely determine the shape of the managers' careers. Individual managers have many different reasons for choosing their own routes across their frame or between different ones. But that does not interfere with the basic observation, which is that each organization has its own distinctive underlying *organizational career logic*, the formal label I shall use for career cultures.

The implications of this are intriguing. Managers, it is widely believed, are very much the products of their career background. People will argue that, for instance, X's background as a salesman caused him to build the X Corporation as a marketing-based business, and Y's background as an accountant is the reason why the Y Corporation is celebrated for its financial control systems. But as we shall see in chapter 2, the evidence supporting the validity of this view is not much more than anecdotes like these. Although researchers are becoming increasingly interested in explaining the behaviour of large firms in terms of the preferences and interests of their management teams, there has been very little research on the impact of careers on managerial behaviour.

It seems to me that the climbing-frame view of managerial careers has the potential to shed light on this problem. Different climbing-frames lead to different patterns of work experience, from which we might be able to draw inferences about the kind of knowledge and expertise managers moving over them could acquire. We may also be able to predict the kind of managerial culture nurtured by each career climbing-frame. By 'managerial culture' I mean the shared basic assumptions in the firm about what its purpose is and what constitute 'proper' managerial activities. In this way the ideas I describe in the book might be used to explore how career processes affect the way companies are managed.

This explains the book's title. My primary aims in writing it are to develop a theoretical connection between the shape of managers' careers and the structure and growth history of the firms they have worked in, and to show how this connection can be examined empirically. But the very nature of the connection suggests further ideas about the impact of careers on corporate cultures and of cultures on careers.

Much of this book is an exploration of the sources of what makes the organizational career logics, or climbing-frames, distinctive. The earlier chapters are directed specifically at readers who are interested in career theory and research, while the later ones are aimed at a more general readership.

In the remainder of part I the scene is set for the rest of the book by reviewing what we know about managerial careers and the link between careers and managerial behaviour, and examining some of the work which leads the way to the climbing-frame perspective.

In part II the concept of the career climbing-frame is looked at in more depth, moving beyond the level of metaphor to show that at least four different and distinctive career cultures (logics) can evolve from different combinations of types of organizational structure and growth. Next, I discuss the reasons, which I summarize as 'individual career logics', which might lead individuals to take different routes across the climbing-frames open to them.

Each of the four career cultures is expressed as a pattern of distinctive and characteristic career paths. If we are to identify the cultures we therefore need a way of mapping the paths. In part III some of the ways that have been used are described and the method I developed for my own study is introduced.

In part IV the threads of parts II and III are drawn together. First, I show how the mapping technique of part III can be used to distinguish between the different career cultures I described in part II. I illustrate the account with findings from my own study, and give examples which show what it can be like moving over the different kinds of climbing-frame. Next, I turn to a more speculative level, reviewing the four career cultures to see what inferences can be drawn about the kinds of manager and managerial culture each might foster. I close by exploring directions in which the book's ideas might be developed, and their implications for anyone managing their own or other people's careers.

Finally, I need to make some points about the book's scope. The ideas were sparked by a comparative analysis of four case studies. This grounded approach limits the extent to which they can be applied to other organizations, an issue which is a familiar one in the organizational literature. I am certainly not making any claim that they provide a complete account of the influences that shape managerial careers.

This book is about Anglo-American managerial careers and not managerial careers universally. Careers are in a sense pathways through social institutions, which vary greatly from one country to the next. This is as true of business organizations as it is of the wider cultural setting in which the organizations are embedded. Even the words we use to describe careers are culture-specific. We also know that the way people make sense of their careers depends very much on their cultural context. One can find striking differences, for instance, in the way different nationalities view what it takes to get ahead in their firm (Laurent, 1986) or how they measure their career success (Schein, 1986). So cultural specificity poses particular hazards for the study of managerial careers, and comparisons across national boundaries have to be made with great care.

By the same token one must be careful when discussing American and British managers in the same breath. The two countries have different educational systems, social structures and cultures. But the categories that are typically used to describe careers are probably more comparable between the two countries, if only because of the way in which the UK has steadily adopted American ways of organizing and doing business (Channon, 1973).

2
The Study of Managerial Careers

INTRODUCTION

Books and articles about managers' careers tend to begin by pointing out that, since large corporations matter a great deal to the economies of major industrialized countries, the study of how they are controlled is of great interest. Especially since the so-called 'managerial revolution' thesis became current, that corporate ownership has effectively been separated from its control (Burnham, 1940; Berle, 1960; Chandler and Daems, 1980), it has been common to assume that the control is exerted by the corporations' managers, and that the more senior the managers, the more control they exert. So the more we know about the managers, the more, potentially, we get to know about why the large corporations behave as they do.

The 'managerial revolution' thesis has been subject to some criticism of late (Poole et al., 1981: 18–21), but one does not have to accept it in its entirety to appreciate the importance of understanding as much as possible about these managers. The reasoning goes as follows.

There are two common caricatures of the firm, the first seeing it as an economic automaton pursuing rational goals and the second as the passive tool of powerful business leaders, the so-called 'great man' theory of history applied to companies. Somewhere between these caricatures there is a middle ground which recognizes that firms are complex administrative systems and that they are run by interconnected hierarchies of managers, assisted by technicians, clerks and workers. Almost anyone who has stopped to think about the implications of occupying this middle ground has been struck by the need to understand what kind of people these managers are, and what this means for the way they shape the actions of their corporations.

In chapter 1 I referred to the idea that managers are, to some extent at least, creatures of their careers. This is the inspiration behind a great deal of what has been written about managers' careers. Managers' personalities, social origins and work careers have been studied extensively, but, curiously, there is very little evidence to support the idea of a link between their careers and what they do as managers. This is partly because, despite the extensiveness of the surveys that have been reported, we still know surprisingly little about the kind of work experience industrial managers typically have over the course of their careers, and partly because the link itself has not been much explored. In this chapter I shall look at some of what we know about the question, to set the scene for the rest of the book.

A cautionary note is needed first about the career 'literature'. Career studies span such a breadth of organizational phenomena and disciplines that there has been an extraordinary amount of compartmentalization in research and writing (Arthur and Lawrence, 1984). An excellent example of the consequences can be found in two reviews of the literature on the same specialized aspect of managerial careers, mobility within companies (Anderson, Milkovich and Tsui, 1981; Stumpf and London, 1981). Although in their original forms each review cited nearly 100 references, Boehm's (1981) introduction to the pair of papers explains that only four of the references coincided. The literature on careers is both vast and fragmented, so any view of the subject is almost bound to be selective and partial.

With this in mind, let us look at the kinds of thing that are known about managers' careers.

RESEARCH ON MANAGERIAL CAREERS

Managers have been surveyed widely on both sides of the Atlantic, although in America there seems to have been more interest in the careers of top executives, particularly chief executive officers (CEOs). The information that has been collected on them tends to be fairly general (table 2.1). There seems to be fairly broad agreement that senior American managers are becoming better educated. Whereas in the 1930s 55 per cent of top managers had never attended college, by the 1970s and 1980s this figure was now well under 15 per cent. It also seems to be the case that getting to the top is helped by having an elite education and an upper-class background (Useem and Karabel, 1986). Many do not have a very wide experience of different business functions. Of a sample of the presidents of 239 large American firms in the period 1945–64, the large majority consistently had spent over 50 per cent of their pre-presidential career in a particular field (Dommermuth, 1966).

British top managers seem to be more mobile. They are more likely to have started their careers in 'output' functions such as marketing

Table 2.1 Examples of recent surveys of American top managers

Geographical origins	Kerin (1981)
Length of service in current company	Gentry and Hailey (1980); Swinyard and Bond (1980)
Education	Gentry and Hailey (1980); Swinyard and Bond (1980); Useem and Karabel (1986)
Business functions worked in	Dommermuth (1966)
Social class background	Useem and Karabel (1986)

than in 'throughput' functions, for instance accounting, and more of them will have changed their function before reaching general management level (Norburn, 1987).

The point has often been made that CEOs are not the only ones who matter. The so-called 'upper echelons' perspective (Hambrick and Mason, 1984) recognizes that it is teams of top managers, and not just the CEO, who are in charge, a healthy corrective to the common fascination with chief executives. Decision-making and control is not even exclusively a top management prerogative: decisions can be shaped by the choices made by much more junior managers and technicians (Bower, 1970). The way control is diffused throughout the firm also varies with organizational form. For instance, decentralized structures based on comparatively autonomous business units (Chandler, 1962: 312; Whitley, 1980) or matrix structures (Sayles, 1976) result in the spread of general management to much lower levels in the firm than is the case in firms with large functional departments in which each function deals with all the company's business areas.

So it is not just CEOs, nor even top managers, whose careers we should be studying if we are to make progress on the matter of linking managers' careers to the way companies are managed. Further, we need to be able to compare careers across organizations, otherwise we shall not be able to infer anything about why one firm is behaving differently from another in terms of their managers' career backgrounds.

Most of what we know about American managers other than chief executives is about specific career events or particular aspects of their careers. It is certainly the case that sociologists and labour economists have been very interested in careers as a form of social mobility, looking for instance at the way labour markets are segmented by race and sex (Rosenfeld, 1980), industrial sector (Tolbert, 1982), occupation (Smith, 1983) and firm in the sense of establishing which kind of firms have internal labour markets (Baron, Davis-Blake and Bielby, 1986).

Table 2.2   Examples of surveys of British managers

General samples
   national
   regional
	Leggatt (1978)
	Stewart, Prandy and Blackburn (1980)

Manufacturing industry
   national
   regional
	Acton Society Trust (1956)
	Clements (1958); Clark (1966)

Membership of British Institute of Management	Guerrier and Philpot (1978); Melrose-Woodman (1978); Poole et al. (1981); Alban-Metcalfe and Nicholson (1984)
Top managers and directors	Copeman (1955); Fidler (1981); Lee (1981)
Mid-career managers	Rapoport (1970); Sofer (1970); Pahl and Pahl (1971)
Heads of selected business functions	Lockyer and Jones (1980)
Business graduates	Whitley, Thomas and Marceau (1981)
Technical professionals	Hutton and Gerstl (1963); Torrington and Weightman (1982)

But these studies are not concerned exclusively with managers. On the face of it, we know more about the broad spectrum of British managers (table 2.2).

It is not easy to extract a coherent picture of 'the British manager' from the kind of study listed in table 2.2, for a number of reasons. Firstly, they draw on different samples with varying degrees of representativeness. For instance the membership of the British Institute of Management has been widely surveyed, but although it is certainly the case that the sample is national and broadly drawn, it is probably biased towards more senior managers than a 'truly random collection of British managerial, administrative and executive personnel' (Poole et al., 1981: 41). Secondly, the definition that different researchers use of a 'manager' varies considerably; some writers even question whether there is any such thing as an occupation of management (Stewart, Prandy and Blackburn, 1980), or, if it exists, whether any consistent patterns are apparent in managers' backgrounds (Leggatt, 1978). Thirdly, career data are often more ambiguous than they first appear so that concise postal questionnaires are likely to yield less reliable data than in-depth interviews. Certainly the findings from each method will not be directly comparable. Yet the studies have used data collection methods ranging between both of these extremes.

Nevertheless a view comes across of people who come from a broad range of social backgrounds with perhaps a bias towards the higher end. They are better educated than the general population, yet only 20–30 per cent of them have a university degree (Poole et al., 1981: 47). It is possible that they have become more mobile: 33–40 per cent of manufacturing managers in the 1950s–1960s had worked for only one employer, whereas the more recent studies of the British Institute of Management have found that this is the case for only 10–17 per cent of the membership. Older managers seem to be less mobile than younger managers, which could simply be a function of the period of exploration that young people go through before they settle down (Poole et al., 1981).

It is often believed that the classic managerial career is one of working up through the ranks of a functional department until, if all is going well, the manager is promoted to the level of general management. But there is an alternative view, which is that managers 'spiral' to the top through many different business activities (Watson, 1964). Although, as we have seen, it seems that British top managers have 'spiralled' more than their American counterparts, the evidence on other British managers seems somewhat equivocal.

Over a quarter of the managers studied by Clark (1966) had changed functions. Almost half of the changes had been into production work, followed in frequency by moves to sales. The largest single category of moves out of a function was away from technical and development work, in most cases resulting in a move to production. Top managers were less likely to have moved out of their specialism before the age of 39, but more likely to have done so thereafter. Directors were more likely still to have changed functions. Associated with this was the finding that top managers and directors were slightly more mobile between firms as well as within firms than lower-ranked managers. There seems, then, to be some support here for the view that spiralism is associated with success in the UK, and that too much specialism is bad for the ambitious manager.

But not all other studies have found the same amount of movement (e.g. Lockyer and Jones, 1980). Another group of authors were very cautious about reporting any statistics at all on moves between functions 'because of the difficulties of distinguishing certain types of changes, particularly those between departments within the same function, and because the information is incomplete' (Acton Society Trust, 1956: 12). Although there are often broad similarities between findings it can be difficult to make comparisons because each study tends to use different categories for business functions (Clark, 1966). In general, most researchers seem to agree that production, marketing and finance deserve treatment as separate functions, but from there the lists diverge.

To make things more difficult, writers rarely define what they mean by each function, taking it as given that everyone knows and agrees on, for instance, what a 'production' or a 'finance' manager does. Yet there is no reason for this to be the case. It is not at all surprising that if we rely on simple statistics which enumerate, for instance, the number of functions managers have worked in, we end up not really knowing very much about their work experience.

Overall, then, our knowledge of the kinds of career and work experience that managers get in American and British companies is not at all extensive or detailed. We know even less, it turns out, about the effect managers' careers have on the way they manage.

MANAGERIAL CAREERS AND MANAGERIAL BEHAVIOUR

A theme which runs through a great deal of writing on managers' careers is the idea that their work experience is a central part of their personal development. There are a number of reasons for expecting this connection between career and behaviour.

One reason is that managers characteristically have too much information to process, which forces them to be selective. They cannot canvass every possible opportunity on every occasion, so the search process they go through to find an appropriate course of action tends to rely on tested formulae within a feasible set built up through experience (March and Simon, 1958). The narrower their experience, the more restricted the range of solutions they will look at: 'executives' career experiences partially shape the lenses through which they view current strategic opportunities and problems' (Hambrick and Mason, 1984: 200). For instance,

> Although members of a firm's dominant coalition — especially the chief executive — are presumed to have a generalist's view, each brings to his or her job an orientation that usually has developed from experience in some primary functional area. This functional-track orientation may not dominate the strategic choices an executive makes, but it can be expected to exert some influence. ... If an entire top management team has risen solely through the organization, it is likely that it will have a very restricted knowledge base from which to conduct its 'limited search' (Cyert and March, 1963) when faced with an unprecedented problem such as a deregulation, intensive competition from imports, or a radical technological shift. (Hambrick and Mason, 1984: 199–200)

A second reason for expecting careers to influence behaviour starts from the well-established idea that firms have cultures with distinctive managerial rationalities reinforced by the way in which their managers are acculturated and educated into the firm's way of doing things. Because career systems and personnel choices are such central and visible parts of firms' rewards systems, they condition managers to think and behave in the 'appropriate' way for the organization (Whitley, 1987a).

There does seem to be some evidence to bear out these predictions. For instance analysis of published data on a sample of American corporations showed that, the broader the variety of experience represented in the membership of a company's board, the more that company was likely to have diversified (Bouchet, 1976). An influential study of the development of four giant American corporations notes that while the 'organization builders', the managers who turned the companies into decentralized, divisionalized structures, had not had much experience outside their firms, they had nevertheless had 'more outside experience than their successors or the professional executives of today' (Chandler, 1962: 315). For thirteen out of a small group of fourteen managers working their way into new jobs, 'their initial actions were in areas where they had had functional experience, and the most significant changes they made during the three years [of the study] also were in the areas where they had experience' (Gabarro, 1985: 116). It also seems to be the case that someone's occupation can affect their personality, which may in turn alter the way they behave at work. A group of 750 American men showed evidence over a ten-year period that their jobs affected such things as their self-confidence, authoritarianism, anxiety and conformism (Kohn and Schooler, 1982).

But we do not know much more about the effect careers have on managers' behaviour than this. Sometimes, even, the evidence is not what it first seems. For instance when a group of managers on a course were given a general business problem to analyse their approach was strongly coloured by their current job (Dearborn and Simon, 1958), and this has been cited as evidence that careers affect behaviour (Hambrick and Mason, 1984). Yet the study did not take career data into account. The situation is summed up nicely by Hall (1987: 307):

> There is probably a socialization process at work ... the longer a person stays in a certain field, the more he or she will be socialized to fit the occupation better.

It is hard to see how one could be any less tentative than this.

We may not know much about how careers affect managerial behaviour in general, but there has been a considerable amount of activity looking at the related question of how much managers need to know about their industries and organizations in order to be effective. The focus here is on the value of the knowledge that is acquired by managers over the course of their careers.

THE IMPORTANCE OF INDUSTRY AND ORGANIZATIONAL KNOWLEDGE

For many years there has been a great deal of speculation, and some research, examining the specialist—generalist debate to which I referred in chapter 1. The controversy is closely linked to the question of the extent to which management is a transferable skill. An outstanding example can be found in the British Civil Service:

> One side says: a man must administer *something* and a knowledge of that something is a necessary qualification for high administrative rank. The other side says: at the higher reaches of administration, work is largely of a general character. (Ridley, 1968: 206)

This debate often appears in another guise, as the so-called 'insider—outsider' issue. 'Insiders' are managers, especially chief executives, who have stayed within a company or an industry, and 'outsiders' are managers who come into companies from quite different backgrounds.

For a long time conventional wisdom seems to have been that management was a transferable skill, a profession, the members of which could run virtually anything (e.g. Brown, 1970; Chapman, 1970; Clee, 1970; Jennings, 1971; Katz, 1971). There is evidence that the picture may be changing. In an influential article published in 1980, Hayes and Abernathy delivered a broadside against what the authors labelled the 'gospel of pseudo-professionalism', arguing that it has been responsible for much of the USA's decline as a business success. We hear in this an echo of the concept of the firm as an administrative organization (Penrose, 1980), which suggests that the growth of a firm is limited by the rate at which its management team can absorb change. Expansion cannot be achieved simply by hiring more managers from outside because they will not have the necessary knowledge of the business nor of the rest of the team to be effective.

If one analyses the managerial role carefully it is hard to avoid the conclusion that managers' skills must be very firm-specific and that managing will never be a true 'profession' in the Anglo—Saxon sense (Whitley, 1987b). It is often argued, for instance, that there is no such thing as a general-purpose manager who can run anything, and that a change of business strategy may call for a change of top manager (Porter, 1980: 252—3; Szilagyi and Schweiger, 1984). This may not always be desirable or possible, however, when consideration is taken of managers' developmental needs and uncertainties over which strategy might be best in highly unpredictable contexts (Gupta, 1986).

But the evidence to support the conclusion that effective managers must be industry or company specialists is decidedly thin. A study which has often been cited in this context is of the work behaviour of fifteen senior American managers (Kotter, 1982). Kotter describes them as 'experts' in their business, making heavy use of their knowledge of their industry's specific products, competitors, markets, customers, technologies, unions and associated government regulations, and of their company's people, organizational procedures, history, specific products and so on (p. 39). He concludes that because they were a group of successful managers they needed this detailed knowledge to be successful. But because there was no comparison sample of managers who were not experts in their business, there is no way of telling whether he is right.

In another small-sample study (Gabarro, 1985) it did prove possible to compare the effectiveness of insiders and outsiders. 'Failed' managers were defined as those who were fired within three years of starting the job in which they were being observed. Three of the four failed managers were new to the industry, while six of the ten successful managers were not. This looks impressive until one calculates the chi-square statistic and finds that the result is far from significant (using Yates' correction for small cell numbers, chi-square $= 1.4$ with one degree of freedom; $p > 0.2$).

There has been rather more research activity on the question of whether CEOs are better replaced from within or outside the firm (the insider−outsider issue). There seem to be two main reasons for this focus. The first is simply that the data are accessible: if one studies large public corporations the succession event is public, and there is usually a great deal of published information available not only on the companies and how well they did out of the change but on the CEO in question. So it ought to be comparatively easy to measure the value of both insider knowledge and the generalist expertise of the outsider. The second reason is the generally held, but not universally accepted, view that the CEO is the most important manager in the company, which means that the investment world in particular is very interested in the impact of different kinds of CEO on stock market values.

The kind of questions that have been investigated include what predisposes firms to replace their CEOs, if they do so whether insiders or outsiders are put in the job and what differences are apparent between the performance of firms with insiders and outsiders at the helm. As one might expect there is some evidence that the replacement of the CEO is predicted by bad business performance and a volatile environment (Pfeffer and Salancik, 1978; Osborn et al., 1981). But bad performance also means that the new CEO is more likely to be an outsider, perhaps installed by the firm's financial backers (Allen and Panian, 1982; Schwartz and Menon, 1985; Reinganum, 1985a,b). However if the corporate results have been too bad the trend seems to reverse: insiders again become preferred, presumably because the board fear that an outsider will simply fire them all (Dalton and Kesner, 1985).

Larger organizations show a greater tendency to appoint insiders to the CEO post (Grusky, 1961; Helmich and Brown, 1972; Dalton and Kesner, 1983; Tuckel and Siegel, 1983), and the same seems to be the case for older organizations (Helmich, 1975a).

A number of studies have looked for differences in the impact of insider and outsider CEOs on corporate performance, with contradictory or equivocal results. One might expect to find in highly technical industries that insider knowledge is important, and this was indeed found to be the case in the minicomputer industry (Virany and Tushman, 1986). Here, CEOs with a background in electronics ran more successful companies than did CEOs without this background. In a more general study of companies from a range of industries (Shetty and Peery, 1976) insiders seemed to produce better business results, although the evidence is not very convincing. The only figure quoted concerns the companies' return on capital invested, and it does not distinguish significantly between the performance of insiders and outsiders ($p > 0.5$), although it was the case that the one 'successful' outsider did come from a related industry. Other studies have pointed to the *disadvantages* of using insiders. Two insider chief executives in succession, for instance, are associated with lower growth rates (Helmich, 1974).

The interest of stock markets in corporations' top management has led to a number of studies of the effects of CEO succession on stock prices and systematic risk (the beta coefficient in the widely used capital asset pricing model), with equally equivocal results. Sometimes there is no difference between insider and outsider successions (Beatty and Zajac, 1987), while sometimes there is, especially when one differentiates between companies in trouble and companies doing well. It seems to be the case that financial markets look for new directions for firms in trouble but do not like too much change of the kind that an outsider might bring to firms that are doing well (Trifts and Winkler, 1987). Small firm behaviour is more complex (Reinganum, 1985a,b) but can be explained in terms of consciousness of financial markets about what they think of as 'management depth'. If a small firm appoints an outsider the market infers that it does not have this depth, but an insider appointment reassures the market on this point (Dyl, 1985).

Because the event of changing the chief executive in a public corporation is so observable this line of research seems to lend itself to comparatively simple hypothesis-testing. But it is bedevilled by the possibility of many competing hypotheses, so that one can usually explain almost any result any number of ways. In particular, it is often very hard to identify the direction of causality.

For instance, it is well established that the appointment of an outsider leads to more changes amongst the rest of top management than if an insider takes over (Gouldner, 1954; Helmich and Brown, 1972; Helmich, 1975b). But without knowing the inside story there is usually no way of telling why these changes have happened. It could be because the old top management are clearly incompetent so that new-comers have to clean the Augean stables. Alternatively the changes may be a consequence of the newcomers' insecurity which leads them to build a wall of 'strategic replacements' around them, people they have worked with before they joined the company and whom they trust (Gouldner, 1954: 91–3). They do this either to insulate them from the firm's unfamiliar, hostile environment or to make them less obviously different from the rest of the management team. Being less different is a sensible survival strategy, because it makes one less vulnerable to being eased out again (Wagner, Pfeffer and O'Reilly, 1984).

So although it may seem as if one can measure the value of insider knowledge or generalist expertise by looking at outcomes like stock prices, the changes that one observes may be reflecting many influences other than just the knowledge and expertise of the new chief executive. One obvious way in which insiders and outsiders can differ, and which is not really only about insider knowledge or generalist expertise, is the kind of networks of contacts to which they have access and the way they build up their reputations for effectiveness.

NETWORKS AND REPUTATIONS

It is sometimes said rather sourly that people succeed not because of what they know but who they know. To a great extent managing is about operating networks of contacts, and there is plenty of evidence that these networks and their concomitant power relations are ex-tremely important in the corporate world (Pfeffer and Salancik, 1978). For instance it is known that family connections between a chief executive and board members controlling significant proportions of voting stock help the CEO stay on through good times and bad (Allen and Panian, 1982). Practitioners, certainly, are given clear advice on the subject:

> Directors and recruiters agree that no board will ever accept a new member that they don't know. And the man or woman they will accept must be someone they are comfortable with. So the would-be director has to get to know the chairman or some other board member through an influential third party. Among the most likely intermediaries are bankers, investment bankers, lawyers and consul-tants. (Perham, 1985: 52)

There is plenty of evidence for the pervasiveness of these networks. A so-called 'core corporate elite' has been identified in the USA, for instance, consisting of people who served as directors of four or more of the 200 largest non-financial and fifty largest financial American corporations. What one writer calls 'a disproportionately large and relatively constant' section of this elite are individuals affiliated with financial institutions (Allen, 1978: 510). These connections between boards have sometimes been called 'interlocking directorates', and although it is not always clear just how they affect the way the corporate sector is managed (Palmer, 1983) they have been much studied (see, for instance, Pennings, 1980; Useem and McCormack, 1981; Bazerman and Schoorman, 1983; Roy, 1983; Scott and Griff, 1984; Useem, 1984; and Stokman, Ziegler and Scott, 1985).

By the same token it is clear that networking is a key aspect of a successful career within a firm. Managers spend a good part of their working lives dealing with people up, down, across and between firms (Sayles, 1964; Stewart, 1976; Kanter, 1977; Kotter, 1982) and developing their networks of contacts in the so-called 'liaison' role (Mintzberg, 1973: 63–5). Studies have shown how the networks help managers set and implement their agendas. One writer refers to them as an 'incredible information-processing system' which, he believes, is far more effective than formal or machine-based systems at keeping managers in touch with their responsibilities (Kotter, 1982). Not surprisingly, networking activities have been shown to be one of the features which distinguished successful from unsuccessful managers (Luthans, Rosencrantz and Hennessy, 1985).

These networks can be built up in a number of ways. Having the right social background clearly helps (Useem and Karabel, 1986) and so does a good mentor (Shapiro, Haseltine and Rowe, 1978; Zey, 1984) in the early stages of a career. Mentoring is usually thought of as a helpful device for developing young managers by means of links formed with superiors (Kram, 1983) or peers (Kram and Isabella, 1985), as well as a useful strategy for reducing control loss in organizations (Evans, 1984). The early stages of a mentor relationship are to do with initiation and 'cultivation' (the actual mentoring). But typically the pairings break up after a few years and are redefined in terms of friendship and 'sponsorship from a distance. ... The senior manager continues to be a supporter of the young manager and takes pride in the junior colleague's successive accomplishments' (Kram, 1983: 620), which is very much to do with network-building.

Moving from place to place plays an important part in building networks, too. It has been found that the more reasons there are for expecting collusion between firms in a given industry, for instance if the number of firms in the industry is not too big or the industry is experiencing rapid technological change, the more top managers move between its member firms (Pfeffer and Leblebici, 1973). There is evidence that international transfers of managers not only build communications networks within the multinationals (Ondrack, 1985) but also socialize the managers into the ways of the firm, increasing its control over its operations as a result (Edstrom and Galbraith, 1977).

So career processes are clearly important in building and maintaining networks of contacts, quite apart from what they might do for managers' technical and managerial expertise. But it is not only who you know, it is what they think about you that matters in building these networks and getting ahead in a career.

There is a lot of evidence that a key factor in the way promotion decisions are taken is personal, sometimes subjective, knowledge of candidates (London and Stumpf, 1984; Lee, 1985b). Indeed a longitudinal study of Japanese retail managers showed quite clearly that getting on with the boss helps someone's career as much as high aptitude does (Wakabayashi and Graen, 1984). The greater the number of different groups within a company who think that someone is effective, given that each group is likely to have their own idea of what they look for in an 'effective' manager, the more successful that person is likely to be (Tsui, 1984). It is no surprise then that, given the extent to which successful careers depend on successfully packaging and selling one's reputation (Gowler and Legge, in press), candidates for promotion spend a good deal of their time developing and polishing their 'image' (Lee, 1985b).

Political dimensions like these arise because managers depend on complex webs of relationships to be effective. This means that managerial effectiveness is not a straightforward concept. This has important implications for the kind of careers managers can have in organizations because it is the managers who are thought of as 'effective' who are the ones most likely to have successful careers in their organization. I return to this point in chapter 3.

Effectiveness is not the only problem one encounters when studying managers' careers, however. As we have seen, the apparently simple way of describing managers' experience in terms of 'business functions' can cause ambiguities in interpretation. This is also true of other variables, making it hard to study careers in general, and in particular to find ways of comparing career patterns between organizations.

STUDYING CAREERS

Some of the problems which make managerial careers difficult to study arise because careers are difficult phenomena to characterize, while others have their origins in the inaccessibility and complexity of much of the data.

It is not easy to find robust ways of describing careers which allow us to compare managers from different companies. We have already encountered briefly the problem of describing careers in terms of business function. The concept of 'functional area' raises some tricky definitional questions which dog career researchers, whether or not they are aware of it.

Business functions are simply the outcome of the division of labour and control within the firm. To assume that all firms are divided along similar skill and knowledge boundaries, especially firms in quite different kinds of business, is clearly foolish. There is, in fact, great confusion amongst academics and practitioners over the use of the term 'function' (Woodward, 1965: 96ff.; Mintzberg, 1973: 114−18).

We know perfectly well that there are great differences between the ways in which firms are organized, and the basic point underlying the so-called contingency school of organization theory is that these differences are not necessarily the result of some firms being better managed than others. There may still be a lot to argue about concerning, for instance, how relations between organizations and their environments are conceptualized (Lawrence, 1981; Astley and Van de Ven, 1983), but there does seem to be pretty general acceptance by now that there is no one best way of organizing. It depends on a great many contingencies, for instance the kind of business, its technologies and its environment.

Knowing what we do about the variety of organizational forms that exist, we need, in fact, to reverse the direction of the argument. Instead of assuming that there are basic common forms which managerial work takes and using this as a framework for comparing managers' jobs and careers, we must look for similarities and differences in the way in which managerial work is defined in different contexts, regardless of how it is labelled. For instance, instead of following the careers of 'marketing managers' in different firms and seeing how many of them reach 'general management', we must examine managers' work in the different firms and see which patterns of experience are typical. We may find that in certain firms it is more likely that top managers have had experience with a certain group of activities, and it may also turn out that many of these activities are related to the sort of things listed in a marketing textbook. That is quite a different matter from assuming that because they were once called 'marketing managers' we know what they did then. Job titles are notoriously unreliable guides to what managers do (Stewart, 1976: 19).

There are at least two other commonly used categories which raise methodological problems: the number of times managers change employer and the way their seniority is measured.

It is hard to think of a simpler descriptive category than the number of employers someone has worked for. But how, for instance, does one count the very common situation in which managers stay working for the same company but the company is acquired by, or merged with, another firm? Technically, and quite possibly in a very practical sense, the employer has changed, but by no means everyone who has experienced this thinks of themselves as working for a new employer.

We can also run into trouble when trying to measure seniority, prestige, status and other indicators of success. If we infer relative seniority or success from structural information such as how far up the organization chart someone is, we are implicitly assuming a model of organizing which equates wide-ranging responsibility with seniority or success. This is not so much a way of measuring success as of defining it, and we have to allow for the possibility that the definition may not apply to particular firms or particular individuals. It will probably be no help at all when comparing managers working for different companies with different structures. It is just this problem which has given rise to the technology of job evaluation, which tries to paper over the theoretical cracks by imposing on everyone the same ideology about how to measure the value of managerial work.

These are not the only problems one encounters when trying to find ways of describing managers' careers in enough detail to be able to compare managers' work experience across companies. Careers describe a path through social structures over time, which has at least two consequences. First, one needs to collect a lot of information about what the managers have done, often going back many years, and this in itself is a substantial task with major methodological problems (Carroll and Mayer, 1986). Second, representing these paths through social space and time in a way which allows one to look for similarities and differences between the careers of individuals and between groups of individuals presents a major data-reduction problem.

Careers, then, are difficult to study and map, because the categories that are available for organizing the information are far from robust, one needs to collect a great deal of information going back many years, and the sheer complexity of the information is hard to handle. It is easy to criticize past work on careers, but much more difficult to do something about it. Later I shall describe the approach I took to tackling these problems which, I shall argue, is a step forward. But like any way of mapping careers it concentrates on some aspects of careers and ignores others, and the aspects on which it focuses are those which emerge as important from the theoretical analysis which is the subject of part II of the book.

The issue of firms having different structures does not just make it hard to find robust categories for describing managerial careers. The way firms are organized defines the structure of opportunities that managers have in them, in other words, the kind of careers they can have. Once we get away from describing careers simply by counting the numbers of employers and business functions people have worked for or in, we must expect to find substantial differences in career pattern from one kind of firm to the next. It could well be that a major reason for the difficulty researchers have had in coming up with clear, consistent pictures of career shapes across national samples is simply that for the most part they have ignored the structures of the firms in which the careers were being made. In the next section I look at what we know about this issue, setting the scene for the rest of the book.

ORGANIZATIONAL FORMS AND MANAGERIAL CAREERS

Managerial careers, by definition, are made by moving through a succession of posts in organizations. In chapter 1 I referred to the way one could look on firms metaphorically as climbing-frames or jungle gyms over which managers 'scramble' to make their careers. The metaphor has its limits, of course, because the 'climbing-frame' can for instance change shape over time, but it nevertheless provides a vivid picture of the link between organizational form and career pattern.

Whether or not the climbing-frame metaphor is novel, the idea that organizational characteristics can shape mobility patterns certainly is not. Over thirty years ago Martin and Strauss (1956) put forward this suggestion in a paper which, as with so much in the 'field' of careers, makes points which have been remade many times since. They proposed a way of looking at managerial careers in which job moves can be either vertically up the hierarchy or laterally across. Many of the moves may represent what they call 'quasi-training': managers are given a new job not just because it needs doing but also because it will give them useful training for later, and because they can be observed doing the job and their potential evaluated. Martin and Strauss related the range of moves open to managers, in my terms the shape of the climbing-frame, to the technology of the firm. Simple technologies allow people to make lateral moves, while for complex technologies this is more difficult and vertical moves up a specialist hierarchy should predominate.

This suggestion has caused a certain amount of interest over the years (see, for instance, Vardi, 1980; Anderson, Milkovich and Tsui, 1981), and other ideas have come forward, for instance looking at the relationship between individual and organizational performance (Jacobs, 1981). Some organizations can be badly affected by poor individual performance but exemplary performance does not make much difference. Here, people are likely to be developed by the organization with great care so that careers will begin at the lowest level and progress slowly upward as, for instance, in the British Fire Service in which everyone starts as a fireman. On the other hand if exemplary performance can help an organization but poor performance will not make much difference, the organization will probably hire a lot of people and keep only a few in the way that universities do, especially in North America.

Curiously, however, not very much has been done with Martin and Strauss's original suggestion (Anderson, Milkovich and Tsui, 1981). '[Career] experience cannot be understood without reference to the environment in which it took place ... [so] ... if environment is so important why has it been overlooked?' (Arthur and Lawrence, 1984: 3–4). One suggestion is that the problem lies in the way that 'any cursory inspection of the established literature [on careers] shows that this subject has received by far the most attention from the psychological perspective, the discipline traditionally least concerned for environmental factors' (p. 4).

There is some indication that Thompson's (1967) taxonomy of technologies explains something of the relationship between organizational mobility and organizational structure, at least in a largely non-managerial sample (Vardi and Hammer, 1977). As Martin and Strauss predicted, the less routinized and the more intensive the technology of the firm, the fewer the lateral moves that take place.

There may be a relationship between career patterns, in terms of 'cross-functional' moves, and the extent to which a firm is diversified, where diversification ranges from simple single-product companies which are run by 'functional specialists' to global multiple-product corporations which depend on managers with interfunctional, interdivisional and international experience (Galbraith and Nathanson, 1978). It is not entirely clear from the way the authors present their evidence (largely based on case studies), however, whether the relationship has been found or whether that is the way things ought to be in their view.

Firms which diversify by internal development as opposed to acquisition have divisional chief executives who are much more likely to have worked in more than one division (Pitts, 1977). For internal developers this may be because it makes sense to share, as much as possible, resources such as top managers between divisions. There are good reasons for firms growing by acquisition not to do this. An important part of the package that is bought along with a company is the expertise of its managers, so acquiring companies prefer not to interfere too much with their acquisitions in order to minimize the chances of key executives from the acquired companies resigning because they resent the loss of their former autonomy.

The research area in which there has been the greatest activity in looking for connections between organizational form and career patterns is that of organizational demography (Pfeffer, 1985). This involves studying flows of people through firms using a variety of internal labour market modelling techniques. Researchers have been most interested in what determines promotion chances and which 'career lines' go highest in the organization, as for instance in White's (1970) study of how vacancies 'pull' people through the structure. Vacancies may be caused by a variety of demographic phenomena (McCain, O'Reilly and Pfeffer, 1983), but perhaps the most obvious are organizational growth, contraction and reorganization. The ways in which these processes are interlinked can be very complex:

> staff assignment involves the continuous renewal of organizations .... As new jobs are created or old ones become vacant, the manager may choose to reallocate these distributions and hence change the organization's design; the manager also selects new occupants who may change the character of the jobs as well as the performance level. (Stewman and Konda, 1983: 639–40)

These systems can behave counterintuitively. Promotional chances vary with level in the firm, but not necessarily monotonically so that bottlenecks ('venturis') can develop in the middle ranks of organizations, with greater chances of promotion both below and above (Stewman and Konda, 1983). On the other hand it was found that the careers of managers in a large American corporation could best be modelled as a kind of tournament in which early success was a prime predictor of later success, so that 'winning' early rounds was necessary for being allowed to 'enter' later rounds (Rosenbaum, 1979; 1984). It is not always as simple as this. In what was believed to be a more technically based firm the tournament model only partly explained career movements. For instance technical people did better than their non-technical colleagues, and it also helped to have held more posts within the firm (Forbes, 1987).

Analysis of lateral as opposed to vertical movement is less common, although Markov models have been used to demonstrate the existence of clusters of jobs characterized by the fact that both lateral moves and promotion are more common within the clusters than between them (Mahoney and Milkovich, 1973).

From a practical point of view, demographic studies like these clearly help executives concerned with human resource management and succession planning. The models often carry implicit advice for anyone concerned with managing their own or other people's careers, because of the way they connect features of organizations such as size and growth with promotion chances. From an individual point of view the 'vacancies' perspective emphasizes how chancy the process can be. For instance a cohort study of people in large American governmental bureaucracies showed that 'success is a matter of being in the right place at the right time. Hence the questions raised concern place in the organization; time in the life history of the individual, the organization or the society; and the circumstances under which the two are right for each other' (Grandjean, 1981: 1061).

But from the point of view of trying to understand the kind of work experience gained by managers over the course of their careers, such research has not contributed very much understanding. Demography takes the structure of the firm as given, without enquiring into what managers do in each part of it or how these activities fit in with what they have done before. The climbing-frame perspective represents an attempt to move from these highly quantitative models to a more qualitative and, in this sense, informative approach to relating organizational form to the patterns of managers' careers.

SUMMARY

The aim of this chapter was to set the scene for the ideas I shall describe in later chapters.

Given that large corporations are now extremely significant to the economies of countries like Britain and America, the question of how they are managed is also of great importance. This means that it is important to know who their managers are and how they think and operate. Managers' careers might affect the kind of managers they are, in turn affecting the way their companies are managed, although we really do not know enough either about managers' careers or about the effect of careers on managerial behaviour to be sure about this idea's validity.

Very little is known about the kind of careers managers have, and in particular about their detailed work experience. Moreover, it is not just the topmost managers who need studying, because control in large corporations can be diffused extensively throughout the organization and to varying degrees depending on its structure. Although managers' careers have been studied reasonably extensively, no very clear pictures emerge beyond some fairly general and sometimes contradictory statistics. The closest one typically gets to understanding managers' work experience is the number of 'business functions' they have had experience of, although not all writers have found this experience easy to describe or analyse.

There are a number of reasons for expecting managers' careers to affect the way companies are managed. These range from the way experience conditions them to adopt approaches they have found in the past to work, to the way promotion systems teach them what is 'acceptable' within the culture of their firm. There is some evidence for this connection but, surprisingly, not very much.

More interest has focused on the so-called specialist–generalist debate, sometimes called the insider—outsider issue when the managers in question are incoming CEOs. This concerns the value of the knowledge managers acquire over the course of their careers. Although it has become fashionable to argue that specialists, people who know a lot about their businesses, make better managers than generalists, the evidence is at best thin. Most of the research on this issue has concentrated on chief executives, the results have often been far from conclusive, and it can be very hard at times to identify the cause of the effect that is being observed.

One important complicating factor is the way managers depend on networks of contacts. Their effectiveness, in other words, may depend as much on who they know as it does on what they know. There is a great deal of evidence that these networks, which span organizations, industries and, probably, economies, matter a great deal to the operation of the corporate sector. One important way in which networks can be developed is by judicious career moves.

A second complicating factor derives from the way these networks operate. Successful careers depend to a large extent on reputations for being effective, although it is not always clear how these reputations relate to objective performance. The way effectiveness is defined in firms plays an important part in shaping managerial careers.

Many of the limitations to our knowledge of managerial careers may simply be traced to the fact that careers are hard to study. If one is to avoid being trapped by vague and shifting categories which depend very much on the way individual firms are organized, such as 'function', 'number of employers' and 'managerial level', one has to collect detailed information going back over many years. The data represent passages through social structures over time, and depicting and analysing this is a far from trivial task.

A further reason why our knowledge of managers' careers is as partial as it is arises because so little research has recognized that, if structures vary from firm to firm and the structures define the way jobs fit together, career shapes must depend on organizational form. Despite the obviousness of this point and the fact that it was made in one much-quoted paper at least thirty years ago, little progress has been made. Most of what we know about the link between careers and the structure of firms comes from work by organizational demographers, who are mainly concerned with measuring the size of the flows of people up and across firms and not with the actual work the managers do and the experience they gain in the process.

The study of careers and corporate cultures needs a two-pronged approach. It needs a theoretical framework which links the shape of managers' careers to the organizations in which the careers are made. At the same time it needs a way of describing and mapping career paths which allows comparisons to be made between careers in different kinds of organization. These lines of attack can then be combined to explore the different ways in which corporate form affects the careers of corporate managers.

Part II
Analysis: the Climbing-frame Perspective

In part II the theoretical framework underlying the book is developed. In chapter 1 I introduced the idea of 'career climbing-frames' as a metaphor for the structure of career opportunities that organizations provide for their managers. I likened the process of making an organizational career to that of moving over such a frame.

This involves looking at careers from an organizational, as opposed to an individual, perspective. In chapter 3 I distinguish between these two levels of analysis and show why one might expect organizations to develop their own distinctive career cultures. Next, I explain rather more precisely what I mean by the climbing-frame metaphor, using an analytical tool I call 'organizational career logics'.

The remainder of part II is taken up with a description of organizational career logics, of how they might vary from firm to firm (chapter 4) and of the 'individual career logics' that describe individuals' reasons for choosing different paths across their climbing-frames (chapter 5).

3
Managerial Careers from an Organizational Perspective

INTRODUCTION

The key to the climbing-frame concept is to understand careers as organizational phenomena. This is more difficult than it seems. It is very common to come across references in the literature to an 'organizational' perspective on careers, when what is really being described is individuals' occupancies of a series of posts in an organization. But careers have quite different meanings at organizational and individual levels of analysis, and the distinction is basic to the study of managerial and organizational careers.

For instance, retail bankers tend to move from job to job in banks at regular intervals. These patterns of job moves come about because the people in question are making their careers in the bank, developing, if all goes well, into more competent, experienced and senior bankers. The individual level of analysis is concerned with the jobs they hold and their personal development. The organizational level of analysis looks at the bank as a whole and examines the patterns of moves from job to job made by the population of managers.

Two main starting-points for understanding organizational careers, which we could broadly call macro and micro, can be discerned in the literature. The macro-starting-point is the context in which the careers are being made: the economic system which gives rise to business organization and the society in which it is embedded, the economic units called firms which result and the way in which they reproduce their management structures. It aims to provide general explanations for how the particular chains of opportunity (White, 1970) which result from all this produce openings for particular kinds of people who pass along the chains, turning into other kinds of people controlling the economic units.

The micro-starting-point is the individual joining the system and climbing a firm's hierarchy. People have certain needs, some of which can be generalized about and some of which cannot, which the career goes some way towards satisfying, and their needs change as they mature and develop. The firm itself has certain requirements for skills and expertise which people either bring with them or develop on the job, and the extent to which the firm's needs and the individual's needs and competencies fit together determines how they climb the hierarchy (Hall and Nougaim, 1968; Schein, 1978; Evans and Gilbert, 1984).

The two approaches are indissoluble, a point nicely made by Hughes (1937):

a study of careers − of the moving perspective in which persons orient themselves with reference to the social order, and of the typical sequences and concatenations of office − may be expected to reveal the nature and 'working constitution' of a society. Institutions are but the forms in which the collective behaviour and collective action of people go on. In the course of a career the person finds his place within these forms, carries on his active life with reference to other people, and interprets the meaning of the one life he has to live.

Similarly, Grandjean (1981) views the career as being at 'the inter-section of societal history and individual biography', as does Mills (1959): 'The facts of contemporary history are also facts about the success and the failure of individual men and women. ... Neither the life of an individual nor the history of a society can be understood without understanding both' (p. 3).

This duality is a particular example of the general issue of the relationship between macro- and micro-frames of reference in the social sciences (Knorr-Cetina and Cicourel, 1981). Giddens (1981, 1984), for instance, describes 'an opposition between theories which emphasize human agency or "action" on the one side, and theories which emphasize "institutional analysis" or "structural analysis" on the other' (1981: 162). He argues instead for what he calls a *duality of structure*, in which 'action and structure stand in a relation of logical entailment: the concept of action presumes that of structure and vice versa' (1981: 171).

The idea is not, of course, original. It has sometimes been called the 'Janus effect' (Koestler, 1967: 48): any part of a hierarchy can also be thought of as a whole in its own terms (Beer, 1979). The idea is particularly applicable to a managerial role in the sense that all managers other, presumably, than chief executives both lead and are members of hierarchies (Bartolome and Laurent, 1987; Willmott, 1987). The roles are two sides of the same thing, and neither can exist without the other. To focus on wholes to the exclusion of parts or parts to the exclusion of wholes is understandable and to an extent inevitable, but it limits our understanding of how social systems work.

This study is an attempt to take the middle ground between macro- and micro-approaches to managerial careers. I aim to produce an explanation of why particular kinds of career patterns occur in particular kinds of firms. I shall take into account both the opportunities the firms provide and individuals' different abilities and ambitions. The unit of analysis is the organization as the meeting-point of economic arrangements on the one hand and individual behaviour on the other.

In this chapter I set out in rather more detail what the organizational level of analysis means from the point of view of the managerial career, contrasting it in chapter 5 with the study of careers at the individual level of analysis. I shall be dealing at a fairly abstract level for the moment, picking up many of the themes introduced in chapter 2, but in chapter 4 I will bring things down to earth rather more by showing how the ideas introduced in this chapter can be used to predict the basic logic of careers in different kinds of organization.

THE ORGANIZATIONAL LEVEL OF ANALYSIS: RENEWING MANAGEMENT STRUCTURES

In order to make sense of careers at the organizational level of analysis it is helpful to view firms as open systems (von Bertalanffy, 1968). Physical open systems exchange materials and energy with their environments, and the exchanges going on across the boundary involve the things that make up the system itself. For instance, a flame is simply a pattern of chemical reactions arranged in space. It looks and feels like a physical object, but the materials which make it up are changing constantly. Similarly, we look and behave like solid, persisting objects, although our component parts are in a constant state of flux: if we stop eating and drinking we literally waste away.

Organizations have many of these characteristics. They persist over time only because there is a steady intake of recruits to cope with growth and to replace people lost through accident, illness, old age, incompetence and a host of other reasons. So one could say that organizations have structural properties, even though they may not be physical structures (Giddens, 1981). Indeed it is tempting to use natural structures as analogues for organizations (Astley and Van de Ven, 1983; Astley, 1985), which of course raises the danger of reification, of treating them as 'things' even though they only exist in the minds of people, constraining and enabling action (Giddens, 1984: 172−3). The difference does not lie in social systems' dependence on continuous reproduction as some authors maintain. Giddens (1981: 169), for instance, argues that what makes social systems different from natural systems is that 'A society which ceases to "function" — to be reproduced across time and space — ceases to be': but so do flames and people. The difference can be found in the way in which

> social systems, unlike natural systems do not exist independently of the activities they govern, of the agents' conceptions of what they are doing in their activity, that is of some theory of these activities. Because such theories are themselves social products, they are themselves possible objects of transformation and so they too may be only relatively enduring (and autonomous). (Bhaskar, 1979: 48)

We can think of a people flow through a firm quite separately from its workflow in the sense that, for instance, Exxon is still recognizably Exxon ten years later even though it is being run by a different group of people. The people flow can be a very complex set of movements up and across the managerial hierarchy. To the extent that firms tend to fill vacant jobs, other than those at the bottom, from within they can be said to have internal labour markets (Baron, Davis-Blake and Bielby, 1986) which provide people with organizational careers. From an organizational perspective we are simply talking about a process of renewal, the process of the firm reproducing itself. It is more accurate to refer to this as the process of the firm producing itself, for which Maturana and Varela (1980) have coined the term autopoiesis, because 'reproduction' is usually reserved for the business of spawning offspring. In this book I shall use both terms interchangeably (producing and reproducing) since 'social reproduction' is a commonly used term in the social sciences.

Demographic techniques (Pfeffer, 1985) provide tools for modelling the people flow, showing population effects on such things as turnover and succession and bringing out the importance of organizational growth for career chances. But these techniques depend on concepts such as organizational career ladders and on clear measures of attributes such as cohort size and individual success. All these can be very complex and muddled in practice, especially in firms which do not have vast internal labour markets. In this study I shall take one step back, to try to understand some of the phenomena which demographic models take for granted.

Organizational renewal involves selection, which raises the question of who gets selected for advancement and on what basis. A tradition deriving from Weber's analysis of late nineteenth-century German public bureaucracy holds that, in Western society, hierarchies are renewed by people who are technically qualified to be promoted to fill vacancies. The qualification is a key part of the new manager's legitimacy in the sense that just being a son or daughter of the firm's owner is not. The extent to which this model dominates thinking today is underlined by the awkward situation in which family members can find themselves in medium-to-large family firms.

Qualification for office, then, becomes a key legitimating feature of hierarchies in bureaucracies. The next question is: what might this qualification be?

The kind of hierarchy is obviously important. Some, which Offe (1976: 26) calls 'task-continuous', involve clear graduations of skill and knowledge so that each successive step up the ladder needs the same expertise as the lower one, only more of it. The medical hierarchy, for instance, assumes that a senior physician has a wider medical knowledge and greater skills than a junior physician, so that the senior can both work unsupervised and supervise the work of the junior. Offe's point is that managerial hierarchies are not like this. There may not be much overlap between the work content of jobs successively higher up the ladder, which is why he labels them 'task-discontinuous' (p. 26).

Task-discontinuous hierarchies present us with the problem of discovering what the technical ability is which qualifies people for promotion. It is almost as if something called 'managerial skills' would have had to have been invented even if they did not exist, because of the need to provide a legitimate explanation for certain people having the right to occupy powerful positions in managerial hierarchies. Sofer (1970) identifies the same point: 'It is ... clear that every placement and promotion system will carry with it ideologies that function to stimulate ambition, to explain why things are as they are and to reconcile people to career disappointment' (p. 24).

For instance, a man who has over the past few years occupied a succession of highly visible chief executive posts remarked privately to me that the only criticism which really hit home to him was of his abilities as a lawyer. Not only did he think he was a good lawyer but he had a very clear idea of what that meant, while the idea of a good manager was too fuzzy for him to take critical comments to heart. It is not difficult to see why this should be so. Managers are so dependent on other people and on the course of events that it is very hard to define effective management with any precision.

A classic analysis of the problem is provided by Offe (1976). The effective manager tends to be thought of as someone who contributes effectively to the goals of the enterprise. This is the usual meaning of the term 'track record', which is to do with achieving results which by definition are good, at least after the event. But the concept is fraught with difficulties. For one thing, the idea that organizations have unitary goals has long been under attack. It is inadequate to propose firms as simple profit-maximizers because there are many other outcomes, such as maximizing sales revenue or growth rate, which may figure in managers' motivations (Loasby, 1976). Further, people may have goals but organizations do not in the same way (Cyert and March, 1963).

There may be many things people in firms want to do which may not be compatible and which are likely to be the subject of political infighting between competing coalitions looking for power. As a result firms are likely to seem to have multiple, contradictory goals which change from time to time.

There are two other difficulties. The first is that — even if we were clear about what the firm's goals were so that we could evaluate its performance — it is hard to identify any one person's contribution to overall performance if the organization is of any size. There are just too many other things going on to be able to isolate his or her part. The second difficulty is that managers do not work in isolation: they are dependent on other people for getting things done (cf. Mintzberg, 1973; Stewart, 1976; Kotter, 1982). Identifying one person's contribution to the goals of the enterprise is rather like trying to listen for the sound of one hand clapping. That does not mean that individuals are not identified. Rather, it means that the identification process has to be more complex than a simplistic definition of effective management, that which delivers the goods, would suggest.

Offe concludes from this that it is simply not logically possible for individuals in large organizations to be rewarded in terms of their contributions to overall goals. Rewards presumably go instead to people conforming with organizational norms. Anyone concentrating on the core, technical aspects of their job rather than on what Offe calls 'peripheral, extra-functional' elements, for instance the social side of the role to do with making the institution work, is liable to become an immobile specialist (Offe, 1976: 60–3).

For instance, in his study of managers in two large UK manufacturing companies Sofer (1970: 230) found that specialism was seen as the equivalent of a blocked career. In the French case this is carried to the extreme that promotion to top jobs is only available, in general, to people with the 'right' educational background from one of the *grandes écoles*. Job performance seems to be almost irrelevant (Granick, 1972: 59). In British and American organizations it is often remarked that while qualities such as aggressiveness and initiative are admired in the abstract they can be very disruptive in organizations and that the way to get ahead is not to 'rock the boat' too violently (Stewart and Stewart, 1976).

Further evidence of the force of Offe's argument comes from the way in which studies of managerial qualities always founder on the problem of measuring managerial effectiveness. Almost invariably the measures that are used are really of organizational success, for instance promotion record, salary, global nominations or rankings of success (Campbell et al., 1970), which is not, of course, the same thing. An influential study on Shell managers (Muller, 1970) explicitly deals with factors necessary to advancement in a large group. It is not uncommon

still to find studies in which the measurement problem is simply sub-
contracted to the organization's managers without any apparent recognition of the problems this raises (e.g. Gillen and Carroll, 1985).
Researchers are often aware that it is very hard to come up with
objective performance measures but duck the theoretical difficulties by
concentrating instead on a complex mixture of 'hard' and 'soft' factors
without being explicit about how much weight they are giving to each
(e.g. Kotter, 1982). Indeed the more writers refuse to face the problem
and try to define effective management with still greater precision, the
longer their definitions tend to get (see Stewart and Stewart, 1976, or
Levinson, 1980, for a number of examples).

As the example of the lawyer—chief executive I cited above suggests,
managers themselves are very aware of this difficulty. The construct of
effective management is a complex one in the perceptions of managers
(Mahoney, 1967), far from something which is easily measurable along
one or a few simple dimensions. People know whom they admire as
good managers but find it hard to be specific about why. An easy way
to test this is to ask a group of executives to identify their best
subordinates and then to list what these subordinates do to make them
stand out. They rarely have any trouble listing key individuals, but the
kind of actions on the list tend to focus on two factors. Both refer to
the executive compiling the list. The subordinates may be 'reliable',
that is, they go away and get on with the job without bothering the
executive and come back with the kind of result which he or she would
have achieved if he or she had done it. Alternatively they are a
'complement': they complement his or her weaknesses. In my own
study, for instance, when I asked managers to say what essential
background or experience they would look for in their successors there
was a strong tendency for them to list their own. Sometimes this was
done quite unselfconsciously, sometimes with a wry grin, and on one
occasion a manager burst out laughing and replied: 'A clone!'.

It may be more fruitful, therefore, to regard concepts about 'effective
management' as the outcome of social processes (Burgoyne and Stuart,
1976). This way of looking at managerial effectiveness sees it as a
social construct which lies at the heart of the process of renewing the
firm's management structure and not as an objective variable that can
be measured in the same way as the manager's age.

If so, then there is a potential circularity in the way managers are
picked for promotion. Because it is so hard to come up with objective
standards for effective individual performance, ideas about good performance are likely to evolve in companies in the way shown in figure
3.1, based on the heuristic used by Campbell et al. (1970).

Figure 3.1 shows an important aspect of the process of the firm
renewing itself. Organizations differ greatly, which means that so do
the contexts (1) in which managers operate. These contexts give rise to

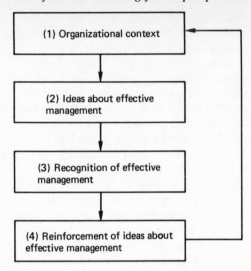

Figure 3.1   The renewal of managerial structures

different ideas about effective management (2). For instance, in some firms great emphasis is placed on solid engineering values, in others financial performance is the main area of interest, while in yet others the main thing that matters is market performance. As we have seen, people find it comparatively easy to recognize good management (3) even if they find it hard to say why, and this leads to certain people being picked out for promotion. As these managers acquire positions of power everyone else draws their own conclusions about what it takes to get ahead and the loop is closed (4), reinforcing the dominant image in the firm of effective management.

The consequences of this circularity can have unfortunate results for promotion systems, resulting in situations such as 'the tautology that the evidence of success is speed of promotion, and speed of promotion is secured by evidence of success ... because evaluation of perform-ance is impossible in large complex organizations' (Hall, 1968: 61). But the central point is that managerial effectiveness emerges from this analysis as a dependent, rather than an independent, variable with the implication that it will be defined differently in different firms. Ideas about effective management − about what the 'right' kind of manager is − play a crucial role in underpinning the organizational renewal process because they legitimate the selection of particular people for promotion to senior positions. Managerial careers are at the core of this renewal process.

We cannot generalize about how conscious the process shown in figure 3.1 might be: this must remain a matter for debate and empirical investigation. One can imagine a range of options. At one extreme it is presumably possible for groups of executives to get together and decide how to write the rules in their favour so as to exclude other groups from power. At the other it might be that everyone is unaware of what is going on, but an observer can see quite easily that people are adjusting the way they present themselves to their colleagues and bosses so that they fit the dominant image of success. There are all kinds of intermediate possibilities including cynical exploitation of one's unaware colleagues (nicely parodied in the musical *How to Succeed in Business Without Really Trying*), dim awareness that one is having to conform with the firm's way of doing things in order to make any progress, the formation of cliques and coalitions who try to establish their ideas in order to help the firm and thereby do well for themselves, and mentoring relationships in which junior managers use social links with powerful seniors to get ahead (Kram, 1983).

The rise of the belief that management is a generalizable, transferable skill is easily understood against this background. People at the top of firms almost invariably find themselves in charge of business activities which they know little if anything about. In this situation their position might well be legitimated by arguing that they possess uniquely 'managerial' skills which have little to do with the specifics of the jobs of the people for whom they are responsible. Once admitted, managerial skills can then become the means for legitimating what could be called the 'professional manager', that is, the individual who can manage anything at all, because someone who has these supposed skills can claim to be qualified for top jobs wherever they fall vacant.

In view of this analysis it is little wonder that effective management is such an emotive topic. Indeed a striking feature of much writing on the subject of good and bad management is the conviction of the authors in the 'rightness' of their view of what makes an effective manager. It is almost as if they are stating the obvious, with which no reasonable person could possibly disagree. 'Obviously,' one author writes, for instance, 'the idea that a good manager can manage anything is nonsense, as much contemporary divestiture shows' (Levinson, 1980: 119).

Figure 3.1 also suggests that promotion patterns in a firm may be resistant to change because of the model's closed loop. The firm itself may behave like an open system with respect to its people flow, but the renewal model shows one of the control subsystems which account for its tendency to persist in recognizable form over time despite the throughput of people. The system is remaking itself in its own image, something, as we have seen, organizational members are usually aware of even if they do not always admit it openly.

Successful people develop big stakes in the status quo, and this can be the source of some anxiety because of the way careers represent a form of deferred gratification (chapter 5). Careers can be thought of as an organizational device not only for rewarding people whose performance cannot easily be measured on a minute-by-minute basis but also as a means of buying their loyalty over the longer term in industries where productivity depends on the application of knowledge rather than energy. Unless firms do this, they run the risk of losing the people on whose developing knowledge they depend (Stinchcombe, 1965; 1983). The corollary of this is that the managers have to put their trust in the career development system of the firm to an extent which at times can be disquieting, so that they accept new postings of various kinds not because of their intrinsic merit but because in the long run the move will pay off in career terms. In organizations such as universities no one really pays much attention to what an industrial human resource manager would recognize as a career development system. Here it can be very hard to persuade anyone to take on major jobs which might help the institution as opposed to them personally. Even in an industrial context the tension can surface in many ways. In particular, people tend to be rather cynical about the nature of the real career development process the firm operates as opposed to the official one.

The model in figure 3.1 therefore provides an explanation for the persistence of organizational culture at least as it affects management structures. But if the loop is broken, say by the imposition of new top management from outside as a result of some corporate crisis, the new success model might bring about profound and rapid change in the career culture. I shall return to this point in the next chapter.

If we can expect to find characteristic and comparatively stable patterns in the way managers are selected for promotion in firms, these patterns being unique to that firm or kind of firm, we need an analytical tool for exploring them. The tool I shall be using I call 'career logics'.

ORGANIZATIONAL CAREERS AND LOGICS OF ACTION

Returning to the open system metaphor, we can see that patterned flows of people through an organization will give an impression of concreteness to the extent that the pattern persists over time. This is the origin of the climbing-frame metaphor I introduced earlier. People are continually entering the frame, usually, but not always, at lower levels, and moving from rung to rung as rungs fall vacant. Sometimes the rungs are higher, sometimes they are at the same level but in a different part of the frame and sometimes managers have to dive for a lower rung for the sake of finding any rung at all.

The power of the metaphor comes from the way it helps make sense of career processes. For instance, it exposes the inadequacy of the commonly used idea of career 'ladders': one metaphorical dimension is simply not enough to capture the richness of organizational careers. It also leads us to expect that different firms will have differently shaped frames depending on how they are organized and managed.

In addition, the metaphor provides a framework for the examination of careers at the individual level of analysis because it is not deterministic: people can choose how and whether they climb. Rungs may be blocked off to them either because the rungs are already occupied or because the workings of the social reproduction process have labelled the managers as unsuitable for that kind of rung. For instance, they may be seen as either unbefitting further promotion or lacking the skills for the job. Even when managers are presented by their bosses with a choice of just one rung, for instance a move to another location or promotion to a post at the next level up in the firm, they can always decline the offer.

I shall elaborate on the way in which the climbing-frame metaphor connects with the study of careers at the individual level of analysis in chapter 5. First, I need to place the metaphor on a sounder theoretical basis before turning, in chapter 4, to its connections with organizations and organization theory.

So far the discussion has been at a very general level. It has been, so to speak, about a contingency theory without any consideration of the contingencies. Its primary purpose has been to introduce the concept of careers viewed at the organizational level of analysis as part of a process of organizational renewal, but it clearly needs taking beyond the point of general abstractions for it to be of any help in making sense of managerial careers. We need an analytical tool for distinguishing between the forms the renewal process can take in different firms. This tool must provide a way of visualizing careers at the organizational level of analysis which pictures them as something other than just an abstract autopoietic mechanism.

Karpik (1978) introduces the idea of *logics of action*, which is his label for forms of rationality and which he uses as a tool for analysing the strategies of large corporations and groups within and without the corporations. The central concept is to do with the exercise of managerial will. Strategies are not determined solely by market structures or economic situations but through the exercise of discretionary power by managers given the strategic resources available to the firm. When discretion is exercised in different ways it is because different forms of rationality are at work. Logics of action are 'an analytical instrument constructed by the observer, designating forms of coherence among objectives' (Karpik, 1978: 46).

Karpik uses the concept for two purposes: to establish similarities and differences between actors who may be socially dispersed, and to demonstrate the relations that exist between the organization and its members. They provide an indispensable link, he argues, between collective aims and private ones, in so far as these constitute a particular solution to a set of economic demands. Weiss (1981) compares the concept with Perrow's (1963) *operative goals*, which are goals actually pursued by a dominant coalition and which Perrow differentiates from *official goals*, that is, goals which are not necessarily implemented. Logics of action describe the intentions of goal-seeking activities, seen from the point of view of the observer rather than the actors.

Logics of action can be used, without borrowing the rest of Karpik's epistemology, as an analytical tool for modelling managerial careers. *Organizational career logics* are inferred from what the observer sees of the way the firm renews its management structure, and different logics represent different solutions to the problem of ensuring the continuing existence of the firm. We have already encountered them in metaphorical form as the climbing-frames over which managers move during the course of their careers, where the shape of the climbing-frame provides the basic logic for the shape of their careers. I shall use the two labels – organizational career logics and career climbing-frames – interchangeably.

A firm's organizational career logic may not necessarily be obvious to its managers. They will be more aware of the process as a succession of promotions, sideways moves and demotions happening to them, although people seem to be surprisingly resistant to recognizing that they are in fact being demoted (Veiga, 1981). But an observer looking at the organization as a whole will probably see a pattern to these moves. Demographers describe these patterns in terms of, for instance, promotion rates and the chances individuals have of rising through the hierarchy (chapter 2). They explain them in terms of age structures, rates of growth of the firm, spans of control and the occurrence of vacancies as a result of deaths, retirements and other kinds of departure. Others may describe the logics in terms of particular promotional ladders, for instance the so-called 'dual ladder' which provides a career path for non-managerial technical specialists in many companies (Dalton, Thompson and Price, 1977; Gunz, 1978; Goldberg and Shenhav, 1984; Mainiero, 1986).

Because we are observing these patterns from outside the organization we can only infer the reasons that lie behind them, which is why I use the term 'logics of action': we are trying to make intelligent guesses at the intentions of the actors who are bringing the patterns about. But because we are dealing at the organizational level of analysis, relating the patterns to what we know of the organizations as opposed to the individuals working in them, the logics are organizational. They are the logical outcome of a particular set of organizational arrangements. I shall come to how one observes these patterns and thereby infers the logics in parts III and IV of the book.

People make choices about which of the opportunities organizations present to them they wish to take. *Individual career logics* are an observer's reconstruction of their motives in making these choices and picking their routes across and between climbing-frames. Individual logics provide much of the explanation for why organizational career logics predict general tendencies for career paths but not what happens in every case.

SUMMARY

In exploring the dual nature of managerial careers, one must distinguish between organizational and individual levels of analysis. The organizational level is to do with the process of the firm renewing itself, where the object of interest is what I called the 'people flow', in contrast to the workflow, resulting from the firm's need to recruit staff to cope with growth as well as to replace those lost. In so far as firms fill positions from within they have internal labour markets which make it possible for people to have organizational careers. The shape of the labour markets are an important determinant of the patterns the careers can take. The individual level concerns the way people make sense of where they fit into this organizational process.

The internal labour market's workings can be very complicated and far from a simple matter of allowing the 'best' managers to get to the top. 'Best' is a difficult concept in the field of management practice, and the most that one can say is that it will depend very much on the kind of firm under consideration. It follows from this that firms will develop their own distinctive career cultures, based on the kind of manager defined in them as 'effective'.

I use Karpik's (1978) idea of logics of action as an analytical device for identifying and characterizing the distinctive organizational career logics that come about as a result of different organizational contexts. Metaphorically, organizational career logics are the climbing-frames over which managers move to make their careers. Individual career logics describe the motives people have for choosing their own routes across and between climbing-frames. Taken together, organizational and individual career logics provide an account of the pattern of managerial career paths that can be observed in corporations.

4
Organizational Career Logics: The Climbing-Frames

INTRODUCTION

Career logics can be formally defined as the intentions an observer infers to be lying behind managerial career paths. Metaphorically, organizational career logics can be thought of as the shape of the climbing-frame over which managers move to make their careers. In this chapter I shall describe a model of organizational career logics which uses three organizational dimensions to predict the shape of a particular firm's career climbing-frame.

Organizational careers involve a series of transitions between a number of posts over time. The organization's structure defines the kind of posts that managers can move between and how the posts relate to each other, so it provides the basic framework for their patterns of moves. The first of the three dimensions I select concerns the firm's structure. The series of transitions takes place over an extended time. But organizations also change over time, and the two processes − managers' careers and organizational changes − are likely to be closely linked. The remaining dimensions concern the way the firm has grown, and the way it has changed.

Organizations which differ in their structure, the way they have grown and the way they have changed can be expected to have distinctively different organizational career logics (climbing-frames). This in turn leads us to expect that they will have distinctive career cultures, with distinctive patterns of managerial mobility. The organizational logics may be unique to particular firms, or they may be typical of particular industries, especially in situations, for instance, when managers make careers across several firms (Grandjean, 1981).

Large corporations have highly complex structures and their different parts can develop in different ways, so we might expect to find more than one kind of organizational logic in any one firm. So even at the organizational level of analysis we do not expect every career in a particular firm to be the same. The closer we move to the individual level of analysis the more reasons we can find for further variation in career patterns, a theme I return to in chapter 5. But in any one firm one organizational career logic will probably predominate, and I shall call this the firm's *modal* logic.

The three dimensions on which the model of organizational career logics is based are relatively independent of each other and describe different kinds of organizational structure, growth and central continuity. Selecting dimensions is always a dangerous business, and it is worth emphasizing at this stage why I am doing it. I am not trying to construct a new theory of organizational form or growth: this would be a very different book if I were. I am searching for some simple explanations for the bewildering complexity to be found in managers' careers, in particular the complexity I found in the research study from which this book sprang. In order to do this I have been forced to be very eclectic, picking ideas from the literature on organizations which seem to be most relevant to my purpose.

THE DIMENSIONS: STRUCTURE, CHANGE AND CENTRAL CONTINUITY

Organizational structure

If we view a career as a passage through a series of posts in an organization, careers in different organizations will be distinguished by the way in which the posts are related to each other, that is, by the organizations' different structures. Whatever one's starting-point in the study of business organizations, one usually arrives at an account of the way in which firms internalize market processes in a hierarchical arrangement (Chandler, 1962; Pollard, 1965; Franko, 1976; Chandler and Daems, 1980). The factory system took over from craft industries by exploiting the scale economies of production and selling which flowed from complex divisions of labour. Combinations of erstwhile competitors made competitive arrangements amongst themselves which gave them collectively greater control of the remaining markets, and these arrangements gradually took the legal form of yet bigger companies. Individual firms insulated themselves from the vagaries of the marketplace by integrating backwards and forwards to secure their supply lines and their distribution outlets (Harrigan, 1983) and by diversifying horizontally to add strings to their bows. The large corporations which are the upshot of these processes vary enormously in their structures, although a number of researchers have pointed to a general trend towards a decentralized, divisionalized arrangement in which the divisions are supposed to be something like quasi-independent companies supervised by a central banking and planning authority.

Divisionalization, however, can be achieved in many different ways. Sometimes the divisionalization stops with a group of very large divisions, each the size of a substantial company in its own right but having an internal structure based on traditional business functions such as production, finance, marketing, R&D and so forth. Sometimes the decentralization proceeds further, so that the divisions of the parent company are a mixture of functional departments and mini-divisions with many of the functions an independent company would have. Sometimes each division is itself a group of divisions of subsidiary companies. Within a subsidiary division or company all kinds of arrangements may be used to regulate dealings between functional departments, from simple liaisons to quite complex matrix structures. Divisionalization, in other words, is no guarantee that a company will be free from the complicated cross-linking arrangements which divisionalization is supposed to do away with.

Careers made within large companies, then, are likely to be quite complex affairs. Previous work on careers has tended to use traditional functional labels to describe the paths managers follow (chapter 2), but this assumes that functional labels mean the same thing at different levels within a hierarchy, let alone in different hierarchies. Jobs vary as one climbs the kind of task-discontinuous hierarchies which are a feature of business firms (Offe, 1976: 26). For instance salesmen do a very different kind of job from sales managers, who in turn have tasks perhaps only partially overlapping with the responsibilities of marketing directors.

Some firms have simpler divisions of labour than others, so that the logic of a career made in these simpler structures is likely to be different from that made in a more complex one. The difference to which I wish to draw attention is the extent to which the structure of the organization is *recursive*. I am using this term in a similar way (although rather more loosely) to that used by Stafford Beer in his 'viable system' model (e.g. Beer, 1979), to mean organizations in which similar-looking structures are nested one within another rather like a set of Russian dolls. A traditional military organization has elements of recursion about it: starting from the top and ignoring specialized commands, each unit consists of fairly similar-looking subunits each in turn made up of yet smaller subunits, and so on. The Church is typically divided into arch-dioceses, dioceses and parishes. The nineteenth-century American industries of transportation and mining, with their low proportion of professional staffs, are further examples (Stinchcombe, 1965), as are service industries such as chain stores and retail banks. A recursive organization is based on similarities. If each unit in the firm is made up from several similar but smaller units it follows that there must be a lot of similar managerial jobs in the company, and the lower one goes in the hierarchy the more similar jobs there will be.

Most organizations have at least some element of recursion about them but in some cases it is far less marked or it applies only to parts of the organization. A big manufacturing company, for instance, may have a large recursive distribution and service system with national, regional and local service centres. But it may also have a non-recursive headquarters structure with staff units — some very large — serving the recursive hierarchies. An R&D laboratory may provide central facilities used by many subsidiaries, a finance unit may act as banker for all the subsidiaries and so on.

There are many reasons why structures are recursive. They may be the result of a strategy of buying competitors to create a single large unit with great market power, such as happened in many parts of the British textile industry. The resulting large companies found themselves with a great many similar mills which needed organizing into groups each processing, for instance, a particular fibre or quality of fibre, and the groups themselves needed collecting into larger divisions. Recursive structures can, alternatively, come about as a result of the spreading of a particular service throughout the country which requires a large hierarchy to coordinate it as happens with most of the major utilities, posts, telecommunications and retailing.

Recursion can be inhibited by factors such as vertical integration, diversification into very different kinds of activities, and complicated functional structures with lateral, matrix-type linkages of the kind often found in the chemical and oil industries. Proliferation of 'element' functional departments such as personnel, planning, control and main-tenance, as opposed to 'task' functions such as finance, R&D, manu-facturing and marketing (Woodward, 1965: 96ff.), probably impedes recursion because it means that some of the activities which are common to many of the firm's basic tasks are split off and centralized.

There are two features of recursion that are important as far as careers are concerned: the number of similar managerial posts, and the nature of the firm's coordinating mechanisms. I shall take these in turn.

First, the number of similar posts: the more recursive a structure, the greater the number of similar managerial posts. This means that it is possible for an internal labour market to build up around the posts so that when one falls vacant there will be a pool of managers in similar posts potentially available to fill it without the need for learning new skills. The less recursive the structure, the more likely it is that vacancies have to be filled by promotion or by someone being transferred laterally from a different kind of post. Both of these mean a change for the new manager in more than just location. Of course the pool of similarly skilled managers in a recursive structure has to be replenished by people being promoted into it. But unless the rate of turnover in the pool is very high, the more recursive the structure, the greater the chances that a vacancy can be filled by someone who knows the job. Chandler (1962: 312), for instance, makes the point that when his four companies decentralized and adopted divisional structures the number of 'general management' posts increased, providing a proving-ground for preparing general managers and testing them for top positions.

The second point concerns the nature of the coordinating mechanisms between the parts of the firm. The less recursive the structure, the more complex these are likely to become and the more important it might be that managers who are intended for top jobs get experience of different parts of the firm so that they understand how it works.

The structural feature of organizations I shall concentrate on is their recursiveness. The more recursive the organization, the higher the proportion there will be of similar managerial posts; conversely, the less recursive, the greater the variety. I shall discuss the significance of this distinction for career logics after bringing two features of organizational process into the model.

Organizational growth

The Weberian concept of the career in a bureaucracy carries with it the implication that the flow of people up the hierarchy is entirely independent of the workflow of the organization. Office-holders do their jobs impersonally according to rule, regulation and precedent and are promoted on the strength of their technical qualification for the next post up.

If that were true life would be a very dull thing indeed. In practice, of course, the workflow and the people flow of an organization are intimately bound up together, and the games that get played can be complex and subtle in the extreme. People make beelines for posts that are associated with growth and avoid those that are part of decline. Special assignments as aides to top executives to evaluate new business opportunities are coveted, association with a major project may be seen as a good thing but not if it goes on for too long, and so on. Equally, managers might be given a particular job simply to give them experience rather than because they are qualified for it, as part of their development for some other quite different post.

The relationship between organizational process and career is brought to a head most forcibly in the matter of growth of the firm. Growing firms need more or different managers, shrinking firms need fewer, diversifying firms may expose areas of weakness in terms of particular knowledge or skills and firms in crisis may need charismatic leaders or hatchet men. In each case the question of who identifies which 'need' is far from trivial, and the answers which emerge can powerfully influence the careers of the managers involved. Even the simple demographics of an organization subject to varying conditions of growth can be a complex matter to understand, and the results of such an analysis can be quite surprising in terms, for instance, of identifying unexpected bottlenecks in the promotion structure (Stewman and Konda, 1983). It sometimes feels, especially to the managers involved, as if careers are only realistic possibilities when firms are growing. However, it is the nature of the growth to which I want to draw attention in this model, since firms grow in many different ways.

In his analysis of organizational change in the companies he studied, Chandler (1962: 284) pointed to the significance of the distinction between two kinds of change: creative innovation and adaptive response (Schumpeter, 1947). Creative innovation, which goes beyond existing practices and procedures, was exemplified in Chandler's view by the corporations' jumps into decentralized, multidivisional structures. Adaptive response may well involve major change, but it stays within the range of current custom, such as when the corporations grew their existing structures into more complex forms.

Stripping these labels of their overtones of change as environmental adaptation, one can recognize a distinction which is often to be found in the strategic management literature, namely that of growth into familiar and into unfamiliar territory (Abell, 1980: chapters 7–8; Quinn, 1980; Miller and Friesen, 1984: chapter 4). Growth into the unfamiliar resembles Astley's (1985) concept of 'quantum speciation'. All growth involves some form of step into the unknown but some types of growth step further into it than others, and of course growth which starts by looking familiar can take on a very different aspect later. For instance increasing sales of existing products would count in anyone's book as staying within the familiar, except that at some stage it may involve having to adopt radically new ways of organizing because the old structure simply cannot cope any more. The distinction, in other words, is between growth for which a *pattern* already exists in the organization and growth for which *no pattern* existed previously and which produces a new kind of organization with different survival chances.

To take a biological analogy, patterned growth resembles ontogeny, the development of an individual according to its genetic code. In patterned growth the organization is developing pretty much in the way that people expect it to. Unpatterned growth resembles phylogeny, the evolution of plants or animals: it results in organizations which are qualitatively different from their 'parents'. I do not mean to imply a crude functionalism by this: organizations are far more subtle things than biological analogies admit, but the analogies do bring out certain

differences in the way firms grow which have very direct implications
for the careers of their managers.

Patterned growth does not, in principle, involve new skills or knowledge, although that is not to say that everything about the growth need
be completely familiar. Embryos, after all, change dramatically as they
develop. A supermarket chain will most probably have a well worked
out system for opening new stores which will define how to go about
handling the unknowns of the new location such as geography, demography, competition, city government regulations and the local labour
market. Similarly, oil companies are systematic about building new
refineries or expanding existing ones. Here, however, the process is
less algorithmic because fewer refineries are built than retail outlets
and the size of the investment is orders of magnitude greater. In both
examples the firm grows by drawing on an existing pool of skills,
expertise and experience to define the tasks that need to be done and
circumscribe the areas of uncertainty and ignorance. By patterned
growth I mean growth which is rooted in the familiar for which formal
or informal procedures exist and from which fairly well-defined ranges
of outcomes are expected.

We can expect patterned growth to have a number of consequences
for managerial careers. A firm undergoing this kind of growth might
well have to recruit managers or other staff from outside, but they are
likely to be more of what it already has. The people involved in the
growing may not themselves have all the necessary skills and expertise
that the firm collectively has built up. Such projects are often used as
training experiences for the staff, perhaps even forming part of managers' long-term development plans.

Unpatterned growth involves something rather more profound. For
reasons which can range from a well-planned diversification programme
to serendipity, firms get into new activities which mean that parts of
the firm look qualitatively different afterwards. It may be, indeed, that
a new division or other offshoot has been formed as a result of the
development. For example when oil companies moved into chemicals
they were taking a step into the unknown. Superficially the technologies
were similar: both involve similar chemical engineering processes. But
the feedstocks, the nature and variety of the chemical processes and
their physical complications, the range of intermediate and finished
products, the markets and the nature of the competition were all
radically different. A second example concerns the recent worldwide
shift from electromechanical to electronic telecommunications exchange
equipment. Manufacturers of this equipment have existed for a long
time in a comparatively stable environment, making much the same
kind of product mainly for national telecommunications organizations.
The shift to the novel electronic technology using stored programme
control and digital transmission techniques has involved changes as

profound as those faced by the Swiss watch industry, whose traditional skills were rendered obsolete in more or less a tick of the clock, an example of what Kay (1982) calls 'technological mugging'.

This kind of growth means that new skills are needed in the firm. As with patterned growth, one cannot easily predict whether they will be developed from within or acquired from outside: this is very much a matter of choice for the people involved. It would take too much space to discuss here the issues involved in such choices, except to point out that they are some of the most sensitive in strategic management.

For instance, acquisition is often seen as a quick and safe option but is also criticized for being much more difficult to manage afterwards than is usually imagined, and predicted results rarely come about (Lubatkin, 1983). Within the past few years, for instance, a great many UK firms have tried to enter the US market by buying American firms and have found that this was far more difficult and fraught with danger than they realized.

Growth from within may result in a more firmly rooted structure as more of the company's management learn about the new business and feel more ownership of it. But it can make it harder for unpatterned growth to take place at all. For instance the incremental change that flows from the policy may make the firm blind to what is going on in the marketplace, as Facit found to its cost when the market for its mechanical calculators fell away dramatically (Starbuck, 1983).

I have identified two kinds of organizational growth which I have called patterned and unpatterned. Crudely, these involve leaps into the comparatively known and the comparatively unknown. I have chosen this distinction primarily because of the implications it has for the skills and know-how in the company. Patterned growth implies not very much novelty, while unpatterned growth needs something entirely new. This, in turn, is likely to have important consequences for the careers of the firm's managers.

The examples I have been using of different kinds of growth have mostly been at the margin of the firm. Oil companies moved into chemicals, for instance, but the bulk of their assets continued to be in their existing oil businesses. In these situations people can be given the job of getting on with managing the new offshoots comparatively independently of what goes on in the rest of the firm. But sometimes, as with the Swiss watch example, the change is not peripheral at all: it strikes at the heart of the firm causing major upheavals through the organization and the careers of its managers. My third dimension, then, is to do with organizational change and the central continuity of the firm.

Organizational change: central continuity

Both patternedness and unpatternedness, as I have used them here, are different forms of growth and imply *central continuity* of the overall organization in the sense that a lot of it carries on as it has been doing and that the changes, however profound they may be for the people directly involved and however they may reshape the organizational climbing-frame on which managers make their careers, are at the margin. It can happen that this continuity is interrupted and the organization goes through some kind of catastrophe, often with traumatic results. I am using catastrophe here in the special sense of catastrophe theory to mean discontinuities in events, '*sudden* changes caused by *smooth* alterations in the situation' (Poston and Stewart, 1978: 1), rather than in the more everyday way in which for instance Kay (1982) uses it to mean a phenomenon which precipitates decline and obsolescence of a product.

By 'central' I mean the administrative centre of the organization in question which forms in effect the apex of the existing managerial career system, for instance the Group Chief Executive and Board or their divisional equivalents if a separate internal managerial labour market can be distinguished. The extent to which the 'centre' takes all the important decisions regarding the management of the firm's strategy or operations does not matter for my present purposes. I am isolating events for attention which shake people's faith in the firm's management, where the 'people' in question may be, for instance, the financial world looking for assurances about the firm's 'management depth' (Dyl, 1985).

In this kind of catastrophe the top management involved − of the company if the crisis affects the company as a whole and of a part of the company if the trouble is more localized − suspend normal business while some kind of major re-evaluation is carried out, and almost anything can emerge. Typically the outcome of bad business results, these crises can be triggered by external agents such as financial backers losing confidence in the company's management or predator companies making takeover bids. Indeed one of the benefits claimed for the takeover system is the shock of being a target: the upshot can be dramatic improvements in the firm's management.

The essential feature of catastrophic change is that it is publicly proclaimed that the present state of things cannot continue and that something is going to have to be done about it. The outcome may be growth of a patterned or an unpatterned kind; it may be radical surgery, major reorganization or simply a determined public relations effort to try to assure the world that things are not as bad as they seem. It is rarely without consequences for the management structure (Pfeffer and Salancik, 1978; Osborn et al., 1981).

Because the change affects top management it is potentially the kind of event which can have a profound effect on the firm's career system. I showed in chapter 3 how dependent the process of getting ahead is on the way effective management is defined in firms. Catastrophic change shakes basic assumptions in the firm's managerial culture and calls into question conventional organizational wisdom about whom ambitious people should be modelling themselves on. The results are unpredictable, ranging from a whole new breed of manager taking over, through some of the existing management carrying on but in a different way from before, to a resumption of business as usual if the culture proves especially resistant to change.

Summary: Structure, growth and central continuity

To sum up, I have isolated three dimensions with which to distinguish between different organizational career logics:

1 the *recursiveness* of the firm's structure;
2 the extent to which the firm's growth is *patterned* or *unpatterned*;
3 the extent to which change in the firm affects its *central continuity*: I use the term 'catastrophe' to describe a central *dis*continuity in the firm's operations.

The three dimensions are relatively independent of each other. This is perhaps easier to see in the case of dimension 1 than it is for dimensions 2 and 3, and some examples might help to clarify my point (table 4.1). A firm might grow at the margin into unfamiliar territory

Table 4.1   Organizational growth and central continuity

		Organizational change	
		Central continuity	Catastrophe
Organizational growth	Patterned	Ford	British Leyland
	Unpatterned	Hewlett Packard	Rolls-Royce

(unpatterned growth) without affecting its existing operations to any great extent (central continuity) in the way that electronics firms such as Hewlett Packard have done. Alternatively it might grow to a pattern and run into a crisis as a result after the manner of British Leyland (Williams, Williams and Thomas, 1983: 217–283). Equally, unpatterned growth such as Rolls-Royce's move into a new technology for the RB-211 engine might be one of the triggers of a catastrophe. Finally, until recently Ford has with few exceptions been careful to stay with the familiar (patterned growth) and — Edsels apart — has on the whole avoided Chrysler-like catastrophes.

In the next section I use these three dimensions to distinguish between different organizational career logics.

ORGANIZATIONAL CAREER LOGICS

The three dimensions I have proposed (structure, growth and central continuity) potentially define eight different kinds of organizational career logic. As we shall see, one cell in the $2 \times 2 \times 2$ matrix is by definition not very likely and four others effectively blend into one, so the upshot is four logics with which we can work. The logics themselves resemble ideal types in the sense that they are theoretical constructs aimed at making careers intelligible by revealing or constructing their internal rationalities (Aron, 1970: 207).

Table 4.2 shows the relationship between the structure and growth dimensions under conditions of central continuity. It defines three logics (constructional, command-centred and evolutionary) and one 'empty' cell. The empty cell in table 4.2 must combine recursion with

Table 4.2   Organizational career logics under conditions of central continuity

		Organizational structure	
		Non-recursive	Recursive
Organizational growth	Patterned	Constructional	Command-centred
	Unpatterned	Evolutionary	(Empty)

unpatterned growth, which is a difficult condition to meet. Such a firm would, in effect, be imposing a common structure on all its business units, whatever their business area.

On the face of it, this does not seem a very viable course of action. It is well known that successful firms match their structures to the kind of business they are in (Woodward, 1965; Burns and Stalker, 1966; Lawrence and Lorsch, 1967), so units in different kinds of business ought to be organized differently. If, however, they are not, it is likely that this is because there is a dominant belief in the corporation controlling the business units that managing is the same wherever it is done and whatever is being managed. In this case the career logic will resemble a form of command-centred culture.

Table 4.2 refers to the situation under conditions of central continuity. For catastrophic change (central discontinuity) the picture is somewhat different. While we could draw a similar 2 × 2 matrix it would be misleading because for the duration of the upheaval the present structure and how the firm has grown previously are almost irrelevant. This is not to say that even in the most catastrophic situations there may not be islands of calm which can be fitted into table 4.2. For instance it may be important to keep contacts going with customers and suppliers if at all possible, so subsystems doing this would be left alone for a while until a new organization is worked out. But while the major discontinuity which catastrophe implies may not stop firms being recursive or non-recursive, handling the catastrophe is likely to be totally absorbing for the managers affected by it. The distinctions drawn by the dimensions of structure and growth are likely to blur for a time, and I shall consider the four potential cells as one. The logic which arises I call 'turnaround', which, as we shall see, is very much a between-organizational rather than a within-organizational career logic.

Constructional career logic

Constructional career logic is a logic of building a cumulative structure of experiences over a working lifetime, to fit managers for jobs which call on the experiences they have accumulated. In metaphorical terms one can think of the constructional logic as an engineering or an architectural process: careers are things one puts together from components called experiences acquired in different parts of the firm. The effect of combining the experiences may be additive, so that experience in posts A and B qualify managers for a job consisting of A + B. Alternatively they may be synergistic in the sense that they help managers understand the firm's coordinating mechanisms and informal networks. Synergy is to do with diverse experiences gained from A and

B qualifying managers for a job consisting of A + B + C + D. The diverse experiences may even help managers put together general theories about the job of managing which they can use in unfamiliar settings. The result, at least in theory, is top managers who have a broad understanding of the business they are responsible for and a good knowledge of the people with whom they need to deal.

Galbraith and Nathanson (1978) describe something very much like this at Dow-Corning:

> Almost all managers [on business and product boards] are chemical engineers. In addition, the career path is multi-functional, providing experience on both business and functional sides. This career system gives board members a sound understanding of other persons' problems and facilitates general all-around communication, so that people are less concerned with territory or turf. (p. 99)

The essence of the logic is that it can only occur when the organizational structure is non-recursive: the variety of kinds of organizational subunits and hence management jobs is high by comparison with any recursive structure. In order for the managers' earlier career experiences to be of some use to them later in their career the organization should not change too dramatically, so the structure needs to be fairly stable in the sense that it shows central continuity and growth which is more likely to be patterned than unpatterned. That is not to say that the opposite kind of growth may not occur, but the more it does, the greater the risk that individual managers' earlier experiences become obsolete or relevant only to a smaller and smaller part of the firm. The more that that happens, the more likely it is that current notions will be upset about what one needs to gain experience of in order to get ahead.

The constructional logic, then, implies making a career within and across a relatively stable, differentiated structure, putting together a set of experiences which mirror those in the organization overall (Martin and Strauss, 1956). Lee (1981: 91) reports that it was the directors of the larger firms she studied who had had the broadest functional and product experience. Of course, only in the simplest of organizations could anyone do this completely, which is perhaps why Galbraith and Nathanson (1978: 88) refer to their products of multi-functional careers as 'renaissance people'. Normally the process must be highly selective. Not only that, but the experiences one has gained early in one's career are likely to be somewhat stale and obsolete by the time one reaches a senior post. Nevertheless it is the logic behind the pattern of moves that is important to the argument here, since it is what fuels moves from job to job. The extent to which it actually works, or, conversely, to which it merely lulls people into a feeling that fully rounded managers are emerging from the process, is something on which I shall speculate in chapter 9.

One consequence of the logic is that people labelled in the firm as 'high-flyers' are likely to be moved around more than those who are not. This is because of the greater breadth of experiences that it is necessary for them to put together in the construction process in order to fit them out for top jobs. Rate of movement, in fact, is a simple and direct informal index of success (Hall, 1968; Veiga, 1981). The corollary of this is that people who want to get ahead will get worried if they are not putting together a wide breadth of experiences in a constructional logic. Being involved in an interesting, challenging job is fine but not if it goes on for too long, not because it has got boring but because one ought, for career reasons, to be moving to something else. As one manager put it to me, in answer to the question 'what can stop able people from getting ahead here?': 'Being in the same job for too long ... being seen to be indispensable in a job'. Equally, people may take jobs they dislike in order to get the right kind of experience (Bartolome and Evans, 1980).

The problem with non-recursive structures is that it can be difficult at times to tell which job is more 'important' than which, making it harder to see who is doing well and who is not. Job evaluation systems clearly play a part here, providing an apparently 'scientific' success scale. These grades can even sometimes be shown on organization charts, as if to underline how hard it can be to deduce from the job's function how important its incumbent is. The breadth of experience managers have acquired therefore becomes a further index of success: the more successful managers are those who have been given a wider range of experiences than their less successful colleagues, who will have been restricted to perhaps one specialist area. A manager working in such a culture commented revealingly to me on this phenomenon:

> I don't know if I'm on the magic [that is, high-flyer's] list: an indication of what they think of me will be what they do with me next. If I'm in the same grade as now, then I'm not on the list; if it's something fairly wild [to a very different kind of job] or more than one grade up, then I am.

Command-centred career logic

Command-centred career logic depends on moving between a series of similar managerial posts, differing mainly in terms of the size of their responsibilities and so in prestige. The analogy with a naval career is compelling, of getting one's first command and then moving from command to successively larger command if all is going well until one gets a squadron of ships and eventually becomes admiral of the fleet. It was this feature of the logic which gave rise to the name I picked. Managers make sense of the way in which their careers are progressing not in terms of how a diverse set of experiences fit together but in terms of the way in which the commands fall into a hierarchy of prestige. Lee (1985a: 4–5) describes a very similar process in a distribution company ('Promco'):

> It is common for branch managers to move from small to large branches. Such moves, whilst not involving changes in title, do involve increases in salary, status and responsibility. They demonstrate ambition and are an important feature of the promotion hierarchy at Promco. There exists an informal league table of importance of branch, related primarily to turnover and profits.

The command-centred logic does not have to be limited to one firm: it is entirely possible to think in terms of an industry career logic in these terms (Baron, Davis-Blake and Bielby, 1986). Technical specialists often have careers like this, but the same can be seen in the careers, for instance, of production managers in the textile industry.

The prime structural requirement for such a career logic is recursion, so that there are the numbers of similar posts available for climbing. As with constructional logics, but probably to a greater extent, there is the need for stability, in other words for the organization to experience central continuity and to grow to a pattern. If either of these conditions does not hold, the possibility of progress through a nicely graded series of commands is likely to be upset: experience in one post may not qualify one for experience in the next in the same way.

The aptness of the naval metaphor for the command-centred logic is illustrated by the way in which so often the most prestigious unit in the firm is informally called the 'flagship'. Career success, or lack of it, is highly visible: it is defined in terms of how big the command is and how it compares in prestige with one's previous command.

Evolutionary career logic

The research study from which this book sprang was of managers' careers in four large manufacturing companies. The fourth of the firms I visited, International Systems Engineering (ISE), gave me the kind of salutary experience which all researchers should have, and which incidentally brought out the dangers of relying on structured questionnaires for exploratory research. Indeed if I had used such an instrument I would probably have missed the evolutionary logic completely.

ISE was my last fieldwork site, and by then I was pretty confident that I knew how to interview managers about their careers. In the first three companies I had got into a well-worked out routine: one asked the managers to describe each post they had occupied, when it had started, what the responsibilities were, to whom they had reported and so on, filling in a neatly laid-out form while they talked. They would describe a succession of posts and of events which caused them to move from post to post, but the events were not usually associated with the actual work they were doing in the posts they were leaving and they were always able to give a very good account of the organizational structure into which they had fitted.

To an alarming degree many of the ISE managers found it very hard to give me the information I thought I wanted. Typically having started work as R&D engineers or scientists on development projects, their accounts were stories of how their projects had developed and how this had affected them. The interview notes looked quite different, sprawling over the boundaries of the form in all directions. While these managers were always very clear in their minds about what was happening to their projects at the time they were speaking of, they were often vague about the organizational context, especially in terms of who was formally in charge of what and what their job titles were. Indeed the titles that were remembered were often rather misleading. For instance at one point one manager inherited the title of Chief [product] Engineer, which in reality meant that he was in charge of contract negotiations with overseas customers. The title itself was an obvious relic of an earlier stage in the organization's development, although the organization itself had grown to the point where it was no longer a very good description of the responsibilities attached to the post.

The essential feature of the logics of these careers was that the managers had been involved in something new to the firm and to the market which had totally captured them. They had started work on an idea, at some stage they had started selling the idea to customers, then selling enough so that they had full-blown production facilities under them together with the necessary sales and service functions, and so on until in some cases they found themselves running subsidiary companies of ISE itself. There was a sense, not of a conscious putting-together of necessary experiences which would make them good managers in the long run (the constructional logic), but of an organization evolving and the managers evolving with it. Evans (1986) describes a very similar situation − albeit one consciously chosen by a firm's management − in what he calls 'steady state careers'.

On the face of it the evolutionary logic seems to be associated with organic structures as opposed to mechanistic ones, if only because of the strong impression of organizational mayhem that the biographies gave. But it is entirely possible to think in terms of the managers growing their organizations in rather more mechanistic ways, and one manager in the study had done just this, using very traditional methods of structuring his division as it grew rapidly in size. Indeed it is often striking to see how R&D workers try to filter some of the uncertainty surrounding their situation by adopting highly formal reporting structures.

The essential organizational feature which gives rise to the evolutionary logic is an unpatterned mode of growth. A growth project which is novel to the company means acquiring new knowledge, skills and expertise, and whether or not they are learnt by current organizational members or bought in they result in a part of the overall organization that is different from the rest. The sense of being special results in a close personal identification between the staff and their project as they mutually evolve. By definition the structure must be non-recursive. It is most likely that the firm is experiencing central continuity because growing into the unknown requires a fair amount of confidence on the part of those funding the growth. Sometimes, however, this form of development can be a response to a crisis, if the firm prospects for new business to replace its existing, failing areas of business rather than trying to defend them (Miles and Snow, 1978).

The form organizational success takes is subtly different from that in constructional or command-centred career logics. It resembles the command-centred logic in the sense that it relates partially to the size of the organization that has evolved. But it is not so much just the size of the organization that matters as the project's significance, in terms of how much interest it still generates, how novel the work going on in it is and, conversely, whether it has got to the stage of routine production and selling with no further development. Promotion is rather more vague than in the comparatively tightly structured constructional or command-centred organizations. As an ISE project engineer described his career within a large defence project: 'Promotion was not well designated. You drift up the grades as you get more useful.' Managers in these logics tend to stay with the project if they can during its 'building' stage, and leave rapidly when it loses its excitement at the so-called 'harvest' stage (Gupta, 1986).

Turnaround career logic

The turnaround logic is a very public kind of career logic almost by definition, and I include it because the first three have one major requirement, that of comparative organizational continuity. It is necessary to have an organizational career logic which reflects situations where this is not so.

The essential requirement which differentiates the turnaround situation from the previous situations, then, is catastrophic change as I

defined it above, involving a central discontinuity to the firm's operations. Someone, usually external to the organization in question and
quite probably its financial backers, decides that the present situation
is not only bad but, crucially, cannot be allowed to go on: the firm is
absorbing too much cash, or its performance indicators show no sign of
turning up. A chief executive is appointed with the task of turning the
situation round in the short term, and his or her contract is increasingly
likely to be written so that the rewards are closely tied to the financial
out-turn. Well-known examples include the then Ian McGregor's
contract (or, strictly, Lazard Frères' contract) relating to the British
Steel Corporation, Sir Michael Edwardes' with Dunlop and Lee Iacocca's with Chrysler. Once the turnaround has been accomplished the
job of the manager is finished and often he or she moves to the next
catastrophe elsewhere. Turnaround managers are the beneficiaries of
the catastrophe if all goes well, along with those survivors in the firm
whose careers are given a boost by the events.

Because the turnaround logic is usually transient from the point of
view of a single organization it is inter-organizational to a far greater
extent than the other logics. The catastrophe at the heart of the
turnaround logic is characteristically proclaimed by outsiders to the
firm such as its bankers, the appropriate government minister or, if the
'firm' is a part of a larger group, its group head office. The logic of the
situation is that new thinking is needed and that insiders to the firm are
probably too 'contaminated' by knowing how things are done in it. It is
these ideas, the reasoning goes, which are responsible for the firm
being in the mess it is in, and so it is vital to bring in a new broom to
sweep clean. So turnaround logics span companies, often with no
particularly obvious connection between them.

As with the command-centred logic, the success of turnaround
managers is signalled to the world at least in part by the size of the firm
they are rescuing. Outcomes matter too from the point of view of both
their immediate reward, if their contract is written in these terms, and
reputation. Although reputations are always important from the point
of view of managerial careers (Tsui, 1984; Gowler and Legge, in press)
they are particularly so in turnaround logics, given that turnaround
managers are so often recruited from outside the firm by people such
as the firm's bankers or the government.

That, then, completes my account of the organizational career logics
model. Three relatively mutually independent dimensions of organization (structure, growth and central continuity) give rise to four distinct
organizational career logics or climbing-frames (table 4.3). To summarize, the logics are as follows.

1 *Constructional:* acquiring a set of diverse experiences by moving
  steadily across and up a complex, differentiated organization.

Table 4.3   Organizational structure, growth, central continuity and career logics

Organizational logic	Structure	Growth	Central continuity
Constructional	Non-recursive	Patterned	Continuity
Command-centred	Recursive	Patterned	Continuity
Evolutionary	Non-recursive	Unpatterned	Continuity
Turnaround	Either	Either	Catastrophe

2   *Command-centred:* moving across a series of similar organizational posts and then up to the next level in the organization at which one is in command of a group of one's former commands and so on.
3   *Evolutionary:* growing with a particular organization or part of one.
4   *Turnaround:* in which the emphasis is on rescuing failing firms and, having rescued them, moving on to the next rescue.

As we shall see in the next chapter, individual managers can pick their own way across and between their frames, and in part III ways in which these routes can be mapped are described. There is no reason to expect large organizations to be homogeneous in terms of their structure, growth and central continuity, which means that they might have more than one organizational career logic. In particular, we can expect a pairing between constructional and command-centred logics.

The relationship between constructional and command–centred logics

When I introduced the concept of recursion I made the point that most firms will be recursive to some degree. The following two examples are taken from my study.
1   Norchem is primarily organized into a complex matrix structure, with large functional departments cross-linked by business coordination departments. This makes it fundamentally non-recursive, because it is hard to make out the boxes-within-similar-boxes structure that would make it recursive. But it also has a number of large manufacturing locations, each comprising many separate chemical plants grouped into areas. Chemical factories have a great deal in common with ships in the sense that they depend on tight command structures with the emphasis on vertical lines of command, large workforces and clear distinctions between 'officers' and 'other ranks'. These factories form an 'island' of recursion within the overall non-recursive structure of the division.
2   Conversely Prestex, a typical recursive organization, is non-recursive at its lowest and highest levels. Its recursive part consists of a

large number of similar textile plants, but within each plant there are a number of different jobs which form a non-recursive structure in the sense that they are functionally different from each other. At board level three separate functional hierarchies – production, marketing and finance, all of which are represented at each level of the organization – come together, forming a further non-recursive element to the structure.

In both companies, therefore, we expect to find the non-recursive parts giving rise to constructional career logics, although far more so in Norchem than in Prestex. We can also expect to find recursive parts responsible for a command-centred logic in both companies. But because there are a great many more managerial posts in the recursive part of Prestex than there are in the non-recursive part, the command-centred logic is likely to be more a feature of Prestex than it is of Norchem.

There is another way of looking at this. The constructional logic implies building something, but if the structure is too big the individual may not be able to finish putting it together. Many medieval cathedral builders never lived to see their structures completed. So we can expect that while some managers will continue adding experiences to their careers more or less endlessly others will emerge at some stage as 'complete' managers with respect to a recursive part of the firm. They might then perhaps resume the construction process in yet another non-recursive part.

Constructional logics, in other words, can lead over time to command-centred logics. The level of seniority managers have to reach for this to happen depends on the kind of organization in which they are making their careers. Norchem, for instance, has comparatively few identifiable 'commands'. Prestex, by contrast, has a great many commands and most of its middle to senior management has made the transition from constructional to command-centred logic.

Command-centred logics can sometimes revert to constructional logics as managers emerge at a higher level in the structure where several different hierarchies converge on, for instance, general management positions.

There are good reasons, then, for expecting more than one career logic in a firm. A firm with a modal constructional logic, in the sense that this accounts for the greater part of its managers' careers, may have small numbers of managers who for a time experience command-centred careers. Conversely, managers in a firm with a modal command-centred logic will probably also experience comparatively short periods of constructional logic. These islands of non-modal organizational logic are an important source of variance in career patterns within firms.

As we shall see, there are other reasons to expect variance, not least being the managers' individual career motives. But to sum up the last part of the discussion, even at the organizational level of analysis we should not be surprised to find variations in career patterns between different parts of the same firm which can be traced to its structure and growth history.

SUMMARY

Organizational career logics enable us to make a number of predictions about the kind of career patterns that might typically be found in different kinds of company. They vary from firm to firm and can be thought of as defining the shape of the corporate climbing-frame managers move over as their careers develop.

I identified four distinct logics. On constructional climbing-frames managers assemble their careers from a variety of different kinds of experience. Command-centred careers involve moving between similar commands; successful managers in these cultures find their commands getting larger and more significant. In evolutionary logics managers grow with their own business area, while in turnaround logics they move from one crisis situation to the next, rescuing each in turn.

Three dimensions of the firm, each relatively independent of the others, make the modal organizational career logic what it is. The dimensions concern whether or not the structure is recursive, whether or not the firm has grown to a pattern and the extent to which it has experienced central continuity in its operations.

By 'modal' I mean the main organizational career logic for the firm: any large firm will have parts in which different logics are at work. In particular we can expect to find islands of command-centred logics in modal constructional firms, and command-centred firms with the tops and bottoms of the climbing-frames showing a tendency towards constructional logics. At the organizational level of analysis, the climbing-frame perspective predicts both a central tendency for career patterns in a firm and ways in which the patterns might vary. It describes the framework of career opportunities which organizations offer to their managers.

5
Individual Career Logics: Paths Across the Climbing-frames

INTRODUCTION

In chapter 3 I introduced the idea of the duality of organizational careers. At the organizational level of analysis, careers are bound up with the process of the firm renewing itself, which led us to the concept of the organizational career logics I discussed in chapter 4. But organizational career logics are not inexorable. It is not as if the shape of the climbing-frame decides once and for all what the 'people flow' over it will be in the way that a screen army in a Hollywood epic flows dutifully over the landscape in exactly the way the director tells it to. People can choose how they move over their climbing-frame. How they might do this is the subject of this chapter.

I shall be exploring the range of motivations that might account for the different routes people can take over their organizational climbing-frames. First, though, a caveat. My aim in this chapter is to locate individual career motivations within the organizational career logics framework rather than to review comprehensively the vast and fragmented literature on career choice. In the space available I can do no more than give some examples of why we might expect career motivations to vary from one person to the next and over the course of someone's career.

When looking at careers from an individual's point of view, it is important to distinguish between two different kinds of meaning careers can have for individuals. These perspectives are often called 'objective' and 'subjective'.

OBJECTIVE AND SUBJECTIVE CAREERS

At its simplest we can think of an organizational career as a sequence of jobs, perhaps representing a climb up a hierarchy and perhaps not.

Because this process is so visible to the observer it has often been called the *objective career*. One's curriculum vitae (CV) or resumé is conventionally just this: a bald statement of the external facts of one's life in terms of job titles, outputs and constraints. Sometimes in the literature this perspective is referred to as sociological (e.g. Van Maanen, 1977: 7). It is important to recognize the distinction between sociological status-labelling, which this is, and a view of a social renewal process which I called in chapter 3 the organizational level of analysis.

Interviews for jobs give a good indication of how partial this information can be, since their point is usually to try to find out the 'truth' behind the CV. Interviewers probe candidates' accounts of their past in order to see what each job involved, how the candidates interpreted the needs of the jobs and perhaps how successfully they did them, how the succeeding jobs related to each other in terms of experience and prestige, what part the candidates played in changing jobs and why, and what they expect to gain from the job for which they are being interviewed. This is a tall order and of course most of us fail to get the information with any accuracy at all, but it makes the point that the simple objective career only scratches the surface of the meaning of careers to individuals.

In an empirical study of careers it may not be possible for practical reasons to get far below the surface of the objective career. Even if one spends several hours talking to someone about their past, one is hearing only a summary of a story. Much of this story may have happened a long time ago so that memory blurs events, interviewees may prefer not to talk about some of it and they may simply not know about other parts either because they never learned what lay behind certain key events or because they are unaware of what really led them to do certain things (Nisbett and Wilson, 1977). But there is a great deal more to careers for the individual than just a succession of jobs. One can, after all, talk in terms of a career in the absence of any job moves at all in the way for instance that an artist or a free-lance professional may do. The object of interest here is the way in which individuals themselves develop over time, the so-called *subjective career* (Hughes, 1958).

Subjective and objective careers have a similar dual relationship as do careers seen at individual and organizational levels of analysis: they are two aspects of what is ultimately the same thing. They both draw our attention to change, to the transitions individuals go through over the course of their lives (Louis, 1980a; Watts, 1981; Rhodes and Doering, 1983; Mihal, Sorce and Comte, 1984; Nicholson, 1984). These transitions distinguish an organizational career from, say, the career of a chartered public accountant who spends his working life running his own practice by himself. As soon as work role transitions intrude —

such as would happen if the accountant were to join a big international firm of accountants, succeed, and end up as a partner in the business — we can talk about organizational careers.

WORK ROLE TRANSITIONS

Work role transitions distinguish organizational and managerial careers from other careers (Van Maanen, 1977). They connect with both aspects of career at the individual level: they are the points at which individuals move up and across the hierarchy (the objective career) and at which their talents or their need for development, testing or resting are recognized (the subjective career).

For instance newly graduated engineers in England need to gain certain kinds of work experience in order to get so-called 'chartered' status. This means that they may well have to go through a number of transitions because their first postings do not normally allow them to do everything they have to. Objectively they are moving through a series of posts and with luck doing a useful job in each, and subjectively they are developing professionally. It is the kind of transitions they go through which provide clues to what is happening at both levels, as we can see if we go on to imagine a quite different kind of transition in the middle of it all.

Suppose one such engineer accepts a well-paid job selling products for someone else, perhaps relating to his area of engineering expertise. He will probably not get his chartered status, end up in a totally different career from the one on which he was originally launched, and quite probably even seem a very different kind of person from that he would have developed into if he had stayed an engineer. Techniques such as job rotation, which is often recommended as a way of stimulating bored mid-career managers (Bailyn and Lynch, 1983; Hall and Isabella, 1985), and career path planning (Walker, 1976) are directly concerned with trying to exploit some of the effects of different kinds of transition to the mutual advantage of firm and individual.

By focusing on the kind of work role transitions people experience we gain access to both subjective and objective careers at the individual level of analysis. We also have a means of pinpointing the effects of underlying organizational career logics because the transitions are between work roles, which are themselves defined by the organizational structure and how it is developing. Although we might well be able to see differences between characteristic patterns of transitions in different firms which reflect the firms' different organizational career logics, we have to remember that people are not always passive tools of their firms. They have their own reasons for accepting or not accepting moves or perhaps even abandoning their careers with firm A and joining firm B. The reasons are probably a mixture of conflicting motivations which shape their careers as powerfully as do organizational career logics. *Individual career logics* are my label for the interpretation the observer makes of these motivations.

INDIVIDUAL CAREER LOGICS

If organizational career logics are to do with the shape of the climbing-frame managers move over, individual logics are to do with which frame they choose to climb and how they decide to climb it. They may ascend for a while, go sideways, change to another frame they like better or just stop climbing, and the choices will be governed both by what they want and by what they are allowed to do. Individual career logics are the observer's attempt to infer managers' motivations in choosing their route over the frame(s) and which cause managers in similar situations to choose different career paths.

I have just implied that two things influence managers' choices of work role transition: what they are offered and what they want. The offers they get depend on the vacancies that are available, which reflect the organizational career logic, and on how they are evaluated by the firm. But what they want can be the result of many different motivations (London, 1983). These can include the kind of person they are, the stage in life they have reached and how they balance work against other roles involving for instance their children, their partners' careers, public activities and moonlighting. First, I shall look at the 'what is on offer' issue.

OFFERING POSTS TO MANAGERS

As we saw in chapter 3, selecting people for promotion is a murky business and heavily dependent on the part of the organizational culture which specifies 'the kind of manager we like around here'. Firms vary greatly in the ways in which they evaluate their employees, from highly formalized systems to very informal processes. Even a carefully thought-out and detailed performance appraisal system is not always carried out as it should be. In the same firm one can find anything from painstaking observation of the rules to empty ritual. The formal system may be at the heart of the business of picking managers for posts, or it may be largely ignored. Informally, people can be selected for moves and promotions for many reasons: on the basis of their general reputations, because they did something at some stage which got them noticed, as a result of a powerful patron or through sheer luck.

This selection process means that labels are hung around managers' necks, describing them in terms of their potential for promotion and movement to other jobs. Just who hangs the label and how it is done is usually a very complicated and opaque business, indeed so opaque that it is often surrounded by a great deal of suspicion and cynicism, especially by anyone who feels that they have been ignored by 'the system'.

Managers' labels, then, describe how well thought of they are in the firm and affect the kind of career opportunities they will be presented with. A 'high-flyer' label probably means that they will get the pick of the jobs. A 'deadwood' label means that they are seen as having no potential for any job in the firm, cutting off all possibilities of personal growth, as does the label 'has reached his or her ultimate managerial potential'. The label 'useful in his or her current specialist area' may keep open the possibility of rising in a command-centred logic within the current specialist hierarchy but eliminate that of a constructional logic involving moves to other functional areas. The extreme case is, of course, the label which says that they are no longer of any use to the organization by virtue of being incompetent, surplus to requirements or too old.

The evaluation process has the effect of making all or some of the firm's organizational logics available to managers or cutting them off from them. If the evaluation is at all positive managers are likely to be given the chance of following one of the organizational logics, but if it is not then their development, from the point of view of the firm, stops, at least for the time being. In either situation they still have the choice of staying with the firm or finding something else.

People's choices, then, may be circumscribed by the way they are evaluated in their firm. I shall now look specifically at the question of choice. Our understanding of what governs it is incomplete, but two threads can be distinguished. The first concerns the way in which people differ from each other in their career interests, and the second the way in which they develop over the course of their careers.

CAREER MOTIVATIONS

Individual characteristics

There is a tradition which holds that people tend to choose jobs which match their personalities. The corollary is that people who have picked jobs which do not match their personalities will tend to be unhappy and underperform. If we could produce workable classifications of personalities and jobs we would obviously have something that would be very useful in helping people choose satisfying careers and organizations pick the right people. This assumes that we know how to specify them; as we saw in chapter 3, 'right' in organizational terms may simply mean people with whom powerful figures in the firm feel comfortable.

The first job choice (Lipset and Malm, 1955; Holland, 1973) and, for instance, how long the individual spends in it (Veiga, 1983) seem to play a pervasive part in determining the shape of a career. However, the ideas which are perhaps best known in the context of individual differences take one step further back and ask, in effect, what is it about people which caused them to choose that particular first job? Amongst the best known are the following.

Convergers/divergers (Hudson, 1966): convergers are believed to select engineering and hard sciences, divergers the arts and humanities. The operative word is 'believed', because Hudson's work was done on schoolchildren.

Field dependence/field independence (Witkin et al., 1962): this concentrates on people's ability to isolate a phenomenon from its context (its field) and see it in their own terms. Field dependents are particularly responsive to social frames of reference and tend to favour careers which are 'people-oriented' such as teaching or sales and to study in areas such as sociology, clinical psychology and the humanities. Field independents tend to have a definite career in mind when they enter college and prefer jobs which need a fairly impersonal, analytical approach such as science and engineering.

Learning styles (Kolb and Plovnick, 1977): people are classified into four groups depending on their preferred learning style measured in two dimensions: concrete experience/abstract conceptualization, and reflective observation/active experimentation. Early career tends to be dominated by a need to accentuate one's preferred learning style, but later it may be that the opposite happens as one looks for fulfilment, picking jobs which bring out learning styles which have hitherto been non-dominant.

Information gathering/information evaluation (Keen, 1977): again, people are classified according to their cognitive styles in two dimensions. *Preceptive* information gatherers tend to fit information to predetermined patterns while *receptors* are more sensitive to the patterns in the information itself; *systematics* think to a sequential programme, while *intuitives* think more holistically. Each dimension is believed to influence job choice and happiness with particular kinds of jobs.

There have also been a number of attempts to describe how people differ in their long-run career goals, including the following.

Career anchors (Schein, 1978): an anchor is 'a syndrome of motives, values and self-perceived talents which guides and constrains the person's career' (Schein, 1977). Schein identified a number, including ones he labelled managerial competence, technical—functional competence, security, creativity (creating something of one's own) and autonomy—independence.

Internal career maps (Driver, 1979; 1980; 1982): four career self-concepts (linear, spiral, steady-state and transitory) are postulated to be interdependent with certain cognitive styles and to guide an individual's long-term career choices.

Career orientations: Derr (1986) distinguishes between five orientations (getting ahead, getting secure, getting free, getting high and getting balanced) which spring, he argues, from individuals' motives, values, talents and constraints.

The diversity of these models gives a good indication of the state of development of the theory of career choice. Studies of the relationship between kinds of people and the careers they followed are rare and often depend on job titles, which are far from reliable indicators of a job's content. Even Schein's study on career anchors covered only a small sample in order that each person could be interviewed in enough depth.

These models are attractive in the sense that they have great face validity and make helpful-looking predictions on the basis of simple, direct distinctions. Yet a specific test of Holland's (1973) thesis, that people choose jobs that suit their personalities, on a group of mid-career managers showed no support for the idea at all (Thomas and Robbins, 1979). The authors speculate that this was because, by mid-career, work was simply not all that important to the managers they studied. In other words personality may well affect career choice, but so might the way we change as we age. Here again there has been a great deal written.

Developmental models

A number of researchers have applied ideas from child development theory to the continuing development of adults. Some concentrate on so-called 'biosocial life cycles', while others link development to jobs in 'work/career cycles' (Schein, 1978).

One of the best-known biosocial cycle models proposes a multi-stage model in which transitional periods are followed by periods of structure building, in turn followed by another transition (Levinson et al., 1978).

1 Early adult transitional period (age 18—22).
2 Getting into the adult world: structure building (age 22—28).
3 Age 30 transitional period (age 28—32).

4 Settling down: structure building period (age 33—40).
5 Age 40 transitional period (age 38—42).
6 Beginning of middle adulthood: structure building period (age mid-40s).

This particular study stopped at this point, but the authors are sure that chances for development carry on for the rest of one's life. Biosocial models of this kind always read very persuasively, even uncomfortably so as one realizes that perhaps the private anguishes and struggles one has gone through are just symptoms of one's age for which ready-made labels are available, for instance the so-called mid-life crisis (Kets de Vries, 1978). There are a great many of these models. Super (1984), for instance, has a five-stage framework for viewing a life which is, he argues, much less deterministic than Levinson's since he does not believe that the boundaries are as rigidly fixed in time. Other roles, for instance family, can play an important part in deciding how, if at all, people experience transitions such as the mid-life crisis (Farrell and Rosenberg, 1981).

The life stages in these generalized developmental models do not always tie in well with organizational careers, however (Veiga, 1983). The work—career perspective introduces organizational concepts to the description of people's development. One such model of managerial careers (Veiga, 1983) involves the three stages of corporate learning (age 29—37), corporate maturity (age 38—55), and the gold watch or pre-retirement phase (age 56—64). Another (Hall and Nougaim, 1968) comprises establishment (age 25—30), advancement (age 30—45) and maintenance (age 45—65). Yet another, specifically dealing with the careers of technical professionals, has four stages (Dalton and Thompson, 1986).

These models shift the emphasis away from the purely biosocial development process, which is seen as providing the background to a career that is primarily influenced by work-related concerns. But their focus is still on the individual in the sense that they talk about the organizational factors which provide opportunities for or blockages to advancement in very unspecific terms.

The organizational element has been brought in more strongly by means of a model in which individuals cross a variety of kinds of organizational boundary in a series of *rites de passage* (Schein, 1971). Socialization, education and training are believed to reach a peak just before and just after crossing a boundary. The learning includes both new skills and the details of the job. The individual's ability to change things peaks in between boundary-crossings.

It is evident that there is quite a lot of divergence between the predictions of different developmental models. A possible reason for this is that the paradigm completely ignores the way age, as well as being a biological fact, is socially defined: you are as old as other people make you feel (Dannefer, 1984a,b). Age means very different things in different social settings. One cannot make general statements about what people are like at different ages without knowing about the context within which they are growing up. This critique is by no means accepted by all (Baltes and Nesselroade, 1984), and it may be more fruitful to look on human development as the outcome of both biological and social processes (Featherman and Lerner, 1985). There is certainly good evidence for one particular way in which people's apparent age seems to be strongly affected by social context: the matter of career timetables.

Writers have often commented on how acutely aware we all are of these timetables (Roth, 1963). There is nothing better calculated to give one a twinge than the discovery that someone much younger has just won a promotion to a job more senior than one's own. Managers develop clear ideas about relative age grading, and people who see themselves as on or ahead of the organizational timetable tend to feel more positively about their job than those who feel themselves to be falling behind (Lawrence, 1984).

People may build up their ideas of the timetable in many ways. They usually know their colleagues' managerial levels and ages and use this information as a point of reference for what the firm 'really does' think of them, as opposed to what they may officially have been told by their boss. If, for instance, a number of younger managers are reaching their organizational level, or their contemporaries are getting ahead faster than they are, they may infer that they are not in the high-flyer category; people are by no means always told when they are. If they have been promoted recently they are more likely to think of themselves as ahead of timetable, regardless of the actual situation (Lawrence, 1984). The timetables people develop, in other words, are greatly affected by the age distributions at each level of management (Scholl, 1983; Stewman and Konda, 1983). Sometimes the timetable may be semi-official: for instance, in large company groups it is often said that no one who does not reach a divisional board by the age of forty can expect to reach the main board eventually.

I have briefly reviewed some of the research which provides evidence for why certain kinds of people are attracted to certain kinds of career, and how these attitudes might change over the course of their careers. Whether one believes the detailed predictions of the various models on offer is beside the point, which is that work role transitions are not neutral events as far as the people who go through them are concerned. We may not know exactly why someone made a particular move at a particular time, but we might be able to make an intelligent guess. Our guess is what I call here the individual career logic, in the sense that logics of action are the intentions of goal-seeking activities seen from the point of view of the observer rather than the actors.

Just what might lead a particular manager to go through a particular kind of transition is obviously a complex matter, and I have only scratched the surface of the vast field of study which focuses on individual rather than organizational needs and motivations. It follows from this that we have to look for individual career logics by talking to individuals and, if possible, watching them go through the transitions in question. The more we understand of what is going on in the managers' minds, the more confident we can be that we have correctly identified the individual logics at work.

In the final part of this chapter I shall turn to the problem of finding a way of describing these individual logics without getting lost in the jungle of competing theoretical models and perspectives that we have just viewed from a distance. As with organizational career logics, I shall identify a very limited number of dimensions (in this case two) which I shall use to distinguish between three distinct individual career logics. These two dimensions are highly synoptic in the sense that they describe two aspects of people's career orientations to their managerial careers without going into why they are so oriented. My reason for being so parsimonious is simply that the primary aim of this book is to try to understand the relationship between organizations and careers. The purpose of this chapter is to find a way of summarizing the different routes people might pick across their organizational climbing-frames.

THE DIMENSIONS: FUTURE ORIENTATION AND DEVIANCE

There are two ways, broadly, in which one can think of an organizational career. The first is quite simply whether one thinks in terms of a career at all: career implies an attitude of future orientation which not everyone has. Assuming that one does, the second issue to be faced is deciding one's attitude towards the range of careers on offer in one's present firm. I shall take these in turn.

Career is closely linked to deferred gratification (Wilensky, 1960; Stinchcombe, 1983). Younger, mobile managers often have lower salaries than their less mobile colleagues, but this can pay off later for the select few who reach top jobs for whom some mobility is a necessity (Roche, 1975; Veiga, 1981). Anyone thinking in career terms is implicitly looking for two kinds of reward from their present job: the immediate rewards to do with pay and other perks, and the deferred rewards to do with their future in the company, which is what I call here *future orientation*. They may accept a job they do not like because it will lead to something better in future or leave a job they like very much because it is necessary to get experience elsewhere. It is rather like the film star who tries to branch out from a highly lucrative role in order to avoid being typecast or, at least, says so for public consumption. The future orientation of managers can mean that they are so caught up with their future that their current job takes second place in their mind. They become obsessed with getting results which will become evident during their expected time in the job rather than results which might be in the long-term interests of the company (Mant, 1983; Thompson, Kirkham and Dixon, 1985).

Not everyone thinks in these terms, and certainly not all the time. The chances are that future-oriented thinking will emerge, if it is going to at all, at the point when individuals have choices to make. For example, should I accept this job, how should I order the priorities of my work, which conferences or meetings should I attend and which can I safely ignore, who in the firm and outside it should I cultivate? If I am not future oriented in the career sense then, for instance, the job choice question becomes just one of comparing the rewards of the jobs such as pay, conditions, whether or not it involves moving house and how that prospect appeals, the intrinsic interest of the work, and the people I would be working with.

Although I have presented the future orientation variable as binary (either I am or I am not), its salience to anyone is quite likely to depend on the choice they are faced with. For example it is more likely to figure in someone's calculations if they are facing a job change than if they are trying to decide which of two routine meetings to attend. There are times when it may disappear altogether even for the most future-oriented person so that all that really matters is the immediate side of the job. It can happen to anyone that the circumstances surrounding their job become very threatening: their performance is being judged inadequate, a major reorganization is in the wind, or a redundancy programme is looming. The situation could be seen in terms of a rapid descent down the levels of Maslow's hierarchical model of needs so that security and safety dominate, and esteem and self-actualization have to wait for better times.

A discussion of why some people are future oriented and others are not is beyond the scope of this book. Personality variables will obviously be important as will social ones. Self-esteem seems to figure in the personality variables that are important (Gould, 1979), and factors such as parental attitudes towards upward mobility will figure in the social category. For our present purposes, which are to do with a very simple model linking organizational form to career type, we simply have to accept that future orientation is a prerequisite for thinking in career terms. The next question becomes: which career?

I defined organizational career logics as, in effect, outcroppings of the organization's culture. If so, then managers have the choice of either going along with the career culture or rejecting it. This view is strongly reminiscent of Merton's (1968) analysis of social deviance, which is based on a simple typology of individual adaptation to a society's cultural goals and institutionalized means for reaching the goals. Individuals may accept or reject either or both goals and means, and may also seek to substitute their own. Merton specifies five combinations of acceptance, rejection and substitution, giving five possible forms of deviance ranging from conformity to rebellion. So managers who reject the organizational career logic(s) on offer can be thought of as *deviant* in this respect. In other words the question is whether, on the whole, they are prepared to play the game in the conventional way for the firm or whether they are not. One could visualize this in terms of acceptance or rejection of one aspect of the employment contract, namely that to do with the manager's future in the company.

Of course in real life a great deal of negotiation and compromise goes on to complicate the picture. As with future orientation it may for some people be entirely unconscious for most of the time, for others it may surface once or twice at times of crisis, while others may spend quite a lot of their career thinking about their future and calculating their advantage. Again as with future orientation, predicting why some people will accept organizational career logics while others will not involves delving into personality and social variables in a way which space does not permit here. There is often a big gap between the opportunities people think are there and those which realistically are there (Derr and Laurent, 1987), so it is often assumed that the more open a company is with its employees about its career plans for them, the more committed (less deviant) the employees will be. But this only seems to be the case if the plans suit them; if not, it makes it more likely that they will become deviants and look for jobs elsewhere (Granrose and Portwood, 1987). The risk of this happening is presumably increased by the tendency for career decision-makers to ignore the personal wishes of employees (London and Stumpf, 1984). Nevertheless the outcome − whether or not people become deviants − is clearly vital to trying to understand why otherwise similarly placed managers can have strikingly different careers.

THE INDIVIDUAL CAREER LOGICS

The two individual-level dimensions − future orientation and organizational career deviance − can be combined to give a 2 × 2 matrix with four cells (table 5.1). The two bottom cells corresponding to future-oriented managers (building and searching) are comparatively straightforward to distinguish, but the upper two are not. The upper pair describe a situation (subsisting) where managers are not looking to

Table 5.1   Individual career logics

Orientation to organizational career logic

		Non-deviant	Deviant
Future oriented?	No	Subsisting	Subsisting
	Yes	Building	Searching

their career as a form of deferred gratification for the time being at least, so it hardly matters whether or not they are deviant with respect to the organizational career logic. Their work role transitions may or may not fit in with the organizational logic, but that is largely a matter of indifference to them except in so far as the new posts offer better or worse immediate rewards.

Building

Building logic involves building a career within the organization and/or an industry, so that one becomes suited for promotion up the hierarchy. It may involve an enjoyable series of developments as managers move from interesting post to interesting post or a series of self-denials as they give up enjoyable jobs because if they stay in them they worry that they will get stuck. They are being developed in the way that people get developed in that particular firm. Building therefore depends on the managers' being future-oriented in the sense that they are career-minded and non-deviant in that they accept, for the time being at least, the organizational career logic on offer to them.

The building process will almost certainly result from a combination of technical motives to do with learning necessary skills and gaining necessary experience, and political motives involving the formation of alliances and getting noticed by influential figures (Veiga, 1981; Forbes, 1987). I use the label 'political' partly because the process mirrors so well the way public political careers are made and partly because managers' success depends so much on the alliances and networks they have built which they can use to their advantage.

These two sets of motives sound different, but in practice they are almost impossible to separate. For instance someone may talk about a particular move – say, to be personal assistant to a chief executive or to be given a series of special assignments outside normal departmental duties – as a mixture of technical ('the experience was very useful') and political ('I made some marvellous contacts'), but his or her peers might well view it as totally political ('you can't turn a job like that down'). Similarly, getting pulled through an organization by a senior manager who likes to have people he or she knows working for him or her could be thought of as either political, in the sense that networks and patronage are being used, or technical, because the senior manager knows the individuals and can trust their technical abilities. Under the label 'mentoring' it has recently become prominent as a technique for developing younger managers (chapter 2).

In passing I should note that someone can build within any organizational career logic: the connection between building and constructional logics is purely semantic. In other words, if the firm's modal logic is command-centred, then that is the logic within which successful managers build.

Searching

The essence of searching is that individuals are for some reason dissatisfied with their current situation and voluntarily change their occupation for something else (Rhodes and Doering, 1983; Mihal, Sorce and Comte, 1984). The earliest form this takes is the search behaviour in which young people try to find what they want to do, but it can go on quite late in life, for instance in the so-called 'second career' (Levinson, 1983). The organizational career logic, in other words, is not right for the individual and the situation is bad enough to force him or her to do something about it.

It is important to remember that we are concerned here with the logic which lay behind the move at the time, not with how events turned out. Suppose, for instance, someone makes a searching move to a quite unrelated job and it turns out that the combination of experiences in the two posts fortuitously makes him or her ideally suited for yet another post later on. In retrospect it would be easy to reconstruct events so that the searching move is seen as a building one, but that would be to misreport the individual career logic which governed the job move in question. Indeed one comes across cynics who maintain that all building is really a *post hoc* rationalization of moves between jobs which, in retrospect, looked as if they fitted together. This, however, seems to me to throw out the analytical baby with the ideological bathwater.

Searching, then, involves future orientation because the move is made in order to advance one's career. By contrast with building, it involves rejection of the organizational career logic as one's preferred way forward (deviance): individuals reject their current organizational career logic and search for one that suits them better. It is one reason for the distribution of actual career patterns in a firm to depart from the norm, but it is not the only one.

Subsisting

Building and searching both have the implication of personal growth: building within some kind of organizational career logic; searching for an organizational logic that feels right. But there are a great many people for whom this future orientation is no longer relevant. People who may well fit this description include those who have reached their career 'plateau' (Carnazza et al., 1981) and who choose not to search for something else, perhaps because they are virtually unemployable elsewhere as can happen to people in mid-life. If they have chosen not to search they may be moved around, left where they are or sacrificed rather like a chess piece so that the main strategy – organizing management succession, in which they no longer figure directly – can be seen through. Their own personal development is not really of interest to the company except in so far as it is necessary to keep them motivated enough to perform acceptably in their current job (Ference, Stoner and Warren, 1977; Hall and Isabella, 1985).

I have made subsisting sound very hollow, but this is by no means necessarily the case. A number of studies of managers on the career plateau have found that people can be quite satisfied with their situation (Evans and Gilbert, 1984; Near, 1984; Slocum et al., 1985). There was more than one manager in my own study who was clearly very happy with this position even though in organizational terms he knew he was a relative 'failure'. He may, indeed, have been a great success by comparison with his original reference group, having risen, for instance, to factory manager from the shop floor. One such man started work as a motor mechanic, joined a textile mill soon after, and in the mid-1940s became its manager. The mill is in the middle of beautiful hill country where the manager can watch kingfishers from his office window: not surprisingly, he has resisted all attempts to get him to move away. It is easy to dismiss such findings as examples of people trying to reduce their cognitive dissonance, but that is irrelevant to the present discussion. For whatever reason, these managers are prepared to live for the moment. They have either been abandoned by the system or have themselves lost interest in getting ahead: work and career are no longer their central life interest. The individual career logic becomes one of subsisting, of making a living for the sake of it.

Subsisting, then, can come in many forms. Three others which have been identified are that followed by the 'careerless' and those induced by the 'uncareer' or the 'non-career' (Hearn, 1977). The 'careerless' are those who cannot make a career for reasons beyond their control. The 'uncareer' is followed by those who do not want to make a conventional career because they have more important concerns to do with changing the social order in which conventional careers are embedded. Finally, the 'non-career' is followed by people who do not want to make a career because work simply is not important enough for them. In its most extreme form subsisting is a logic of survival: any job, so long as it is a job. It may be a phase in a career in which things have gone wrong because the manager's performance is seen as unacceptable. There might have been a traumatic reshuffle, reorganization, corporate collapse or redundancy exercise. Managers typically describe this kind of experience with phrases such as 'going near the edge of the precipice' and its end as 'rejoining the system' or 'coming in from the cold'.

Managers who are subsisting may or may not be deviants. This dimension is probably irrelevant because if the organizational logic has rejected them it really does not matter what they think of it. The essential feature of subsisting is that it is present-oriented, which distinguishes it from searching. People who are unhappy with their present position and who are looking for something better have, to some measure at least, a future orientation. But we do have to be careful imputing motives to people in situations which may in reality be confused or blurred. There is a particular danger of confusing a subsisting move *post hoc* with searching. It can often turn out unexpectedly that jobs people are forced to take, perhaps as a result of being fired, suit them much better than they had expected and they begin building within the new logic (Latack and Dozier, 1986).

For instance a highly successful executive in my study had developed a crippling disease some years before I met him and had been treated compassionately by his company. He had been moved from senior production management into an administrative post serving the Board, and much to his surprise he found himself much preferring the new role to the one he had just left. The move was really governed by a subsisting logic but, because he was now developing well as a company secretary, anyone who did not know his medical history could easily mistake the move in retrospect for searching.

Sometimes managers leave their firm because they find themselves in what they see as an impossible position, without actually being dismissed. This almost certainly means rejecting the firm's organizational logic, but it is not always easy to say whether it involves future or present orientation (searching or subsisting). One manager in my study had at one point in his career been recruited by his new employer's chairman without the agreement of its managing director, who had it in for him as a result. Another felt his authority undermined when his chairman fired one of his subordinates behind his back. The upshot was that both managers left their respective firms because neither felt they could carry on as they were. Their prime need was for a job with which they could live, so to that extent their moves were subsisting. Yet their careers did continue thereafter, very successfully, and neither of them lost their future orientation in the long run. So in retrospect, and especially without any knowledge of the unhappiness that lay behind the moves, they could easily be thought of as searching.

These examples simply emphasize the point that career logics are ascribed to the individual by an observer: we do our best to make sense of what has gone on, but in the final analysis we cannot be sure that we have got it right (Wagner, Pfeffer and O'Reilly, 1984). As we get to know more about what was in the mind of the individual making the job move, it is quite likely that we might change our view of the kind of logic that lay behind it. As with searching moves which look in retrospect like building, we need to remember that it is the logic prevailing at the time which matters in the reconstruction. There is no reason, indeed, why subsisting could not represent a transient stage in a manager's career.

The three distinct individual career logics, then, are as follows.

1 *Building:* staying within the modal organizational logic, in other words following the dominant career model in the firm, which probably implies being on a successful career path.
2 *Searching:* abandoning the modal organizational logic and looking for something that is closer to what one wants to do.
3 *Subsisting:* abandoning, or being abandoned by, the modal organizational logic and looking on one's job as simply something necessary for survival.

The different logics have important consequences for the shapes of managers' careers. In part III the question of what exactly I mean by 'shape' in this context is opened up by examining work role transitions in greater depth.

SUMMARY

In this chapter managerial careers were looked at from an exclusively individual-level perspective. At the individual level of analysis, managerial careers can be seen from a variety of points of view. These ranged from subjective, to do with the development of the person, to objective, to do with the posts the managers pass between.

Organizational careers are characterized by a sequence of work role transitions from post to post. These conceptually link the organizational and individual levels of analysis because a work role has the same duality of meaning as does a career. Focusing on transitions draws out the point that organizational labour markets form only half of the explanation for career patterns. They may provide the climbing-frame on which managers can make their careers by setting out opportunities from which they can choose. But the range of choice is limited by the way in which managers have been evaluated by their superiors, in the sense that only those who are well regarded will be offered the jobs which go with a successful career.

In order to understand how managers make their choices we need to understand something of their own motivations, which can be a function of their age, the kind of person they are and their personal circumstances. The research literature on career choice is fragmented and incomplete, and so for my present purposes I adopted the 'logics of action' perspective to summarize career motivations into three broad groups which I called building, searching and subsisting. These individual career logics account for the way managers make choices about which route to take up, across and between organizational climbing-frames. I distinguished between these individual logics by means of two dimensions concerning people's orientation towards their career: (1) future orientation and (2) deviance with respect to the firm's organizational career logic. The logics describe individuals' motivations at the time they made their choice rather than in the light of what might have happened afterwards.

The career logics model has now been developed to the point where it makes a number of predictions about the kind of career patterns that might typically be found in different kinds of companies and about some of the individual factors which might cause the actual career patterns of the managers to depart from the expected ones. It can be summed up as follows.

Organizational career logics are a function of firms' structures and modes of growth, and can be thought of as defining the shape of the corporate climbing-frame managers move over as their careers develop. I identified four logics: constructional, command-centred, evolutionary and turnaround. The organizational career logic is only available to managers who are well thought of in their firm. If the organizational career logic is available to someone, they have the choice of three individual logics: building within the organizational logic, searching for something else or subsisting. If the organizational logic is not available to them, they only have the choice of searching or subsisting.

The career logics model is about intentions and modes of rationality, but it says nothing about what the managers' careers actually look like. I turn to this in part III.

Part III
Analysis: Mapping Career Paths across the Climbing-frames

So far I have been evasive about how one might recognize a career logic, apart from where I talked generally about the 'patterns of work role transitions' that arise from it. If the framework is to be of any use it has to be rather more specific than this. We need to know how to go about recognizing these career patterns in practice.

The method we use has to be able to cope with both individual and organizational levels of analysis. This suggests a demographic type of approach in the sense that one looks for individual phenomena which can be aggregated to give organizational measures, rather than identifying organizational variables and deducing from them the consequences for individuals. In part III a way of mapping careers which has these properties is described.

In chapter 6 I introduce career mapping and the approach I take here. It is based on analysing managers' work experience, and focuses on work role transitions as the event which gives careers their shape. In chapter 7 I describe the mapping technique itself and outline a number of ways in which the maps can be represented and analysed.

Part III, then, paves the way for the final part of the book in which I put the two halves of the picture − career logics and career maps − together.

6
Mapping Experience: Background

INTRODUCTION

The career climbing-frame perspective makes predictions about the kind of careers which might be typical of particular kinds of firm, and about the individual variations that are possible within this framework. But it says nothing about how we might look for these differences. A way of mapping managers' career paths is needed which allows us to compare and contrast the career patterns of managers, as individuals and as groups, from different firms.

Unfortunately there is no obvious, ready-made approach already available. Career researchers have taken many different approaches to the problem of mapping careers in response to the three basic difficulties which have already been introduced (chapter 2). The first difficulty is that the descriptive categories or attributes which can be used for the maps are far from robust. The second is that an enormous mass of data has to be collected, typically relating to what happened many years previously. The third difficulty is that this mass of data has to be reduced to reveal patterns, a problem which is exacerbated by the need to compare the careers of groups of managers from different firms.

This chapter introduces the way I shall describe career paths in the book.

MAPPING CAREERS: METAPHORS AND VARIABLES

Careers are difficult to visualize. Not only does one have to find a way of conceptualizing the organizational climbing-frame on which managers make their career, but both climbing-frame and managers change over time. The problem is closely akin to having to work within a space-time continuum where the space is defined by the climbing-frame, except that one is not necessarily limited to four dimensions. It is no surprise to find that people adopt powerfully metaphorical languages when they talk about career issues.

There seem to be two common kinds of metaphor used to describe careers: horticultural and spatial. The horticultural metaphor dramatizes careers as autonomously growing things which need taming. For instance, talent is home-grown or implanted, deadwood is pruned, bad apples are discarded, ranks are thinned or experience is grafted on. All of these have in common the idea that people in the organization are somehow under the control of the gardener and that they can be changed in the way that the gardener wants to change them. The increasingly common use of the term 'human resources' for people is very revealing in this context. It implicitly labels people as things to be used or acted on, instead of treating them as collaborators in the process.

The spatial metaphor, akin to Gouldner's (1957) geometric metaphor, deals with the space within which this action takes place. One talks about vertical moves, lateral moves, broad responsibilities, narrow experience, moving to the centre or to the periphery, reaching one's level of incompetence, high-flyers and so on. The reason for this is obvious. Organizations are such complex entities that it is hard to avoid using devices such as the organization chart to represent them. The chart then becomes the map across which people move, and we have a helpful and convenient conceptual framework for a language of career.

A spatial language naturally lends itself to graphical representation, with the dimensions of the picture coming from the metaphors in use. Four main dimensions tend to be used:

1   organizational level;
2   organizational activity such as business function or business division;
3   centrality to the source of power in the organization;
4   time.

There are many examples of how these dimensions can be used. One can visualize a cone in which the vertical dimension is organizational level, functional activities are shown as sectors of the horizontal circular slices and centrality to power is represented by closeness to the central vertical axis (Schein, 1971). Organizational level can be plotted against time, which makes a useful teaching tool to help managers understand what has happened to them over their careers (Thomas, 1981). Level can be plotted against 'occupational field', in order to show how the content of each succeeding job relates to its predecessor (Watts, 1981). Matrices of transition probabilities between posts in the firm have been suggested as well (Milkovich, Anderson and Greenhalgh, 1976).

There are, of course, other ways of viewing transitions from post to post, in particular approaches focusing on the effects of the change on the individual. One way of looking at this is to distinguish between the extent to which individuals experience personal development from the transition, and the extent to which they develop the role they move into (Nicholson, 1984). Another is to assess transitions from the point of view of the number and intensity of the changes involved (Hall, 1979). The list of possible changes includes, in increasing order of intensity, change of job alone, of organizational level, function, occupation and occupational field (for instance from engineering to management). The magnitude of the transition is a function of both the number and intensity of the changes it involves. This scheme has been used to study career coping strategies (Latack, 1984).

A further distinction can be drawn between inter-role transitions, when a new and different role is actually taken, and intra-role transitions, when a new and different orientation is taken to an old role (Louis, 1980a: 332). Transitions also vary in the extent to which people experience surprise at and make sense of their new and unfamiliar settings (Louis, 1980b).

The spatial metaphor is a direct and useful starting-point for mapping careers, and I shall use it here. But it is important to choose the dimensions of the 'space' carefully. As we have seen (chapter 2), dimensions such as 'business function' and 'managerial level' are potentially misleading because organizational structures vary so much from one firm to the next. The work that goes on in a particular function can be quite different in different firms. Similarly, comparing levels between firms is such a complex matter that an entire industry, job evaluation, has built up around the problem. Selecting these two dimensions could make it extremely difficult to compare career patterns in different organizations, or even to draw maps for people who have changed companies. A bad choice of dimensions, then, could hide the patterns we are looking for.

So far I have done little more than point out how hard it can be to map careers. The time has come to take a more positive line and to explain my approach, which involves mapping individuals' work experience.

MAPPING EXPERIENCE

Why experience maps?

In part II the concept of organizational career logics was anchored to organizational structure and the way it develops. The metaphor of a climbing-frame brings this out by focusing on the simple image of a structure which gives shape to the paths of the people moving over it. Moreover in chapter 5 I argued that work role transitions are the distinguishing feature of organizational careers. It follows from this that a mapping technique for individual careers which is sensitive to different kinds of career logic should have two features. It should map (a) transitions between posts, against the background of (b) the division of labour in the organization.

The information the maps are drawn from can only really come from one source, the managers themselves. As there are no universal rules governing functional divisions in organizations, we cannot infer much from just listing the names of the departments in which managers have worked. There is no substitute for asking managers to explain in some detail what they did in each post over the course of their careers. Happily, most people enjoy doing this: telling your life story to a stranger can be quite a therapeutic experience. And it can also be fun for the researcher. Certainly my own experience of collecting well over a hundred detailed career histories suggests that there is hardly ever such a thing as a dull biography. Even one which superficially looks dull has its fascination. There are usually reasons explaining why things turned out as they did, often quite unconnected with work, which make an intriguing story in themselves.

The upshot of this biography-collecting process is a collection of stories which detail the managers' work experience. The stories are much more than bald accounts of the functions someone worked in. Let us take an example, a manager who, when I met him, was in charge of the Treasury function of the multinational manufacturing group Cemco. The kind of 'bald account' which could be obtained from a postal questionnaire or résumé might describe his first three posts as follows.

Post 1: training as a public accountant, Hepplethwaite & Co.
Post 2: accountancy trainee with Supersuds Inc.
Post 3: accounts department, Cemco Plc.

This looks like a fairly conventional beginning to a career, and in many ways it was. It suggests that he spent his second and third posts using his training as an accountant and − in some unspecified way − broadening his experience. There is something of a question-mark hanging over his move from Supersuds to Cemco, but nothing of any great interest apart from that. It sounds like the beginnings of building within a command-centred career, moving from post to post, where each post was similar to the previous one but more demanding. But we really do not have enough information to be sure.

Let us now look at a summary of the way he described these moves in the interview.

The manager trained as a clerk in a small local chartered accountancy firm in the north of England (Hepplethwaite & Co.) and then, when qualified, joined a multinational detergents group (Supersuds Inc.). For eleven months he went through a further training programme. He spent time at a factory location, then in the Head Office central costing department and finally in the forecasting department examining short-term profit and costings for industrial products. By now he was bored stiff, so he moved to Cemco Plc, where his first post was a Headquarters job consolidating Group accounts and reporting on operational results of the Group's subsidiaries.

This story is, of course, itself incomplete. Even so, the picture emerging is not quite what it appeared from the résumé list we first saw. For instance the move to Supersuds looks much more like a false start to a career, an unfortunately typical experience of a company training programme. Management development managers are commonly very proud of this kind of programme, but it was usually remembered by the managers I interviewed with emotions ranging from boredom to loathing. The Supersuds post involved quite different work from that which he would have come across in Hepplethwaites, which would have involved mainly personal and small company taxation work and auditing. His move to Cemco was clearly a searching one, not a building one. Although superficially his first post with Cemco probably used skills he had learned as a trainee with Hepplethwaites, it is likely that most of this would have been picked up from course textbooks. Consolidating the accounts of multinational groups is a world away from the kind of business that small local accountancy firms deal with.

There are still questions we would like to ask. For instance, what kind of operational reporting systems did he use at Cemco? Did Cemco use simple financial accounting techniques of the kind with which he was familiar from Hepplethwaites, or was this his first experience of some more sophisticated methods? Did he really leave Supersuds because he was bored, or was there more to it than that? Was he, for instance, incompetent?

However much is learnt of someone's biography there is always more that stays hidden, but we have to stop asking questions at some stage. The interview data which I summarized are much richer than the résumé account from which we started and are quite enough to be getting on with.

This, then, is an example of what I mean by mapping managers' experience. To the extent that the maps come from accounts of the sequence of jobs managers have held they are maps of their objective careers (chapter 5). To the extent that they are coloured by the way the managers tell their stories the maps will also have an element of subjectivity about them.

Work experience is complex to analyse, and I shall distinguish between two aspects, experience of 'locations' and of 'activities'. These resemble the concepts of 'functional' and 'institutional' specialization used in a study of how the career specialization of American chief executives relates to that of their successors (Smith and White, 1987).

Kinds of experience: location and activity

The unit of measurement I shall use to analyse the experience managers get from each succeeding post is the *element of experience*. Table 6.1 illustrates this by comparing two posts which have followed each other in a manager's career. Suppose each post can be thought of as involving responsibility for a number of different tasks. Tasks 1, 3 and 4 are unique to their particular post, while task 2 is common to both. The boundary is fuzzy: in some respects post B involved a break with the past, and in some respects it did not.

Table 6.1 glosses over a number of points, not the least of which is the question of who are involved in tasks 1−4. Take the example of a production manager in charge of a factory making engineering components: there are at least three ways in which we can look at the task experience he is getting in the post. The relevant experience could be manufacturing engineering components, or managing people manufacturing engineering components, or managing people, who just happen to be manufacturing engineering components.

Each way of looking at the post involves a successively higher level of generality concerning the nature of the manager's work. In other words, each takes a step closer to the view that the work of the manager is the process of managing, which is in turn one step closer to the general proposition that managerial work is the same, no matter where it is done. As we have seen, there is considerable and growing scepticism on the part of a great many writers about the idea that managing, or at least managing when it is being done well, could ever be described like this. The other extreme, which is to say that the

Table 6.1

Post A	⟶	Post B
Task 1		
Task 2		Task 2
Task 3		
		Task 4

manager's post is manufacturing engineering components, misses out anything to do with the managerial role altogether. It is highly unlikely that he actually makes any components himself, and it is quite possible that he only understands in principle how it is done.

I shall try to take the middle course as far as possible. This is to say that our production manager is getting experience of managing people making engineering components. This allows us to record two things: (1) what was unique about the factory, and (2) the fact that his responsibilities involved managing people making components rather than making them himself. The finer points about the extent to which he involved himself in the manufacturing process are left out of the description simply because we would have had to watch him managing in order to include them.

The next step is to be more analytical about the type of experience that the manager is getting. We have to find a way of describing this with enough simplicity for us to compare one post with another over the course of a career using data from interviews with busy managers.

So far I have used the word 'task' in a rather vague way to denote elements of managers' posts which can be described in isolation from other elements. Of course, managers do not necessarily think of, or work on, one task wholly in isolation from all the others for which they are responsible. So once again we have to take the middle course, avoiding a number of dangers as best we can. For instance, we must ensure that we do not miss too much of the *gestalt*, the overall shape, of the post. We must also avoid becoming spuriously precise, producing measures so sophisticated that they are impossible to use or, worse still, cease to make any kind of sense at all.

I distinguish between two features of managers' posts: the experience they get of the *locations* at which each post is carried out, and the experience they get of the *activities* each post involves. Very broadly, by locations I mean the features which are specific to a particular post, and by activities I mean the features which can be generalized across different posts.

In other words each of the managers' tasks is broken down analytically into a particular activity carried out at a particular location. For example, the career of a particular textile production manager had followed a classic command-centred logic. At the time I met him he was responsible for production and sales planning across a group of plants which processed a particular man-made fibre. The locations for which he was responsible, then, were the plants. The activities for which he was responsible, using the simple schema I outlined above, were production management and sales planning management.

Locations Anyone who has studied managers' jobs or careers in any detail − by which I mean in more detail than is usually possible in a

Table 6.2

Post	Firm	Product group
1	A	X
2	B	Y
3	B	Z
4	B	Y, Z

postal questionnaire − knows how hard it is to generalize about managers' posts. The concept of location is an attempt to address this side of things directly by identifying the unique features of one manager's post which distinguish it from other managers' posts.

Posts are obviously marked out by their physical location, for instance the factory(ies) or office site(s) the manager is responsible for. But physical location is only one way in which managers' posts differ. The concept of location as I use it here is more general than just geographic. By location I mean all the features of a post which are unique to it. These features include each specific physical location, organization or part of one, role set, product, process and market that the managers deal with in the course of their work. A simple example might clarify this.

Table 6.2 shows a marketing manager who has passed through four jobs. In post 1 he worked for firm A, marketing product group X. He then changed firms to B to market product group Y. Next, his boss moved him to product group Z, and finally he was promoted within firm B to be in charge of product groups Y and Z.

The first three posts each involved responsibility for a single location, while post 4 involved responsibility for two locations. The advantage of describing his career in this way is that we can see the extent to which his experience was carried forward through his career.

His first post move was quite a break. The two jobs had nothing in common other than the activity, marketing, which may or may not be done similarly in the two firms. If the two firms were in the same industry, the chances are that the activities were fairly similar. His second move also involved novelty, since new products could mean dealing with a new group of colleagues in the firm, new customers, new technical concepts and so on. On the other hand his third move to post 4 had a good deal of the familiar about it. The novelty will probably have been to do with the managerial role itself. He was more senior, with broader responsibilities and probably less need to get into detail.

This example shows why I have used such a broad definition of location. Changes of product, of physical location or of company are all different from each other. What is less obvious is how they differ. Ideally, it would be useful to be able to develop categories for each kind of change of location. But in order to do this adequately we would need a robust theoretical framework for managerial work of the kind that does not exist yet, as well as an enormous amount of information about each post in the manager's career. We would next face the problem of how to account for changes over time in, for instance, personnel and organizational structure. There seems a severe danger of over-sophistication in this process. It is important to remember why we are interested in describing locations and activities in the first place. It is in order to map a manager's experience in a way which we can relate to the career logics model of part II, and this provides the criterion for deciding how much detail to go into. I can illustrate this point by considering a particular kind of transition, namely that of change of employer.

Employer changes are clearly thought of by many writers as qualitatively different from other aspects of job change. 'Number of employers' is the one statistic that tends to be common to most studies of managerial careers, sometimes to the extent of being the only statistic used. Obviously there is a practical reason for this. It is an easy question to ask, which is an important point especially when the researcher is limited to a postal questionnaire.

An example of the difficulties in interpretation is given by a manager who worked for a small firm which was bought by the British General Electric Company (GEC), which closed it. He naturally left and joined another firm, where exactly the same thing happened again. Apart from feeling somewhat haunted by GEC, the manager faces a problem when a researcher asks him the deceptively bland question: 'how many times have you changed employer?'. There is a problem of definition: which employer changes are we interested in and which not?

I think that it is necessary to keep an open mind on the question of the primacy of employer changes in analysing careers. For one thing, in countries such as the UK or the USA which have highly efficient secondary capital markets there is a great deal of involuntary employer changing that goes on as companies are bought and sold. Although top management turnover commonly rises after a takeover (Walsh, 1988) this is by no means necessarily true of everyone else in the target company. Indeed, it is a common criticism of acquisitive firms that they tend to buy companies and leave it at that. Quite often, by contrast with the GEC manager whom I have just used as an example, the managers I met in my own study seem hardly to have noticed changes of employer.

There are a number of reasons for arguing that we should at least identify employer changes made by the managers themselves. One reason might be that a change of firm is likely to involve more novelty than if the move had been within a firm. Another might be that the change of post is much more likely to have come about as the result of an autonomous, searching logic decision (chapter 5) by the managers themselves.

It is quite impossible to predict the amount of change associated with a change of employer. It is necessary to look at specific examples. People might change employers to find everything new and unfamiliar. Alternatively they might move into quite familiar surroundings either because they had been dealing with their new employer for some years previously or because their previous post had brought them into contact with their opposite numbers elsewhere. On the other hand an internal move can involve a lot of change (Louis, 1980a). It might involve being transferred to another part of the same firm which is in another country, in another market and which in many ways might be a different firm. Alternatively it could simply mean being relocated across the corridor where hardly anything has changed except the sign on the door.

Furthermore, we should not necessarily assume that decisions to change employer are taken by managers themselves whereas internal moves happen at the behest of the firm. Often, the idea of changing firms never occurs to people until they are surreptitiously made an attractive offer by a competitor or a head-hunter. How different is that, in terms of the exercise of initiative, from the case of someone offered the chance of a move within his or her firm which he or she is at liberty to turn down? It can also happen that managers are forced to leave their employer against their will and take the only post they can find elsewhere in a subsisting move. This involves about as much exercise of free will as if they had been given the choice of being moved to a different post within the firm or being fired, as happened to at least one manager in my study.

These practical points raise the spectre of distinctions without differences, something that stalks any attempt to classify changes in managers' posts, however it is done. Instead of getting tangled up in the issues we could take a simpler line. This is to avoid distinguishing between types of change, merely saying that change has taken place. Later, when we come to compare managers' career maps, if we need to get more information about the logic shaping the moves we can revert to the stories they told to see what the significance was of different kinds of post changes. This is the broad approach I have taken. But we can refine the mapping technique a bit more than this. It would be an advantage if we could find some way of looking at the similarities and differences between locations. The concept of activity provides just such a means.

Activities   Take two mechanical engineers, A and B, both of whom change posts. Let us suppose that A changes locations to a new project but carries on doing much the same kind of design work that he was doing before. B, however, not only changes locations but also becomes a sales engineer in the new post. On the face of it, A's posts before and after his move have more in common with each other than do B's. Both transitions involve a change of location, but while A's does not involve a change of activity, B's does.

Activities are to do with practising task-focused skills. They can be defined along three dimensions: (a) standardization of tasks, (b) certi-fication of practitioners and (c) degree of specialization (I am indebted to Richard Whitley for this classification of skill).

The first dimension, task standardization, concerns the extent to which the activity is carried out in broadly the same way in any setting (location). The more it is, the more the occupation can be thought of as a 'quasi-profession'. I use the prefix 'quasi-' to try to avoid the noise surrounding the label 'profession', which in Anglo-Saxon societies at least usually implies many other characteristics of an occupational group, such as the way it is organized, controls entry and exerts monopoly power (Saks, 1983), in which I am not interested here. The more an occupation can be thought of as a quasi-profession, the easier it is to identify the activities it involves. It is also likely that people will tend to move between posts involving the same quasi-professional activity.

The second dimension, certification of practitioners, is only relevant to the extent that it helps us understand which kinds of experience can be combined with which in a single career. In the life insurance business, for instance, the duties of an actuary in the UK are defined by statute and cannot be carried out by an unlicensed person. This obviously affects the shape of careers in life insurance companies, in particular the careers of the actuaries themselves.

The third dimension, degree of specialization, is in a sense a softer form of the second dimension. It defines some posts as comparatively inaccessible because of the specialized knowledge they need. The more specialized an activity, the less accessible it will become to laymen, and, other things being equal, the harder people who are trained in it will find it to get a different job.

In their most obvious form, activities are what professionals or quasi-professionals do in the practice of their (quasi-)profession. In other kinds of jobs one cannot by definition be as positive about identifying the kind of activity(ies) involved. For practical purposes it may well be best to avoid being over-purist about the theoretical problem. For instance, marketing may or may not be a quasi-profession within my definition, but it may well be reasonable for the purposes of a particular study to assume, at least until some evidence is found to overturn the conclusion, that different marketing activities resemble each other more than they do human resource jobs.

The approach I take here is to work as far as possible from the managers' accounts of their careers. Suppose, for instance, that in table 6.1 we had listed activities instead of tasks. The kind of transition the manager might have made going between the two jobs would be described in terms of the way he or she talked about the activities 1–4. Activity 2 is common to both jobs because it was described as a common element, while activity 4 is new to him or her because he or she felt it to be new. This means that we have to collect a fair amount of detailed information about each post, so as to be able to gauge the effect of the way firms are organized on their managers' career patterns.

In practical terms we might operate as follows. Take manager Y who, in a short career, has marketed sheeting for firm A and then moved to market biscuits for firm B. The two jobs are both similar and different. They are similar to the extent that she was working on the same activity, and different because she was at different locations. The justification rests largely on the way the labour market seems to work: it is quite possible for firm B to have recruited her as 'a marketing specialist'.

The analysis of similarities and differences can carry on to whatever depth that is necessary. For instance, it might turn out on further enquiry that manager Y's first post had entailed market forecasting and brand management, while the second involved all this as well as sales force management. If we were studying the careers of marketing managers it could be important to go into this level of detail. In a more general study, it may not. All classifications are subordinate to a purpose, and provided one is clear about the purpose it does not prove to be too difficult to decide how far to pursue the analysis of activities. The only danger in going into unnecessarily fine detail is that the patterns may become obscured by noise, a problem which can occur with the use of any instrument.

Relationship between activities and locations

The formal definitions I have given of activities and locations – activities as the generalizable features of a post, locations as the specific features – suggest superficially that the two dimensions are mutually independent (orthogonal). Because of the way in which activities are defined there are limits to the extent to which this is the case. This has both theoretical and practical implications.

Table 6.3(a) shows a post with two activities and two locations. Activity 1 is carried out in both locations, while activity 2 is carried out only at location 2. We can also draw it as a matrix of activities and locations with a Y if that activity is carried out at that location and an N if it is not (table 6.3(b)). It certainly seems as if the two dimensions are orthogonal. Whether each cell in the matrix has a Y or an N in it

Table 6.3

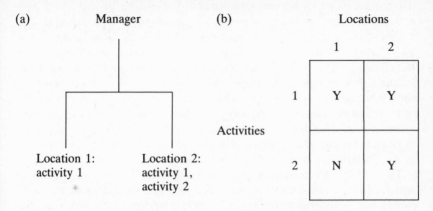

(a)   Manager   (b)   Locations

Location 1: activity 1   Location 2: activity 1, activity 2

Activities

	1	2
1	Y	Y
2	N	Y

depends only on the answer to an empirical question: is that activity carried out at that location?

There are good grounds for expecting the two variables to be correlated, because certain kinds of activity are more likely to be carried out in one kind of location than in others. For instance production management is more likely to be carried out in a factory than it is in a design office. We are not really dealing with two independent measures, since geographical locations are frequently described at least in part in terms of the activities that are carried out there. This becomes obvious as soon as one thinks of examples of how geographical locations might be described in practice, for instance 'domestic sales department', 'factory Y', 'corporate planning group' and so on. Each refers not only to whatever it is that makes the post unique – domestic sales as opposed to Latin American sales, factory Y as opposed to factory Z – but also to the main activity that goes on in the group. The two dimensions can only be formally orthogonal in an organization where activities and roles are completely distinct. This condition might be approached at general management levels, particularly in smaller firms, where people are in charge of a broad range of business functions. In large organizations it is highly unlikely to be found.

There are two main practical consequences of these theoretical considerations. Firstly, we can expect to be faced with tricky decisions from time to time when coding managers' jobs. Secondly, there will be some career patterns which we do not expect to encounter. The practical problems come from the way in which the distinction between generalizable and specific features of a post is to some extent arbitrary. There will always be cases in which doubt exists about whether a move to a new post involves a change in locations only or a change in both locations and activities.

An example of a 'forbidden' career pattern may help to underline the nature of the theoretical problem. It is easy to picture the career pattern of, for instance, a technical professional who stays in one activity for a lifetime but moves at regular intervals between locations. This pattern is so common as to have its own label, 'cosmopolitan' (Gouldner, 1957; 1958). The converse pattern, staying in the same location but regularly changing activities, is much harder to imagine simply because of the way in which I have defined locations. Examples of this kind of transition were very rare in my study, but one concerned a young man who, after a few years as a training officer for a particular group of people, was promoted to be personnel officer for the same group. Normally, a change of activity implies a change of location.

To sum up, the non-orthogonality of the two dimensions (activities and locations) influences the way that one can use them in analysing career data. Patterns which seem to show correlations between the two variables activity and location have to be treated with caution, since one has to exclude the possibility that the pattern is an artefact of the way the variables were defined. So although I shall look at the activity and location dimensions separately I shall also make considerable use of other, derived, dimensions which use them in combination. I shall describe these derived dimensions in chapter 7, where I show how location and activity experience can be used to map and analyse careers.

It is quite possible even at this stage to see the connection between the mapping technique and the different career logics I described in part II. In the final section of this chapter I shall quickly preview some of these connections.

USING DIMENSIONS OF EXPERIENCE: A PREVIEW

We are mapping work experience in order to trace managers' routes across their climbing-frames. The use of the metaphor 'climbing-frame' is a little misleading. It suggests that there is a concrete object which remains in the absence of the people moving over it, but of course this is working the metaphor too hard. Strip away the people, and the organization vanishes. Organizations can be pictured in many different ways (Morgan, 1986) and career patterns give us information about the way people move through them which potentially can add to other data we have. In particular, they can tell us a great deal about how the skills and expertise that are used in different parts of the firm fit together.

Ordinary accounts of organizations are on the whole static. A career perspective is dynamic by definition, because it is about seeing people moving through the organization over the course of their working lives. So the career-mapping technique gives us another way of looking at organizational form. We can see already that certain features of organizational career logics ought to be revealed in particular kinds of work role transition. Constructional logics involve putting a variety of experiences together. We expect to find in organizations with such logics managers who have had experience of a great variety of different activities and locations. Command-centred logics, by contrast, are about doing the same kind of thing (similar activities) in a variety of different settings (locations). Evolutionary logics are a matter of responsibility for a steadily widening set of activities in a steadily widening set of locations. Finally, turnaround logics are probably the least patterned of all, involving a sequence of widely differing activities in widely differing locations.

The activity−location framework for mapping work experience also has the potential for predicting the kind of expertise developed by managers moving over different organizational climbing-frames. It suggests that different frames develop their own characteristic kind of manager, which in turn implies that managerial labour markets might be segmented in ways which hitherto have not been obvious. Experience of particular locations is clearly linked with task and with knowledge of particular organizations or industries and knowledge of what the firm does and how it works, whom to go to to get cooperation and whom to avoid, whom it deals with, who its competitors are and so forth. Experience of particular activities is more closely associated with skills involving the technology of management.

It follows from this that it should be possible to draw inferences about the kind of managers developed by different career logics, knowing something about the patterns of work experience revealed by the experience-mapping technique. I return to this point in chapter 9.

SUMMARY

We need a way of looking for the effects on managers' careers of different organizational and individual career logics. Careers are elusive things to map, which is clearly why there are so many ways of viewing them. The distinction is sometimes drawn between the so-called objective and subjective careers, where the objective career is the series of jobs and posts individuals move through and the subjective career is the way they develop as this is going on. The mapping technique I use in this book has elements of both. In metaphorical terms people are seen as moving through organizational space over the course of their careers, where the space is the organization(s) they work for, that is, the climbing-frame(s).

We cannot draw a map of someone's route across their climbing-frame without having a map of the frame itself. But the problem with organizations is that there is no one standardized way of organizing. Just listing the labels of the rungs the managers have moved over does not say much about what happened on each rung. We have to know what the managers did on each rung, that is, in each post. In other words, we need to map their work experience over time.

Experience is a multi-faceted concept. I distinguished between two partially orthogonal aspects which I called experience of different locations and of different activities. Location describes the features of managers' tasks that are specific to a particular post, not only the geographical ones. Activity describes the features which can be generalized across different posts. Managers' work experience in a particular post can be described as experience of certain activities carried out at certain locations.

Turning this round, we see that mapping managers' work experience potentially can tell us a great deal about the kind of firms they work in. To the extent that the maps reveal firms' underlying organizational career logics they reveal something of the firms' structures and the way in which they have developed. In addition, each dimension of experience has implications for the kind of expertise the managers themselves are developing and for the kind of managers they turn out to be.

7
Experience Mapping in Practice

INTRODUCTION

In chapter 6 I introduced two dimensions of experience — location and activity — which can be used to map managers' career paths over time. We now need to consider how the maps might be drawn.

For many purposes all that is needed is a way of depicting a manager's career so that it can be compared with other managers' careers. For instance, I shall give a number of examples of these maps to show how varied the careers were of the managers in my study and to form a bridge to part IV of the book. If people can draw maps of their own careers, it may help them to make sense of what has happened to them and what the possibilities are for their future.

But we need to take the analysis at least one stage further. The organizational career logics framework predicts that managers have career patterns which are characteristic of the kind of firm they have worked in. We therefore have to find ways of extracting information from the maps so that we can compare the careers of groups of managers from different organizations. This means classifying and coding the features of the maps which distinguish them from other managers' maps.

As we saw in chapter 6, experience mapping allows us to differentiate between the kinds of work role transition expected in different organizational career logics. There are two ways in which we can use the dimensions of location and activity to classify work role transitions.

At the simplest level, we can classify the transitions themselves, ignoring the time at which they happened in each manager's career. We can then compare the distribution of different kinds of transition in different organizations, to see whether they fit the predictions of the career logics model.

Next, we can introduce the dimension of time. A transition which happens at the beginning of an individual's career may have a different meaning for the individual from the same kind of transition happening late in his or her career. We also may wish to differentiate between transitions which happen in quick succession and those which are much more spread out over time. In this way we can begin to build a picture of careers as patterns of transitions, rather than just counting the total number of different kinds of transition that each manager has experienced.

There are, of course, many ways in which each of these steps can be taken. My primary aim is to describe one approach in enough detail so that I can show how experience mapping can be used to distinguish between the effects of different organizational and individual career logics. In so doing, I will have said enough for readers to be able to adapt the technique for their own purposes.

EXPERIENCE MAPS

In order to see how one might draw a map of the experience managers have gathered during the course of their career, let us return to the manager's post shown in table 7.1(b), which is reproduced for convenience from table 6.3(b). This matrix is simply another way of showing the responsibilities of the post shown in table 7.1(a), which can be separated into two locations and two activities. If one post can be represented by a two-dimensional matrix of this kind it follows that a series of posts can be represented by a series of matrices. The problem we face is finding a way of comparing these matrices with each other. If we can, we will have in principle a way of representing the pattern of the manager's career.

We can do this formally by deriving a series of conversion matrices

Table 7.1

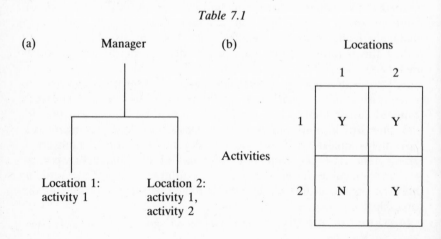

to describe how the matrices of successive pairs of posts relate to each other. All one has to do is rewrite the matrices of the kind shown in table 7.1(b) with the cells occupied by 1 for Y and 0 for N. The conversion matrix describing the way the post is transformed into the next one is a second matrix of 1s and 0s which, when added to the matrix for the first post, yields the matrix for the second. In this way, each transition from post to post is represented by a conversion matrix.

The conversion matrix approach is appealing because it suggests that it might be possible in principle to derive a framework which has the potential to predict managers' next moves, given the kind of moves they have made in the past. But this is less easy than it looks. One difficulty is the limited number of data points which may be available from which to predict. For instance, the greatest number of posts any manager had been through in my own study was sixteen, and they had usually been through many fewer than this. Secondly, the technique would have to be able to cope with discontinuities of many kinds, such as when someone changes to a 'second career'. Moreover there is every reason to expect to find, as indeed was the case, a very complex set of transitions as managers move from company to company, their companies are reorganized or acquired, they move through different career stages and so forth. The mathematics of data series such as these in which both trends and discontinuities can be expected in a small number of data points would be extremely hard to handle.

For these reasons I shall stick to simple graphical ways of relating one activity matrix to another which, although direct descendants of conversion matrices, take advantage of the eye's ability to pick out patterns which are very hard to characterize analytically.

In principle the problem is one of analysing patterns in three dimensions: activity, location and time. Figure 7.1(a) shows someone whose first post involved working on activity 1 in location 1, who then moved to post 2 where he or she worked on activities 1 and 2 in location 2.

It would be a good deal simpler to show this as a pair of two-dimensional maps, one for activities and the other for locations (figure 7.1(b)). In this way we can deal separately with the two aspects of the manager's career, so long as we remember that this is an artificial distinction made for analytical convenience. The benefit of dealing with them separately is more evident if we look at a number of examples.

Figure 7.2 shows the map of what must be the simplest career case one might expect to find. It is, in fact, that of a manager from my study who joined his family textile firm after leaving school. The break in the activity and location lines indicates the point at which he formally became managing director six years after starting work. He has run it ever since in much the same way despite its having been acquired by two successively larger firms. During his career he has been involved in

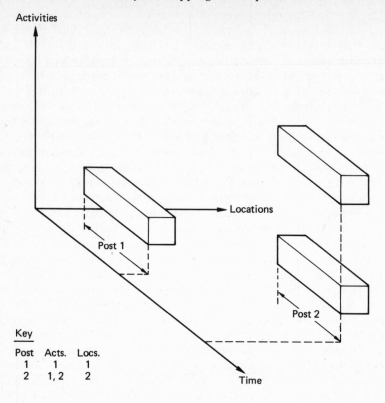

Key

Post	Acts.	Locs.
1	1	1
2	1, 2	2

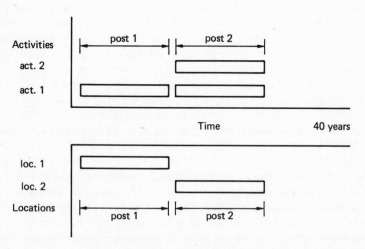

Figure 7.1   (a) Three-dimensional experience map (idealized)
(b) Map (a), drawn as two two-dimensional maps

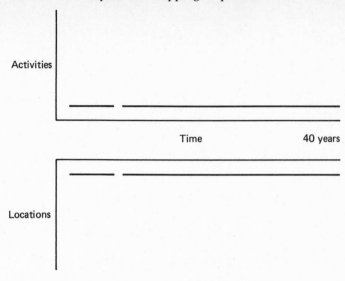

Figure 7.2   Experience map − specialist

one activity, running the business (the top half of the map), at the same location (the bottom half). Although during his early years he was not in overall charge of the business, he apparently worked in all parts of it and, presumably, since it was not large, he did not differentiate between different aspects of his experience at that time.

This picture is of someone who is probably about as much a specialist as anyone is likely to be. His lifelong experience has been with one set of activities in one location. Of course, things must have changed in the firm and with its customers and suppliers since he started work. The firm was a great deal larger, for one thing. But the map shows very clearly a pattern of continuity which contrasts strikingly with other patterns one might expect to find. I shall illustrate this with some idealized examples.

The career of a generalist who has held seven different kinds of job over the course of his career might appear as shown in figure 7.3. Every time this manager has changed posts, he has moved to a new activity and a new location.

This generalist career is characterized by its overall pattern of similar kinds of transition. This is also the case for the cosmopolitan (Gouldner, 1957; 1958) shown in figure 7.4. Here, the seven posts have each involved the manager practising the same activity, but each time in a different location. For instance, he might be a professional engineer or an accountant who has worked for a variety of different companies.

Similarly, the 'pyramid-climber' shown in figure 7.5 has had a career marked by similar kinds of transition. Each new post has involved new

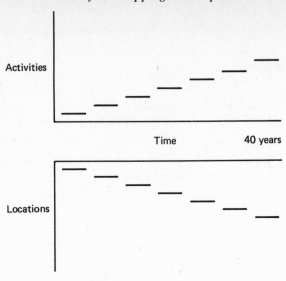

Figure 7.3   Idealized experience map − generalist

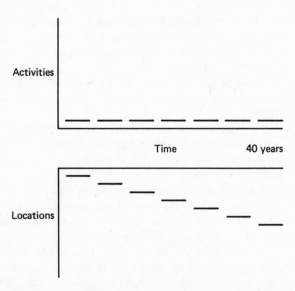

Figure 7.4   Idealized experience map − cosmopolitan

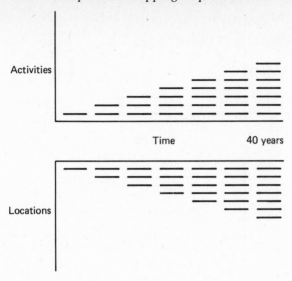

Figure 7.5   Idealized experience map – pyramid-climber

responsibilities on top of those which she already had. This might happen if she had been steadily promoted up a given hierarchy. In practice, of course, the rate of accumulation of responsibilities will not be linear, because the higher someone is in their hierarchy, the bigger each additional responsibility tends to be. For instance a junior production manager might be promoted to run two plants instead of one, while later she might be promoted from factory manager to production director, responsible for many different manufacturing sites around the world.

The 'second-careerist' (figure 7.6) is an example of someone in whose map one particular transition stands out. The first four posts involved pyramid-climbing of the kind shown in figure 7.5, but then he moved to something entirely new where all the locations and the activities were unfamiliar. The 'second career' covered the last three posts, during which the pyramid-climbing started again. Had we seen the map just before the change, we would have classified the manager as a classic 'pyramid-climber'. Again, if the transition had been near the beginning of the manager's working life and he had carried on for long enough in his second career, we might guess that this was just some kind of early-career transitional period of the kind that developmental career models (chapter 5) describe, and that he was indeed a pyramid-climber.

I have called the person whose career is shown in figure 7.2 a specialist and the person whose career is shown in figure 7.3 a generalist,

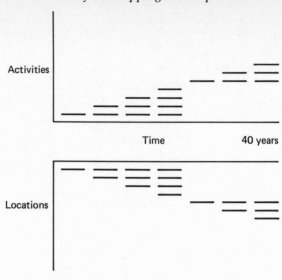

Figure 7.6   Idealized experience map − second-careerist

yet there is nothing in principle to stop specialists in one post becoming generalists in their next one. For example, this would have been the case if the specialist manager had gone to work for another company a year or so before I met him. Equally, had the second-careerist (figure 7.6) made the change to the new environment just before the map was drawn, he, too, would have appeared as a generalist in his current post.

Potentially, then, we can expect experience maps to fall into at least two classes: those in which the outstanding feature is the general trend of transition, and those dominated by a single break in the general trend. Real location−activity maps are, of course, much richer in detail. Any post can involve quite a number of different locations and activities, and each location or activity may or may not be common to both posts, so that there are very many possible types of transition. On top of this, each sequence of transitions is unique to the manager in question, who may have changed career logics − organizational and individual − more than once. This adds up to a lot of potential complexity, and figure 7.7, a selection of career maps from managers in my study, shows some examples. The broken lines designate posts in which the individual was not really a manager, which is why they tend to occur in early career, and the horizontal axes are marked in decades. Briefly, the maps describe the following careers.

1   This manager (figure 7.7(a)), a generalist from the chemical firm Norchem, has built within a constructional logic, changing activities

and locations steadily and at two points (A and B on the map) beginning to broaden his responsibilities for locations before making yet another change.

2 This manager (figure 7.7(b)), another Norchem generalist whom we first met in chapter 5, at one point began consolidating his position by reverting to a previous location (A) but with broader responsibilities for activities (B). His final move (C) was a subsisting one, forced on him by ill-health, and involved yet another complete change.

3 This manager (figure 7.7(c)), from the construction and engineering materials firm Cemco, started in production management in another firm, then moved (A) to research, changing employers twice (B,C) in the process. Later (D) he reverted to production management and latterly was broadening his responsibilities in that area (E).

4 This manager (figure 7.7(d)) has spent his life in textiles, mainly in the kind of technology used in the textile firm Prestex in which I met him, but with brief excursions (A−C) to other related processes. His location map reflects the fact that he has worked for ten different employers, in thirteen different locations, in six different countries.

5 Starting as an accountant with a large manufacturing firm, this manager (figure 7.7(e)) gradually built up his responsibilities before joining Prestex (A) still as an accountant. Four years before I met him he was made deputy mill group manager, a production job (B).

6 This manager (figure 7.7(f)) has spent his career with the electrical engineering and electronics company International Systems Engineering (ISE), first designing and selling large capital equipment and then gaining some broadening experience elsewhere in the same division (A). ISE was hit by a major crisis which had its roots in the capital products he had originally worked on, and the crisis saw him broadening his responsibilities to a different product range (B). Most recently, in a sequence of rapid changes, he acquired several other of the operating company's newly acquired businesses (C,D).

The maps give a vivid picture of the richness of managerial careers and are useful as diagnostic and developmental devices in a similar way to Thomas's (1981) 'career graph'. Managers find drawing their own maps an enlightening experience, simply because the maps capture, on a single sheet of paper, patterns which are not easily seen in the conventional listing of jobs one tends to give when asked for an account of one's working life. The maps can be embellished in all kinds of ways. One can show for instance employer changes, promotions and geographical moves by adding detail to the basic outline.

But the maps also give an idea of the data reduction problem one faces when trying to move beyond the level of simple description. This

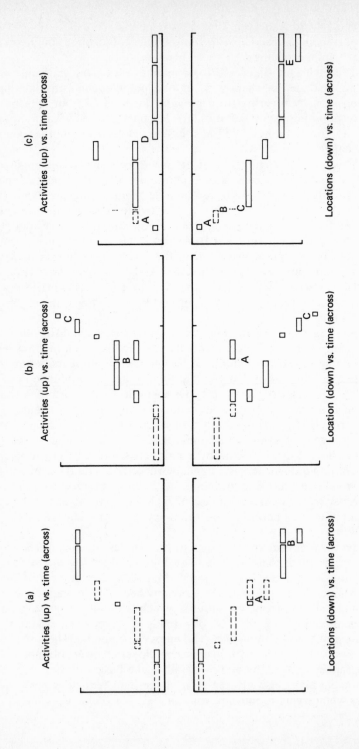

(a)

Activities (up) vs. time (across)

Locations (down) vs. time (across)

(b)

Activities (up) vs. time (across)

Location (down) vs. time (across)

(c)

Activities (up) vs. time (across)

Locations (down) vs. time (across)

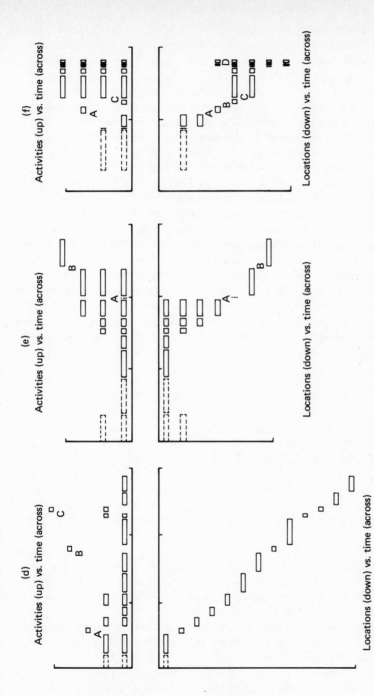

Figure 7.7 Experience maps of six managers from the study

happens when one needs to classify the maps into career types, or, as we shall have to in the present study, to aggregate data from many maps to look, for instance, for systematic similarities and differences between managers from different organizations. If we set out to analyse location—activity maps, taking as the unit of analysis the overall pattern of work role transitions throughout managers' careers, we are assuming that there is a reason to expect overall patterns. We may well find this, and, as I hinted in chapter 6, the career logics model predicts it. But we cannot test the theoretical prediction that patterns will be found by using a mapping technique which assumes that they are there.

We have to find a way, therefore, of extracting information from the maps which we can examine to see whether there is any evidence for the existence of the patterns we are looking for. There are many ways in which this could be done. We could, for instance, abandon the maps and adopt a strictly analytical approach based on the idea that length of experience relates to expertise (McEnrue, 1988), measuring indices such as managers' degree of specialization and how this changes over their careers (Gunz, 1986). The method I outline in the next section makes fewer assumptions and is more direct. It is a means of classifying work role transitions to one of a limited number of types, where each type can be related to the kind of move different careers logic might generate.

CLASSIFYING WORK ROLE TRANSITIONS

In this section I describe the five-way classification of work role transitions which I shall be using to differentiate between the effects of different career logics. Its detailed derivation is not vital to the account because the classes can all be understood at a descriptive level. But they do have formal definitions, the derivation of which needs to be understood if they are to be used to code career data. A description of the derivation can be found in appendix A. Briefly, it consists of three steps.

1 The location and activity transition maps are examined separately. This allows us to classify each work role transition in two distinct ways: in terms of the kind of changes in location it involved, and in terms of the kind of changes in activity.
2 The two classification schemes which come from step 1 are combined so that a work role transition can be classified to one of 121 different transition types.
3 The complexity of the unified scheme (step 2) is reduced to give a simple five-way system which allows one to examine career paths for the influence of organizational and individual career logics.

The greatest variety reduction takes place in the third step. There were three main reasons for selecting the method I used for reducing the large possible number of transition types to five. First, and most important, it allows us to relate transition types to the career logics model. In other words, it makes theoretical sense. Second, using the data from my own study, none of the five transition types was very rare. Third, again using my data, none was so common that it included a disproportionate number of transitions. A category which is too common does not make useful distinctions, in the way that separating animals into groups of quadrupeds and bipeds does not usefully distinguish between different breeds of sheep.

The classification scheme assigns work role transitions to one of five different categories which I called continuity, cosmopolitanism, innovation, iteration and expansion. The first three are comparatively straightforward.

1 *Continuity:* the new post involves a new job, perhaps at a different level of responsibility, but not involving a change of location or activity. If it is a promotion it does not involve significantly broader responsibilities but mainly a change in title, for instance from research fellow to senior research fellow.
2 *Cosmopolitanism:* the new post involves activities which are familiar to managers but in an unfamiliar location. Examples could include a financial analyst moving from one treasury department to another, a production manager moving to a new (to him or her) factory which has familiar production technologies, or a chemical engineer changing from one process plant contracting firm to another.
3 *Innovation:* the new post has very little in common with what managers have done before: it is a novel experience. They drop all current responsibilities and change to ones which are new to them. Examples from my study included a computer specialist who became a plant maintenance engineer, a factory manager who became a machinery salesman and an accountant who became a production manager.

Continuity transitions involve no change of any significant kind. But suppose instead of a continuity move the manager had experienced some kind of reshuffle of his or her responsibilities without anything novel being added, perhaps losing some activities or locations and possibly returning to some he or she left years before. This kind of transition falls into the class which can be called iteration.

4 *Iteration:* the new post has links with the manager's past, but not of the simple, direct kind found in continuity and cosmopolitanism. For instance, someone may return to a plant he had once worked

on, a reorganization may have taken some products from his portfolio and added back others he is familiar with, or his responsibilities
may simply have been cut down such as might happen if he has
reached his 'career plateau' (Carnazza et al., 1981). There is nothing
in the new job that he has not experienced at some stage before.

Finally, it often happens that, instead of continuity moves, managers
experience an expansion of their responsibilities into something new.
Sometimes it can be pure growth in the sense that they simply add to
their portfolio, but sometimes it can be more complex. Transitions of
this type can be called expansion.

5   *Expansion:* iteration, but with the added feature that the new post
    involves something new to the manager. It is a process of acquiring
    new activities or locations while still keeping links with the past
    (which distinguishes it from innovation), as might happen to some-
    one being promoted up a hierarchy to take a job with broader
    responsibilities. For instance a production manager might be pro-
    moted to be in charge of the group of factories which include his
    current one, a business general manager might be promoted to run
    the division in which he works, or a new venture manager might be
    told to develop one of his current projects into a fully fledged
    business.

We have reached the point where, by making a number of simplifying
assumptions, we have a means of classifying work role transitions as
one of five types: continuity, cosmopolitanism, innovation, iteration
and expansion. In the next chapter I shall show how these can be
linked to the career logics framework I put together in part II. But
there is a further feature of experience maps which the analysis so far
has ignored. The significance of particular kinds of transition can vary
according to when they happen in people's careers.
    In my analysis of experience maps I have only considered the two
relatively independent dimensions of location and activity experience.
This means that it is possible to compare the careers of two managers
in terms of, for instance, the total number of continuity and innovation
moves each has experienced so far. But suppose each manager has
gone through roughly the same number of each kind of move: what
does that tell us? If we are comparing large numbers of managers −
say, representative samples of managers from two firms − it may be
good evidence for inferring that the shapes of the career climbing-
frames are similar in each firm. For just two managers, however, it is a
different story. We cannot be sure about how similar their career
shapes are until we know whether the moves happened at similar times
in their careers.

For instance, consider the situation where someone changes post and everything about the new post is new to him. If he were a youngster one would perhaps say that there was nothing too surprising about this. It is simply an example of the kind of searching that goes on early in careers before the individual settles down. If 'he' were a married woman one might begin to suspect some form of subsisting induced by the kind of hidden sex discrimination that is still widely practised. For instance, was she having to take any job that she could find as a result of her partner's being moved by his employer to a new location? Finally, if he were an older man a complete change of post could perhaps be evidence of subsisting as he is shuffled about by his employer to make way for younger people. Or it could be a different kind of searching as he makes a jump into a second career.

For two managers the problem is in a sense trivial: their experience maps can simply be put side by side. But the problem becomes far from trivial if one is trying to compare the careers of large numbers of managers, because floor space for the maps soon runs out. We need a way of reducing the data still further, so that the career maps of lots of managers can be plotted on the same piece of paper. In the final part of this chapter I introduce an alternative way of drawing career maps which makes this possible.

CAREER STAGES AND PATTERN MAPS

Suppose we were to divide managers' careers into arbitrary time bands − say ten-year stages − and then look at the overall pattern of transitions within each stage. If the length of each stage is chosen well, there should be less variety and complexity in the transition patterns within them. If so, we should be able to see for any individual which are the predominant transition types within each career stage. For instance (figure 7.8), someone may have experienced mainly continuity moves in her first ten years at work, innovation in her second, iteration in her third, and predominantly expanding transitions in her fourth ten years at work.

Within any one of these career stages other kinds of transition may have been experienced. For instance in her third ten-year band there may have been one expanding move together with four iteration ones. We have classified her pattern for the third career stage as iteration because that is the predominant, but not the exclusive, transition type.

The unit of analysis in figure 7.8 is not an element of experience (as it is in figures 7.1−7.7) but the pattern of transitions the manager has experienced during a given career stage. For instance, during her first career stage the manager in figure 7.8 had a pattern of mainly continuity moves, in the second a pattern of mainly innovation moves and

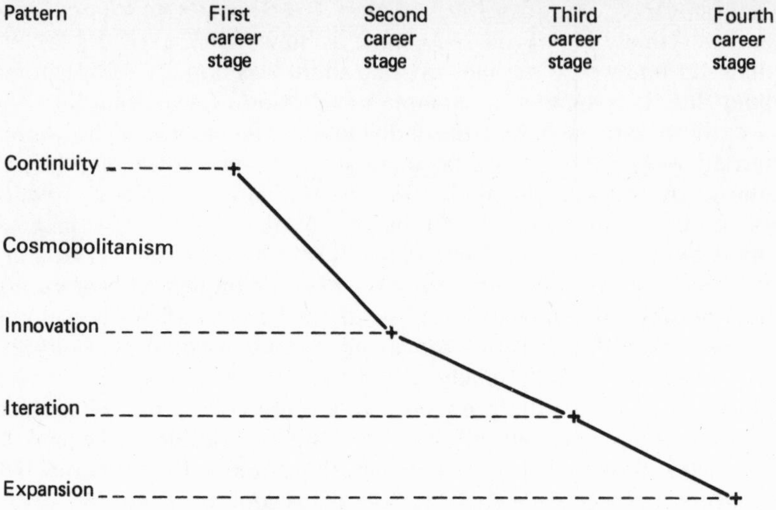

Pattern	First career stage	Second career stage	Third career stage	Fourth career stage

Continuity _ _ _ _ _ _ +

Cosmopolitanism

Innovation _ _ _ _ _ _ _ _ _ _ _ _ _ +

Iteration _ +

Expansion _ +

Figure 7.8   Pattern mapping

so on. For this reason I shall call it the manager's *pattern map*, to distinguish it from the experience maps of figures 7.1–7.7.

If we were to plot the careers of several managers on figure 7.8 we would almost certainly get a tangle of lines. Some might zig-zag all the way across to career stage 4, while others might get only as far as stages 2 or 3, depending on how long the managers' careers had lasted. In principle, the kind of things the pattern maps might show include:

- which patterns represent the more common end-points to careers;
- which earlier patterns are associated with particular career end-points;
- where people starting their careers in, for instance, the continuity pattern tend to end up, and how this compares with those starting in other patterns;
- which factors might be associated with one type of pattern rather than another; for instance, are certain kinds of pattern typical of certain types of career climbing-frame?

The key to being able to draw pattern maps is being able to recognize a predominant kind of transition within each career stage. There are many ways in which we could go about doing this. The patterns could be classified entirely qualitatively by inspection, that is, by sorting the patterns into groups which look similar. Alternatively, they might be classified algorithmically using a set of decision rules of the kind which could be handled by a simple computer program. Finally, more sophisticated methods of pattern recognition could be used. It would take too much space here to go into how one might set about any of these, but some detailed suggestions were made by Gunz (1986). I shall confine myself here to outlining some of the kinds of findings that can emerge from drawing pattern maps like these.

There are two obvious ways in which the pattern maps might be used: to analyse careers by stage, and to look for overall patterns.

On a purely analytical level, the career stages themselves can be used as the unit of analysis by regarding them as a set of 'partial careers'. In the case of my study I used seven-year time bands, because that turned out to yield the most fruitful results. As with using transitions as the unit of analysis, we can see whether the partial careers are distributed in the way that the career logics model would lead us to expect, which allows us to control partially for the length of time the manager spends in a post. It gives us a kind of half way house between transitions as the unit of analysis and people as the unit of analysis. This reduces the effect of the rate of change of post on the results because it ignores the number of transitions within any one career stage. Analysing by transition as opposed to by career stage gives more weight to transitions which have followed each other in quick succession. I describe the kind of findings that can emerge from this approach in chapter 8.

Careers tend not to fit into a small set of easily identified overall patterns. That is as predicted by the career logics model, for two reasons: each firm is likely to have more than one organizational career logic, and each manager at any stage has the individual choice of building within his or her firm's organizational logic, of searching or of subsisting.

Nevertheless, in my study there were some overall patterns that could be picked out. Some managers had a predominance of one kind of transition, and I called them 'persistent' continuers, cosmopolitans and so on. Others had patterns distinctive of, for instance, early continuity or late cosmopolitanism, where 'early' meant during the first two seven-year career stages. The patterns overlapped in the sense that people would sometimes show elements of more than one pattern. Furthermore, within any one career stage transitions of a different type often took place. Despite these complexities, the following kind of observations could be made.

Continuity took three forms: early, late and persistent. Early continuers were those who took time to gain experience of something in depth before setting out on a process of exploration. No significant movement took place at all during this stage, and it was virtually complete by the end of the first decade. The late continuers showed the opposite kind of pattern. If someone was a continuer in their third seven-year career stage, the chances were high that they stayed continuers thereafter. This was sometimes, but not always, an indication that they may have been 'plateaued' by their employers. Sometimes any movement in their late careers consisted of having responsibilities shuffled around or being returned to old ones, but sometimes their responsibilities were noticeably broadened at this stage.

Cosmopolitanism also seemed to take three forms. Early cosmopolitans were those who were developing an area of expertise in a number of different locations before, in many cases, becoming for a time either a continuer or an innovator without any associated cosmopolitanism. In contrast, the late cosmopolitans were those who had become established in their field in mid-career and on the whole stayed with it, moving from one location to another. Sometimes they iterated or expanded, and occasionally they made an innovation move. In addition, there were persistent cosmopolitans, the great majority of whom had started as cosmopolitans and who were, presumably, the classic professionals who had spent most of their working lifetime practising their occupation in many different settings and who might perhaps better be labelled 'craft workers'.

Innovation was far less evenly distributed between the career stages than was either continuity or cosmopolitanism. It was more a phenomenon of early career and often took a transient form. Early, transient innovators were probably those going through an exploratory phase during which they searched for something they wanted to do. Mid–late, transient, innovators were usually those going through some kind of career change from something in which they had been established for some time, corresponding to either searching or subsisting individual logics. In addition there were a small number of managers for whom innovation persisted as a pattern throughout their careers. Usually this pattern reflected the fact that they were building within their organizational career logics rather than searching for something at which they could succeed, and I shall return to them in chapter 8.

It was unusual for a manager to experience no iteration or expansion, and where this happened it was probably a sign that their careers had not been as successful as those of others in the sample. It was certainly the case that those who had neither iterated nor expanded in three or more seven-year career stages were among the least successful, measured using Bass's (1976) salary-to-age ratio. One group of managers for whom it seemed to be a characteristic of early career had not experienced early promotion.

Iteration by itself was usually an extremely transient phenomenon and was associated with other signs of being plateaued, that is, being moved to a subsisting individual career logic. However, there were a very small number of managers who had experienced iteration in three or more career stages, and in two of the three cases this could be related directly to their organizational career logic (chapter 8); they were among the most successful of the managers in the sample.

Expansion, by contrast, was much less transient and not surprisingly associated with a more successful career than was iteration. Persistent expanders almost always avoided iteration by itself, and if they went anywhere at all it was very largely to pure continuity, that is, to an interlude with no change at all of any significance, an indication that they were consolidating their responsibilities.

That concludes my description of how maps can be drawn and analysed. There are many ways in which the techniques might be developed, some of which I have already mentioned and others I shall refer to in chapter 10. But the classifications I have described in this chapter are quite sufficient to allow us to look for differences in career patterns which can be traced to different career logics.

SUMMARY

This chapter had three aims. First, it introduced the experience-mapping technique I shall use in part IV of the book to examine managers' careers for the influence of organizational and individual career logics. Second, it showed how the maps might be analysed, and developed ways of classifying the information in them which I shall use in part IV to show how one might examine managers' careers for the influence of organizational and individual career logics. Third, it formed a bridge to part IV by showing what different career paths can look like using the mapping technique.

I took the concept of experience as I analysed it in chapter 6 and developed a mapping technique for tracing managers' careers across a form of three-dimensional space. The experience maps that come from this technique can range from simple to very complex and are easier to analyse if split in two, so that one plots separately locations against time and activities against time. For many purposes that is as far as one needs to go, because the patterns that the maps display contain a great deal of information about the shapes of managers' careers.

When analysing very complex careers, or comparing, as we shall have to in part IV, the careers of groups of managers, we need to be able to extract information from the maps analytically. I showed how it was possible to classify work role transitions into one of five groups (continuity, cosmopolitanism, innovation, iteration and expansion), which provide a framework for analysing career maps statistically and combining the information from groups of maps.

Finally, I showed how the framework of the five transition types allows us to analyse careers by career stage, which is important because the significance of a particular kind of transition can vary according to when in a career it happens. Pattern maps show how a manager's career develops by moving from one pattern to another as his or her career moves from one career stage to the next. They can be used either to carry out further statistical analysis, this time on career stages rather than on individual work role transitions, or to compare the shapes of groups of managers' careers.

Part IV
Synthesis

Parts II and III of the book have been essentially analytical. In part II a way of looking at the frameworks within which managerial careers take place was described, the so-called organizational and individual career logics. In part III mapping techniques for the careers themselves were developed, together with ways of classifying the kinds of work role transition and patterns of transitions that one sees in the maps. In metaphorical terms, part II was about the shapes of organizational career climbing-frames and the reasons people might have for choosing different paths across them. Part III was about tracing these paths.

In part IV the two themes are brought together. The career climbing-frame model predicts that firms will develop distinctive career cultures and that this distinctiveness can be linked to their structures and the way they have grown. Using the career mapping concepts developed in part III, chapter 8 explores the consequences of these distinctive cultures for the patterns of work role transition which result. In addition, within any organization career patterns will vary as individuals choose their own paths across the climbing-frame. This variance will take predictable forms depending on which individual career logic the manager is following. These predictions can be demonstrated in practice. I shall illustrate this with examples from my study of managerial careers in several large corporations.

Chapter 9 is more speculative. An important reason for studying careers is the widespread belief that different kinds of careers develop different kinds of managers. Although it is very hard for both theoretical and practical reasons to measure managerial expertise, I show how it is possible to make a number of predictions about the kinds of manager developed by different career cultures and by the different paths individuals choose within them.

Chapter 10 concludes by reviewing the contributions and implications of the ideas presented in the book, together with their potential for development. It also draws out some messages for career practitioners.

8
Climbing-frames and Patterns of Work Role Transitions

INTRODUCTION

The career logics model I set out in part II of the book is in essence an explanation of why we might expect different kinds of firm to have distinctive career cultures. We can now explore the consequences of these different career cultures using the methods of mapping careers and analysing the maps which I developed in part III.

The experience mapping technique visualizes managers' career patterns in terms of five kinds of transition from post to post that I labelled as follows.

1 *Continuity:* the new post involves a new job, perhaps at a different level of responsibility, but not involving a change of location or activity. If it is a promotion it does not involve significantly broader responsibilities but mainly a change in title.
2 *Cosmopolitanism:* the new post involves activities which are familiar to the manager but in an unfamiliar location.
3 *Innovation:* the new post has very little in common with what the manager has done before. It is a novel experience for him or her.
4 *Iteration:* the new post has links with the manager's past but not of the simple, direct kind of 1 and 2 above.
5 *Expansion:* the new post involves iteration, but with the added feature that the new post involves something new to the manager as well.

A firm's organizational career logic causes its managers to have careers which, although individually varied, tend to follow a pattern that is characteristic of the logic. These patterns should make themselves apparent as different kinds of transition from post to post. So managers from firms with differently shaped career climbing-frames should have careers with different relative proportions of the five transition types. Furthermore the individual variations in the patterns should reflect the individual career logics of the managers themselves.

It turns out to be quite possible to detect these differences, as I shall show by drawing on illustrations from my own study. There are predictable differences to be found between organizations in the way that managers' work role transitions are collectively distributed between the five categories I have just listed. It is also evident from looking at individual biographies that careers follow different patterns in companies with differently shaped climbing-frames.

But first we must return to the career logics themselves to establish the kinds of transition that should be associated with each organizational and individual career logic.

CAREER LOGICS AND CAREER PATTERNS

The career logics model I set out in part II proposes that any particular firm has a set of career logics corresponding to certain features of its structure and the way the firm has grown and changed. The model also says something about the individual factors which might cause the actual career patterns of the managers to depart from the expected ones. First, I look at the four organizational career logics: constructional, command-centred, evolutionary and turnaround.

Career patterns: different climbing-frames

Constructional climbing-frame   The emphasis in constructional logic is on putting together a wide variety of experiences in a firm with a complex, non-recursive structure so that individuals mirror, as far as possible in terms of what they know and can do, the overall organization. To achieve this they must make a series of complex movements across the firm with the aim of getting as broad a background as possible and without getting 'trapped' in any one business function or product area. Each move to a new set of experiences is likely to involve a break with the past, that is, it is an innovation move. For instance, a research worker being groomed for senior management might be moved to a commercial job, or a sales executive might similarly be given experience of a business development activity. Moves like these should be common on constructional climbing-frames as a result of the managers' building their catalogues of diverse experiences.

Given all this constant movement into new experiences and the severe practical problems of succession planning in complex organizations, it would be surprising if there were not also a certain amount of covering of old ground as well. For instance, it may be that the only way in which managers are to be given experience of particular new activities is to move them to locations they are familiar with. So we can also expect this kind of climbing-frame, more than the others, to lead to a lot of iteration. As we saw in chapter 7, iteration is often associated with being plateaued, as managers are shuffled around to make room for their more successful colleagues. In this case, however, it is not. It is a normal part of a successful career. Furthermore, if managers emerge eventually at the top of a constructional frame as 'complete' managers the logic implies that they are likely to do this by moving into jobs which give them responsibility for many of the things they have worked in before. This, too, is iteration.

A further consequence of this particular logic is that managers will try to avoid being labelled as experts unless the expertise is a particularly key one. So although there is room for the absolutely vital expert in even the most constructional of logics, the other three transition types should not be as common as on other climbing-frames. Cosmopolitanism carries with it the danger of getting labelled as someone who is limited to a particular kind of activity. Worse still, continuity could mark one out as quite immobile. Further, since the logic means the manager cannot afford to stay with any one experience for too long, expansion is not a likely outcome either.

To summarize, innovation and iteration should feature in the careers of people building their careers on constructional climbing-frames, while continuity, cosmopolitanism and expansion should be comparatively rare.

Command-centred climbing-frame The distinguishing feature of command-centred logic is a recursive structure, in which there are a comparatively large number of similar commands. Managers build their careers by moving from command to command, and if all goes well each successive command is larger than the previous one. Managers working for a large retail bank, for instance, whose careers take them from one branch to the next are probably doing a similar job in each branch in the sense that the activities are likely to be much the same. The locations are not, however, and can differ in a number of ways. For instance the size of the branch, the ratio of personal to business accounts, the type of business accounts and how well-to-do the personal customers are may all be different. All of these will make each successive post a different job and more or less demanding than the previous one.

This pattern of similar activities in different locations is a classic example of cosmopolitanism, which we expect to be a strong feature of command-centred careers. We also expect the cosmopolitanism to be interspersed with expanding moves as managers are promoted to successively higher levels in the organization, for instance from branch manager to regional manager. But recursion also means that this type of move probably involves very little change in activity. A recursive structure is so called because it consists of similar organizational units nested within each other. So this expansion will be associated with continuity as well.

Finally, the large number of similar commands tends to result in comparatively 'flat' hierarchies. Even in very large service organizations, for instance, there are surprisingly few levels of management between the basic operating unit and corporate headquarters. This is notorious for slowing the rate of promotion when managers reach senior middle management, reinforcing the likelihood of finding continuity in the firm.

Managers building their careers on command-centred climbing-frames, then, should experience more cosmopolitan moves than on other kinds of frames, but their careers are also likely to show an excess of expansion and continuity.

Evolutionary climbing-frame In evolutionary logic managers grow with their particular organizational unit, rather than spending some time with the unit and getting experience in it before moving to the next one. Careers of this kind feel different from those of the previous two logics because they are not as obviously connected with moves across and up bureaucratic hierarchies. Looking back at such managers' biographies it can often be hard to decide when one post ended and the next began. After a time, the manager just seems to have been doing a broader, more important job. For instance many managers in International Systems Engineering (ISE) who had started as R&D engineers found their work gradually getting more complex, and involving more and more business functions as their projects matured and reached the point of commercial exploitation. Although they may often be formally qualified to move to other parts of their company, people in these cultures tend to stay with the part in which they have 'grown up'. There is often quite an evident emotional link between these managers and the businesses they have helped to develop.

The transitions, such as they can be identified in an evolutionary logic, therefore involve adding locations and/or activities to the manager's post, so having a strongly expansive aspect. To the extent that they are still concerned with the same business, though, they will be coupled with continuity.

Turnaround climbing-frame This logic differs from the other three in that it is a logic of discontinuity from the point of view of the firm. It is a transitory phenomenon which ought to disappear once the catastrophe which sparked it off is past. The firm is likely to be quite different after the dust has settled, so that from an organizational point of view it is hard to know what the new career logic will be, if it is indeed any different from the old career logic. It is probable that there will be some change, if only because existing patterns of promotion are quite likely to have been altered. The appointment of a chief executive from outside is associated with far more change in the ranks reporting to him or her than is the case for insider appointments (Gouldner, 1954; Helmich and Brown, 1972; Helmich, 1975b).

From the point of view of turnaround managers themselves, however, the situation is much clearer. They will probably have been selected and appointed by a powerful outside group, for example a company's financial backers or a nationalized corporation's government department, on the strength of their reputation for having successfully rescued other organizations. Because, in this kind of situation, there is often a strong feeling amongst the group setting up the rescue that the insiders have failed, it is common for the turnaround manager to be a complete outsider. Almost by definition, then, the move will have involved innovation. There may also be an element of cosmopolitanism, for example if there were some kind of link between turnaround managers' successive rescue jobs. For instance, they may have a reputation for being particularly good at turning around firms of a particular kind.

At the organizational level, then, the career logics model makes a number of predictions about the kind of transitions which should predominate in particular kinds of organization. Constructional climbing-frames should have more innovation and iteration and less continuity, cosmopolitanism and expansion than other frames. Command-centred frames should be higher in cosmopolitanism and continuity, evolutionary frames should show more expansion and continuity and turnaround frames are likely to have an excess of innovation and, perhaps, cosmopolitanism.

As we have seen (chapter 4), any one organization can have more than one organizational career logic. The modal logic is simply the main one. There are likely to be islands of other kinds of logic in various parts of the firm. It follows from this that if one looks at an organization in aggregate the predictions I have just listed will get somewhat blurred if the sample includes managers who come from, or have crossed between, more than one of these kinds of logic.

But there are other reasons for expecting blurring of the predictions. So far we have looked only at the effect the shape of the climbing-frame has on managers' careers. There is also the effect of individual choice to take into account.

Career patterns: different paths across the climbing-frames

When I discussed individual career logics − the process of choosing one's path across the organizational climbing-frame − I separated the process of individual career-making into two distinct stages.

The first stage involves people being evaluated by their organizations. This has the effect of making all, some or none of the organizational logics available to them which, in turn, may restrict their choice of individual career logic. If the managers are thought of as worth promoting, that is, if the evaluation is positive, they will have open to them the choice of any of the three individual logics (building, searching or subsisting). However, if the general opinion is that their career prospects are limited, that is, they have been negatively evaluated, they no longer have the option of building. They must choose between searching or subsisting.

The second stage involves choosing an individual career logic – the path across the climbing-frame – from the ones that are available to the manager. Again, each logic has predictable consequences for patterns of transitions between posts. I shall look at each of the three individual logics in turn.

Building   This logic simply means that people follow the organizational career logic which is on offer to them, with the consequences for their careers that I described in the previous part of this chapter. In other words, they are likely to have a typical career for that organization.

Searching   Searching is the logic of looking for something else to do because individuals no longer want to continue building within their current organizational logic. In terms of the framework I set out in chapter 5, they are organizational career deviants but are still interested in building a career because they remain future oriented. They are prepared to accept sacrifice to that end in the short term. Whatever the result of the searching, it is bound by definition to result in a change of location, and since people doing it have embarked on their search in order to find something different to do it is quite likely that the result will be an innovation move. The less they want, or are able to find, a new activity, the more the move will resemble a form of cosmopolitanism.

Subsisting   Subsisting could be associated with almost any transition pattern, since people doing it tend to be moving at the behest of outside forces. At the limit they are looking for any job, so long as it is a job. If the subsisting is of a less extreme kind they are likely to be left where they are or moved around in order to make space in the organization for more promising managers. Again, they might be given some job rotation to keep them from getting too bored. These moves could involve cosmopolitanism if they are kept doing things they are familiar with or innovation if it is thought that a complete change might be good for them. Iteration, too, might be a consequence of the move. In addition, we could expect the rate of movement between

Table 8.1 *Transition types predicted to be associated with each career logic*

Career logics	Main transition types	Subsidiary transition types
Organizational		
Constructional	Innovation	Iteration
Command-centred	Cosmopolitanism	Continuity, expansion
Evolutionary	Expansion	Continuity
Turnaround	Innovation	Cosmopolitanism
Individual		
Building	Pattern(s) associated with relevant organizational logic (see above)	
Searching	Innovation	Cosmopolitanism
Subsisting	Cosmopolitanism, innovation, iteration, continuity	

jobs to slow down and perhaps stop altogether, a special case of continuity. We would not, however, expect expansion because of that pattern's association with career success.

This draws together the themes of parts II and III of the book by showing how drawing experience maps of careers and examining them for continuous, cosmopolitan, innovative, iterative and expansive transitions allows one to 'see the career logics model in action'. The logics model makes a number of predictions (table 8.1) about the kind of transitions that might typically be found in different kinds of companies and about some of the individual factors which might cause the actual career patterns of the managers to depart from the expected ones. The remainder of the chapter draws on illustrations from my research to show how one can go about identifying career logics in practice, how well the predictions I have just made get borne out and what it can be like making careers in different career cultures. But first, I need to give a little background to the research itself.

CAREER LOGICS AND PATTERNS: EXAMPLES FROM RESEARCH

The research study

The study from which these examples are drawn was of the jobs and careers of 115 managers ranging in seniority from lower middle management to board level. More information about the study can be found in appendix B and is given by Gunz and Whitley (1985) and Gunz (1986). All but one of the managers were men, so I shall use the male pronoun when discussing the cases. I interviewed each manager in some depth about his career, yielding information about each job he had occupied and his reasons for moving to the next.

Because my aim was to look for distinctive career patterns within organizations it was necessary to select business units with well-developed internal labour markets. They did not have to be legal entities such as companies or groups of companies. A large division of a yet larger group would do if it behaved for most purposes as though it were an independent firm (Palmer, 1983). This independent behaviour would have to manifest itself as control over its business strategy within very broad limits and an internal labour market which was sufficiently large and self-contained to provide careers for the majority of its managers. Completely closed labour markets are, of course, most unlikely.

I selected business units, either divisions or subsidiary companies, from four large manufacturing corporations in line with these criteria. In two cases (Norchem and Prestex) only one division was studied because of the size of the divisions, while in the remaining two corporations respectively three and two subsidiaries were selected. I introduced the business units in chapter 1 (table 1.1), but I need to say more about them now so that I can discuss their organizational career logics. The organization charts are greatly simplified for clarity.

Norchem Division of Dewar Industries Plc (figure 8.1): Dewar operates in a range of process industries, and Norchem makes specialized performance chemicals. Norchem has a matrix structure with large functional departments, for example research, development, manufacturing, marketing; business groups coordinate all work relating to particular product lines across all departments.

Prestex Division of Grosvenor House Plc (figure 8.2): Prestex consists of a group of some forty geographically scattered plants. It is organized into product-based groups, which manufacture a broad range of textile products to be sold to other textile businesses both inside and outside Grosvenor House. Each director of Prestex is responsible for overseeing the work of his particular functional specialists at the level of the division, of groups of plants and of the plants themselves.

International Systems Engineering Plc (ISE; figure 8.3): ISE owns a group of companies which operate in the electrical, electronics and computer industries. They make a broad range of products from large systems to small components. For my study, three subsidiary companies were selected.

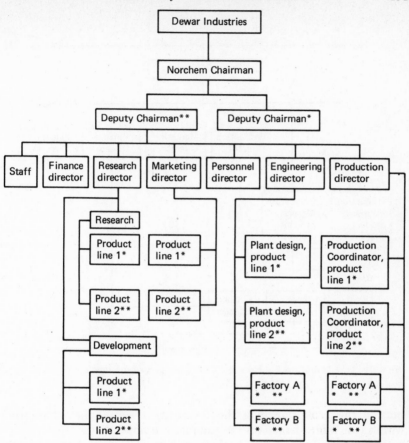

Figure 8.1   *Norchem (this figure is greatly simplified)*
     *   *members of the business group for product line 1*
     ** *members of the business group for product line 2*

Cemco Plc (figure 8.4): Cemco owns a group of companies that make materials for the construction and engineering industries. Historically, it was based on a single technology which hit serious trouble recently, forcing a rapid diversification. Two subsidiary companies were selected for the study.

Depending on how one defines managerial grades, the managers I met represented between 5 per cent and 15 per cent of the management of each of the business units selected. Prestex was towards the higher end of this range, and Norchem was towards the lower. In none of these companies is there much interchange of staff between subsidiaries or divisions. In each case more managers were recruited from

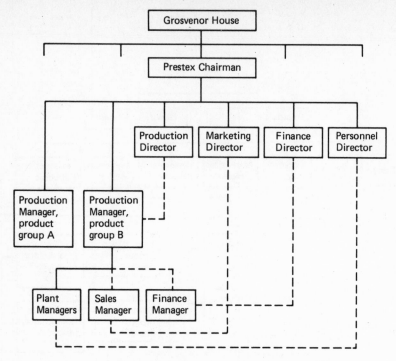

Figure 8.2   Prestex (there are six groups in all)

outside the groups owning the divisions or subsidiaries than from within (for more details on the sample, see appendix B).

We can now look at each business unit in turn, to see how we might classify the shape of their career climbing-frames, that is, their organizational career logics. As we shall see, in three of the business units there is a dominant career logic which I have called modal, and some subsidiary ones. In the fourth organization (Cemco) the situation is less clear.

Shapes of the career climbing-frames

In chapter 4 I related organizational career logics to three features of organizations: whether or not the structure is recursive, whether growth has overall been patterned or unpatterned, and whether or not the firm has experienced central continuity (table 4.1). For clarity I shall keep my descriptions of each organization brief, restricting them to the points most salient to the classification process. More detail is given by Gunz and Whitley (1985).

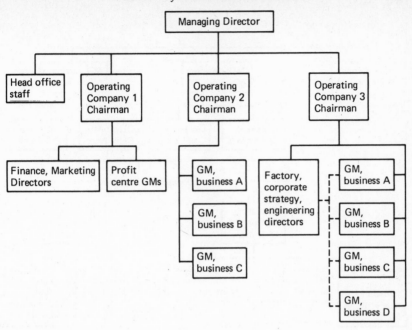

Figure 8.3 ISE. The factory, corporate strategy and engineering directors of Operating Company 3 tend to act as specialist advisors to their Chairman and internal consultants to the Business GMs. The operating companies are all fully incorporated subsidiaries of ISE

Norchem Norchem has a very complex structure, based partly on business function and partly on type of business, that is, product line. The two are connected by a series of matrix linkages (the business groups; figure 8.1). Parts of the structure are recursive, but these islands of recursion are comparatively isolated.

The production directorate is an example of geographical recursiveness. The division has several large factory sites, geographically widely separated. Each site is divided into areas, each area consisting of individual, separately managed plants. The factory sites' physical remoteness from Norchem's head office means that some other Norchem departments organize themselves around this recursive structure. For instance, each has its own maintenance engineering group organized to match the production structure, and simple technical development is done by chemists in development groups attached to each factory site.

Norchem's central research department has product-based recursiveness, organized around product lines. Here, however, the recursiveness is less marked. Each line serves strikingly different kinds of market, so the research groups are organized differently and differ a good deal in the work they do.

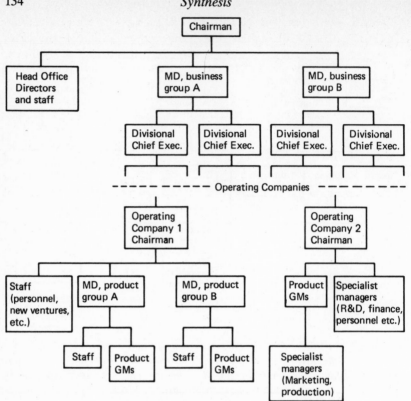

Figure 8.4   Cemco. The operating companies are all fully incorporated subsidiary companies of Cemco

So although there are islands of recursiveness they are limited because
there is no one overall recursive logic to the structure. Broadly speaking
there are two: the logic which comes from the physical layout of the
production plant, and the logic which comes from the products and
processes on which Norchem's business depends. An additional complication comes from the way the production processes are interlinked.
Norchem's products can go through as many as twelve steps in their
manufacture, each involving a different plant. Furthermore some of
the output of any plant can be recycled back to another plant earlier in
the chain or in a quite different chain and perhaps at a quite different
factory site. Finally, Norchem sells both the products that emerge at
the end of the chain and the intermediate products from plants
somewhere in the middle of the chain. This makes for a production
planning problem of almost nightmare proportions and is one reason
for the complicated matrix structure. Overall, then, the structure is
non-recursive.

The division's business position is difficult because its products are tied quite strongly to textiles, but it has not experienced any catastrophe: it has experienced central continuity in its operations. Although it has pioneered some novel business areas in the past this kind of growth is well behind it. It now has well-established procedures for introducing new products and processes and modifying existing ones. Its growth is now far more patterned than unpatterned.

The combination of non-recursive structure, patterned growth and central continuity means that we expect the modal career logic for Norchem to be constructional. However, we do expect managers whose careers take them through recursive parts of the division such as the production directorate to experience command-centred logics for part or all of their careers.

Prestex With forty separate plants, Prestex has a large number of commands which have to be filled. The plants fall into pecking orders of prestige, the most prestigious of which are even referred to as flagships. When someone is moved from one plant to the next, everyone knows from the relative prestiges of the two plants whether this represents promotion, demotion or neither. The plants provide the basic organizing logic for Prestex so that all the three main business functions (production, sales and finance) are represented at the level of each plant, each product-based group of plants and head office. Unlike Norchem, everything is organized around product group. The result is, in effect, three parallel hierarchies, one for each business function, making the structure highly recursive.

As with Norchem, there has been a strong element of central continuity over its recent history. The textile business has been in steady contraction since early in the century so that plant closures and rationalization of production arrangements are almost routine now. Within Prestex there has nevertheless been some growth. New fibres have been introduced, and at the time of the study a number of plants were being re-equipped with higher-capacity machinery to boost output. It has, though, been very much growth to an existing pattern. The textile business has gone through a number of re-equipping phases as new, faster technologies have appeared, and Prestex's managers, most of whom have qualifications in textile technology, are quite used to change of this kind.

This combination of a recursive structure, patterned growth and central continuity means that we expect the modal organizational logic in Prestex to be command-centred. There is also the possibility of a certain amount of constructional logic either right at the start of a career as young managers get experience of a number of departments within their chosen functional hierarchy or at very senior levels in the functional hierarchies.

International Systems Engineering Plc ISE is very much the creation of engineers who would get ideas for something new, develop it and find a market for it. They would sell more and more until, in many cases, they found themselves running large businesses. This happened in areas as far apart as solid state physics and control systems. In the case of solid state physics the result was the formation of a highly successful operating company manufacturing a wide range of electronic components, including a world-beating microelectronic technology, under the leadership of a former university academic originally hired to research the physics of such devices. In the case of control systems, engineers working on a major government contract devised a new control technology which they went on to try in quite different, non-governmental, areas of application. The result was a new operating company working in industrial and consumer markets which were quite new to ISE, managed by the engineers who had worked on the original ideas.

Unlike Norchem, much of this development had happened during the careers of the managers I met, and indeed some of them were responsible for it. Sometimes the driving force behind the project was the needs of a major contract such as the government project. Sometimes the ideas came as spin-offs from existing projects, for example trying the government project technology in a civilian market. Sometimes, as with the solid state devices, they were speculative ventures in their own right. Change, in other words, was unpatterned overall although in individual established businesses a patterned variant had sometimes set in.

The company had hit a major financial crisis not long before I met it, caused by problems in one of its oldest subsidiaries. Its financial backers reacted in the classic manner, bringing in a chief executive from outside the company to run ISE as a whole and a charismatic and energetic engineer from a distant part of the company to turn around the troubled division. This was certainly catastrophic change in the sense I have used the term here, but the effects were mainly limited to the small corporate management structure and the division which had caused the crisis. Most other subsidiary companies were established and successful enough, it seems, to have hardly noticed the change. So in these other subsidiaries, and in the pre-crisis era for the division which hit trouble, the firm had experienced central continuity, which formed the framework for the bulk of the careers of many of the managers in the study.

The result of this growth history is that, overall, the structure is non-recursive. Each subsidiary has gone about things in its own way and in one or two of them some recursion could be seen, but this was not a strong influence. Perhaps, if the rate of change in the industry slows and ISE goes through some years of patterned growth, the picture may change.

The unpatterned growth, non-recursive structure and, in the main, central continuity mean that we predict that the modal career logic for ISE should be evolutionary. But we expect to find islands of other organizational logics. For instance, in places where recursion was visible there should be signs of a command-centred logic at work. Again, at the top of the company and in the division in which the crisis had happened the catastrophic change should have – and did – lead to a turnaround logic.

Cemco Cemco has perhaps the most mixed structure of all four organizations. Historically very successful, Cemco has built a world-wide network of companies based on a particular technology. The older parts of the company have aspects of Prestex's recursion in the sense that they are based on clusters of production units, each making a given product range for a given market. On the other hand there is evidence of a gradual move away from functionally specialist departments. While there are still a great many such departments, there is a trend towards comparatively self-contained business units. This introduces non-recursion because of the differing natures of the businesses. In recent years this has become more marked because of the efforts Cemco has been making to escape from its dependence on its basic, rapidly obsolescing, technology. It has concentrated a lot of effort into diversification, bringing about a considerable amount of unpatterned growth as it has moved into quite new products, processes and markets. This in turn has introduced new business and production units, sometimes on new sites and sometimes within existing factories, emphasizing the non-recursive side of Cemco's structure. But despite the company's undoubted serious business troubles its history up to the time of my fieldwork was marked by central continuity.

It is hard, then, to identify a modal logic for Cemco: there is quite significant variation from one subsidiary to the next. The degree of recursion varies from subsidiary to subsidiary, so we can expect to find a mixture of constructional and command-centred logics. But, in addition, unpatterned growth is a feature of some subsidiaries to a greater extent than others, so we can also expect signs of an evolutionary logic as a result of unpatterned growth where it has occurred. If we were forced to make a choice of modal logic it would probably be that there should be an emphasis on a constructional one, for three reasons. First, the corporation has overall a non-recursive structure. Second, it has not experienced a catastrophe. Third, the unpatterned growth has been somewhat marginal.

Table 8.2 summarizes my descriptions of the four business units and my deductions about the shapes of their career climbing-frames.

Climbing-frames – the organizational career logics – are in them-

Table 8.2 *Predicted organizational career logics in Norchem, Prestex, ISE and Cemco*

Firm	Structure: recursive?[a]	Growth		Predicted organizational career logics	
				Modal	Other
Norchem	No	Patterned	Continuity	Constructional	Command-centred
Prestex	Yes	Patterned	Continuity	Command-centred	Constructional
ISE	No	Unpatterned	Continuity[b] Catastrophe[c]	Evolutionary Turnaround	Command-centred
Cemco	No	Both	Continuity	Constructional, command-centred, evolutionary?	Command-centred

[a] Each firm had a small proportion of the opposite kind of structure, responsible for the 'other' predicted career logics (last column); this was especially true of Cemco (see text).
[b] Pre-crisis.
[c] Post-crisis, most noticeably affecting corporate headquarters and the division responsible for the crisis.

Table 8.3   *Predicted transition types for Norchem, Prestex, ISE and Cemco*

Firm	Predicted modal organizational logic	Predicted transition types (*main type in italics*)
Norchem	Constructional	*Innovation*, iteration
Prestex	Command-centred	*Cosmopolitanism*, continuity, expansion
ISE	Evolutionary[a] Turnaround[b]	*Expansion*, continuity *Innovation*, cosmopolitanism
Cemco	Mixed	All

[a] Pre-crisis.
[b] Post-crisis (most noticeably affecting corporate headquarters and the division responsible for the crisis).

selves invisible. All we can see of them are the paths managers make moving over them, which in part III of the book I mapped in terms of work role transitions. Combining the predictions of table 8.1 with table 8.2, we obtain table 8.3.

For clarity, table 8.3 ignores the additional kinds of transition we expect from the localized organizational features shown in table 8.2. It makes a number of predictions about the kind of work role transition we expect to be more common in each of the four corporations that I studied. For example in Norchem we expect to find more innovation, and to a lesser extent iteration, than the other three transition types. In Prestex, by contrast, we expect to find cosmopolitanism predominating, with continuity and expansion also featuring. Transitions should therefore not be randomly distributed between the four firms but should follow the patterns outlined in table 8.3.

But we also expect to find some variation within each organization, for four reasons. Firstly, the models only predict tendencies. No theory of this kind could ever be as deterministic as to predict that on, for instance, a constructional climbing-frame it is impossible to have continuity transitions. Secondly, there are good reasons for expecting each kind of climbing-frame to be associated with more than one kind of transition. For example, table 8.1 predicts that constructional logics are likely to give rise to iteration as well as innovation. Thirdly, as we have seen looking at the four corporations, it is entirely reasonable to expect more than one shape of frame within a given organization. For instance (table 8.2), we expect Norchem to have a modal constructional organizational career logic, but in addition to have islands of command-centred logics. Fourthly, individual managers can make their own choices about how they move over the climbing-frames, and the three individual logics of building, searching and subsisting can bring about different kinds of transition from that expected of the frame.

Those, then, are the predictions. When I examined the careers of the managers I interviewed in each of the four companies I did indeed find evidence of the kind of transition patterns I expected. In the next part of the chapter I shall draw on some of the results to show the kind of patterns which emerged.

Distribution of transition types between Norchem, Prestex, ISE and Cemco

The 115 managers had experienced a total of 822 work role transitions (appendix A, table A.1), having changed posts anything up to fifteen times each (appendix B). The interviews yielded considerable detail on what they had done in each succeeding post, and I was able to assign all but twenty-four of the 822 transitions to one of the five transition types (continuity, cosmopolitanism, innovation, iteration and expansion). Usually the unclassifiable transitions corresponded to early training periods when the managers had moved around a great deal without doing a 'proper' job in any posting. Appendix A explains the background to the classification process, and table A.3 sets out the formal classification rules. Table 8.4 summarizes the results.

Let us ignore for the moment which business units have more of

Table 8.4   Frequencies and (column) percentages of all transition types, by business unit

	Norchem $n = 197$	Prestex $n = 213$	ISE $n = 207$	Cemco $n = 205$	Total $n = 822$
Continuity	15 (8%)	37 (17%)	34 (16%)	30 (15%)	116 (14%)
Cosmopolitanism	51 (26%)	90 (42%)	58 (28%)	68 (33%)	267 (32%)
Innovation	53 (27%)	26 (12%)	29 (14%)	34 (17%)	142 (17%)
Iteration	34 (17%)	16 (8%)	9 (4%)	23 (11%)	82 (10%)
Expansion	40 (20%)	38 (18%)	72 (35%)	39 (19%)	189 (23%)
Innovation + iteration	87 (44%)	42 (20%)	38 (18%)	57 (28%)	224 (27%)
Unclassified	4 (2%)	6 (3%)	5 (2%)	11 (5%)	26 (3%)

Excluding 'unclassified' transitions, chi square for the frequencies is 63.4 with twelve degrees of freedom ($p < 0.005$).

For specific transition types, comparing the number of each kind of transition with the number of transitions not of that type the following chi squares with three degrees of freedom are obtained: innovation, 16.6 ($p < 0.005$); continuity; 8.9 ($p < 0.05$); iteration, 18.8 ($p < 0.005$); innovation + iteration, 40.8 ($p < 0.005$); cosmopolitanism, 14.8 ($p < 0.005$); expansion, 20.2 ($p < 0.005$).

Table 8.5   Comparison of the distribution of transition types between each pair of business units (chi squares)

	Norchem	Prestex	ISE	Cemco
Other three	36.7***	18.2**	27.7***	1.9
Norchem		32.6***	35.2***	12.0*
Prestex			17.9**	4.6
ISE				15.3**

With four degrees of freedom; *, $p < 0.02$; **, $p < 0.005$; ***, $p < 0.001$.

which kind of transition. Table 8.4 shows clearly that the distribution of transitions across the five classes of transition varies significantly from one business unit to the next. This is in accord with one of the basic propositions of this book: that different organizations should have distinctively different career cultures. What we are seeing here is the effects of the different cultures on the kinds of transition managers in each company typically make from one post to the next.

By processing the figures a little more (table 8.5) we can see that the differences between the business units are not uniform. If we compare each business unit with the other three as a group we see that Norchem, Prestex and ISE are all quite distinctive, while Cemco is not. Its distribution of transition types resembles a mixture of the rest. Taking each pair of business units in turn, we find that, individually, Norchem, Prestex and ISE are all significantly different from each other. Cemco's distribution of transition types most closely resembles that of Prestex, with Norchem and ISE next in line.

This is very much in keeping with what we expected to find. We predicted that the differently shaped climbing-frames of Norchem, Prestex and ISE should produce distinctively different patterns of work role transition in each business unit. We also predicted that Cemco should, in effect, look a bit like a mixture of the other three, and that, too, emerges from the figures.

Thus far, we have not taken any notice of the kind of differences there are between the business units, simply noting that the differences are there. But the differences themselves are also in the directions we expected, as we can see if we look at each business unit in turn.

Norchem The constructional climbing-frame that I identified for Norchem should, according to the predictions of the first part of this chapter, be marked by a high proportion of innovation and iteration moves. This is indeed what we see in table 8.4.

Norchem managers have experienced more innovation overall than have the others: fully 27 per cent of all Norchem moves were innovation.

In other words over a quarter of the moves Norchem managers made involved a change to something completely new, while for the other three business units this was the case for an average of only 14 per cent of all transitions. We can demonstrate that this difference is significant by comparing the number of innovation moves with the number of other types of transition in each business unit (table 8.4).

We do not expect to find much continuity in Norchem, and indeed only 8 per cent of Norchem moves were of this type, compared with the average for the other business units of 16 per cent. Again, the difference is significant.

This pattern seems to be echoed by the amount of iteration which went on in the careers of Norchem managers. Of Norchem moves, 17 per cent were of this kind, while for the others the proportion ranged from 11 per cent (Cemco) down to 4 per cent (ISE). If we combine innovation with iteration we find that Norchem had by far the greatest proportion of such moves. While Norchem managers may not have stayed with particular activities or locations in the short term, they clearly had a tendency to return to them later. This is what we would expect from the kind of modal constructional logic predicted for Norchem.

Prestex   I described Prestex's modal career logic as command-centred, which should lead to a high proportion of cosmopolitan moves. As expected, cosmopolitanism was very much the hallmark of Prestex careers. Prestex managers have experienced a significantly higher proportion of cosmopolitan transitions than the average for the sample. 42 per cent of all Prestex moves were of this type, by contrast with the average overall of 32 per cent and an average for the remaining organizations of 29 per cent.

ISE   ISE is a more complex case because there was the possibility of at least two distinct organizational career logics at work. Of the three subsidiaries I studied, only one was a candidate for the turnaround logic, and many of the managers I met there had spent the bulk of their careers elsewhere in pre-crisis ISE. Most of the managers in the sample had spent most of their careers on an evolutionary climbing-frame, for which we expect to find expansion as the commonest kind of transition.

Expansion was indeed noticeably more of a feature of the careers of ISE managers than it was for the other organizations. It occurred in decreasing order of frequency in ISE, Cemco, Prestex and Norchem.

Cemco   Cemco is the most mixed of the business units I studied, in terms of both its structure and the way in which it has grown. This makes it hard to identify a modal organizational career logic for the company. There are perhaps grounds for putting the constructional logic at the top of the list, which should in turn lead to more innovation and iteration than other transitions. But there are equally good grounds for expecting most of the other types of transition to be present.

This is indeed what we see. For instance, Cemco is second on the list for innovation and iteration taken together, which is what we expect from a constructional logic. However, its overall distribution of transitions (table 8.5) resembles that of Prestex quite closely. This is partly because cosmopolitanism was also quite strongly represented, as would be expected from its command-centred logic.

As we have seen, there were significant variations from one business unit to the next in terms of their overall patterns of work role transition, and this was in the direction predicted by the framework I set out above. The findings show the expected evidence in three of the four firms of distinctive career logics and in the fourth (Cemco), again as expected, evidence of a mixture of career logics.

This analysis took the individual work role transition as the unit of analysis. Next I shall show how analysing the career maps by career stage can provide supporting evidence for the picture that is emerging.

Analysing careers by career stage (pattern mapping)

Analysing career maps by looking only at the total number of each kind of transition tells only part of the story. It ignores the stage in a manager's career when each transition happened. For instance, a high proportion of innovation moves in a particular company might come about simply because most people did their moving around in their first few years. This is why in chapter 7 I developed an alternative method of mapping careers – pattern mapping – which takes as its unit of analysis the pattern of transitions that managers have experienced at each succeeding stage of their careers. Analysis of data like these can get extremely complex. As the aim of this chapter is only to be illustrative, I shall do no more here than pick out some of the more significant findings that emerged from my own study. More detail is given by Gunz (1986).

It turned out to be convenient to divide the managers' careers into seven-year stages. Longer career stages showed less detail, while shorter ones showed too much and ran into the problem that there was an increasing chance that the manager had not changed jobs within them. So the unit of analysis became the pattern of transitions managers experienced in each succeeding seven-year stage of their careers. A manager might, for instance, be an innovator in his or her first seven-year period, a cosmopolitan in his or her second period and so on.

Looking at the career data in this way it is possible to find the same kinds of difference between the four business units that I found when I took individual transitions as the unit of analysis. The distributions of transition patterns in each business unit were significantly different from each other at the 5 per cent level.

It becomes harder to look for the source of the differences between the companies because of the small numbers involved in some of the career stages, especially the later ones. Not all managers had had equally long careers (appendix B). One simple way of analysing the results is to look at the number of managers who experienced each kind of transition pattern as a percentage of the total number of managers in that career stage. Figures 8.5–8.7 show what happens when we plot three kinds of transition pattern in this way.

Innovation   Figure 8.5 shows the proportion of each business units' managers who fell in this pattern. The final two career stages are somewhat misleading in the innovation case because very small numbers of managers are involved. However, during the first 21 years of their careers Norchem's managers have experienced consistently the highest proportion of innovation. This is what we would expect from Norchem's modal constructional career logic.

Cosmopolitanism   Figure 8.6 indicates that after the first seven years, during which time they were usually learning their trade, Prestex managers consistently experienced the highest proportion of cosmopolitanism, again as expected from Prestex's modal command-centred logic.

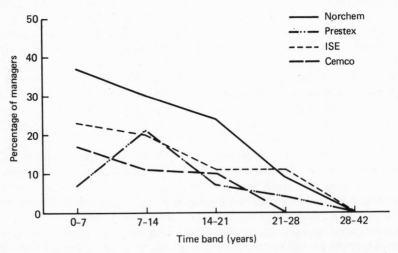

Figure 8.5   Pattern map of innovation in Norchem, Prestex, ISE and Cemco

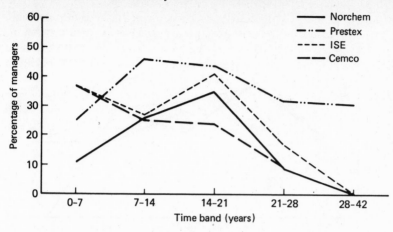

Figure 8.6   Pattern map of cosmopolitanism in Norchem, Prestex, ISE and Cemco

Expansion   Figure 8.7 shows ISE with the highest proportion of managers who have experienced expanding transition patterns after the first seven years, reflecting the influence of its modal evolutionary career logic.

Analysing the pattern maps in this way therefore reveals the kind of patterns that we expect to be generated by each type of climbing-frame. It also shows that the patterns persist over the course of the managers' careers. This provides further evidence that we are seeing the influence of an organizational phenomenon at work.

We can extend this analysis one more step, by looking at the whole-career patterns of individual managers. Pattern mapping lets us identify managers who have spent more time than others in particular patterns. Persistent cosmopolitans, who I defined as having spent at least three seven-year career stages in a cosmopolitan category, are an expected product of building a career on a command-centred frame. Of the 26 managers who could be so described, twelve (46 per cent) were from Prestex, and the rest were evenly split between the other four business units. This difference is significant at the 5 per cent level. There were not very many persistent innovators, but most of these were Norchem managers, again as expected. Persistent iteration was a very rare phenomenon, but of the three managers in this group, two were amongst the most successful managers from Norchem, providing support for the prediction that iteration can be the result of a successful career on a constructional climbing-frame. Finally, of the fourteen managers in the persistent expanders group, half came from ISE, again very much as expected.

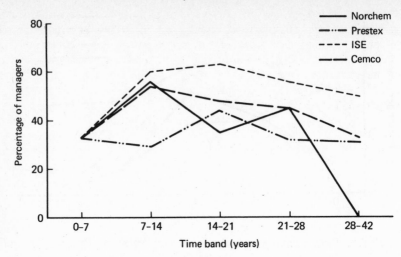

Figure 8.7   Pattern map of expansion in Norchem, Prestex, ISE and Cemco

Analysing careers by career stage is more difficult than simply looking at the distribution of individual work role transitions, but it can provide important supporting information. Both kinds of analysis — transition and pattern — show the predicted effects of the firms' organizational career logics. They also show, as expected, that there is variation in career patterns within each firm. In the final part of the chapter I shall illustrate some of the sources of the variation, by looking at the biographies of managers who have made their careers on differently shaped climbing-frames.

Moving over the climbing-frames: biographical examples

It is easy to forget that the patterns I have been discussing are the results of mapping the careers of real people. Sometimes they follow their organizational career logic, sometimes they do not, but rarely do they fit the ideal types one constructs in a theoretical study such as this. The analysis in this chapter has been about overall influences of career climbing-frames, and I shall conclude it by showing what the frames mean for individuals. For simplicity, I shall restrict the examples to managers who have mainly built their careers within their business units' modal organizational logics, or who have built careers within islands of non-modal career logic.

Constructional career logics   Two senior and highly successful engineering managers from Norchem are good examples of building a career within a constructional framework.

Over the course of a long career the first engineer had worked for only a short time outside what could generally be called engineering. However, this covered mechanical maintenance, civil construction, mechanical construction, theoretical design, method study in design and construction, and project management, all in a wide variety of different sites across Dewar Industries (Norchem's parent company). Not only did these cut across traditional professional boundaries such as the one separating civil and mechanical engineering, but the kind of work, the work environments, the time horizons and the people with whom he dealt all differed greatly from one post to another. It was, in other words, an example of how an organization with a very complex division of labour has a great many organizational boundaries which can be crossed in complex ways. This complexity is not uncommon in technical careers (Ziman, 1987).

The second engineer's career shows how, even within a highly differentiated structure, it is possible to detect a command-centred logic at senior levels. His very early career was marked by a classic example of searching: he joined Dewar Industries, left the company and the country and worked for two other companies before returning to Dewar. He next made a series of building moves, sometimes to new activities (innovation) and sometimes not (cosmopolitanism). The cosmopolitan moves reflected something of a command-centred logic as he was moved through three successively larger factory engineering jobs. Twenty-four years after starting work he made an innovating jump to an entirely unfamiliar business function. Shortly after that he was put on the divisional board with three activities in his portfolio: engineering, the new function, and a cross-functional business area which was part of the division's matrix structure.

The two engineers were also the two successful persistent iterators we met in the previous section of this chapter, managers for whom at least three seven-year career stages had been mainly characterized by iteration. This pattern is more commonly associated with plateauing, but it is also a product of constructional logics. Their innovation moves were accompanied by a considerable amount of iteration, in particular in each of their final appointments. Here, they were both given responsibility for a large number of parts of Norchem in which they had previously worked.

Command-centred career logics   Most Prestex managers' careers had been made on command-centred climbing-frames, some of which spanned companies. Moving between companies was particularly common early in their careers, which for many was when the industry was less concentrated and there were more small firms to move between.

The building process of one of the most successful and senior Prestex managers had had a very clear political as well as technical side to it (chapter 5). He started as a management trainee with Prestex but became so irritated by not being allowed to do a 'proper' job that he got himself transferred in a searching move to become a technical assistant in one of Prestex's R&D units. At that time some new machinery was being experimented with, and he became the company expert on it. The experience and contacts this gave him led to his being invited to take up his first command, setting up a plant using this machinery for another, smaller, company. He soon realized that his promotion chances were limited there so he rejoined Prestex's R&D unit in a further searching move as personal assistant to the unit's head. From there his career turned into a succession of moves from command to command. His boss was promoted to run a plant and then a group of plants. On each occasion he moved with his boss as deputy, so that he was in a very senior position by his early thirties. His last two moves were at board level as production director, first of a smaller sister division to Prestex and then of Prestex itself. He had, in other words, become 'admiral' of the 'fleet' of plants.

Command-centred climbing-frames can, as table 8.1 suggests, cause continuity and expanding moves as well as cosmopolitan ones. A senior Prestex executive experienced cosmopolitan moves in his first ten years at work, during which time he moved across a number of organizational boundaries. These moves included being head-hunted by a competitor and then head-hunted back again by his first employer. Thereafter he continued to build, getting promoted steadily up Prestex's command structure. The remaining twenty-five years saw him rise by means of expanding and continuity moves to a senior and highly respected position in charge of a group of plants without any further cosmopolitanism.

Evolutionary career logics Evolutionary climbing-frames generate career patterns in which personal and corporate growth go together hand-in-hand. Two examples from ISE illustrate this.

A university teacher joined ISE's components business in its R&D department and introduced the technology which subsequently displaced the one which was current at the time he joined the company. The work grew, they started selling some of the new components, the scale of production grew and he grew with it, becoming Chief Engineer. For reasons which were not made clear at the interview an interlude followed. He was put in charge of a business in a completely different product area, but when the general manager of his original business was promoted he moved back to take charge, where he stayed ever since. At the time of my study his original subsection of an R&D department had grown into a highly successful subsidiary of ISE, with him as its managing director.

The head of one of the control systems divisions of ISE had started work with ISE as a development engineer on a major government project in the project's early days. As the organization grew and became more complex the emphasis of his work shifted to match it. He became involved in the development of many spin-offs from the project, including staying up all night writing a paper proposing a new venture which eventually became very successful. These spin-offs eventually led to the formation of a fully fledged subsidiary company. He was responsible for many of the projects within this subsidiary, and both the projects and the subsidiary grew steadily. When the chief executive of the subsidiary fell ill he was the obvious choice to take over. The move seems to have taken him by surprise, although it was an obvious consequence of ISE's evolutionary career logic.

Turnaround career logics The turnaround climbing-frame automatically suggests well-known 'company doctors', that is, people who have become known for their apparent ability to rescue company after company from the brink of disaster. Their careers are too well documented, often by themselves, to need reiterating here. But it is worth recognizing that there are many less well-known managers who are also given this kind of role.

One such was a development engineer for one of ISE's large government contracts who showed himself early in his career to be the kind of person who naturally took charge of things whether or not that was his official role. He grew rapidly with the project and played a large part in turning it into a major business transcending the project itself. When one of ISE's subsidiaries ran into a crisis which threatened to bring the entire Group down, the Chairman of ISE asked him to try to rescue it. He accepted, spent five years rebuilding the division and was then sent to do a similar job for a US subsidiary of ISE. He had clearly made the transition to turnaround manager.

Non-modal organizational career logics Organizational climbing-frames, as we have seen, are not necessarily homogeneous: they can have islands of differently shaped frames. These islands resemble ecological niches within which it is quite possible to build all or part of a career. If the niche is important to the company (cf. Hickson et al., 1971) such careers can be very successful. If it is not, the careers suffer by comparison with those made outside the niche on the company's modal climbing-frame.

We saw an example of a successful niche career in the manager whose experience map is shown in figure 7.3. Six years after joining his highly specialized family firm he became its chief executive. Soon after that, the firm was acquired by Prestex, which largely left him alone. He expanded the business until it was four or five times larger than it was when he first joined it. He had, in other words, operated his own independent evolutionary career logic very successfully within the command-centred logic of Prestex.

There were also examples of successful niche careers within Norchem. These exploited the islands of command-centred logic within its modal constructional logic, most commonly in the important area of production management. For example, a successful production manager had experienced some early innovation moves, building within Norchem's constructional logic. The jobs involved working as a plant chemist and shuttling to and from the central production coordination department before moving into a classic command-centred sequence of posts as senior plant manager, assistant factory site manager and then factory site manager.

Not all niche careers were successful within Norchem, however, because some niches could prove to be hazardous places to occupy. A young PhD chemist joined Norchem to work on a major project which looked like an exciting venture to be part of. It was a rare example of the division growing in an unpatterned way. The product was new to Norchem as was its market, and it involved a joint venture with another firm from a different industry. The climbing-frame model predicts that the project group should have had an evolutionary career logic, which is non-modal for Norchem. The young chemist sensed that this was so and that staying with the project was not the way to get ahead in Norchem. He tried to search for a more mainstream job in Norchem but was persuaded to stay with the project by an attractive salary offer. Eventually the project flopped in a spectacular and highly visible way. Only then did he find himself able to join the modal career logic for Norchem. It was clear that his career had suffered as a result, because he had spent too long trapped within the career niche of the failed project.

The examples I have given are some of the simpler ones I encountered, in that they are mainly the result of people building their careers on the modal climbing-frame offered by each firm. Even so we saw exceptions, such as the young textile manager who lost patience with Prestex's management training scheme and the university teacher who left academic life to join ISE. In my study I met managers who had searched for different kinds of work early in their careers and managers who had searched late, managers who were unhappy with the subsisting which had been forced on them and managers who were entirely satisfied with it. All of these individual routes across the climbing-frames introduced variations to the expectations framed in table 8.1. They help explain why there is by no means always a simple relationship between a given organizational career climbing-frame and the patterns of work role transitions one finds in the careers of the managers who move over it. But − in the sense of exceptions proving rules

– they support the basic concept of this book, that managerial careers have a structural basis.

SUMMARY

In this chapter I drew together the two themes of this book, by showing how the career mapping technique I developed in part III can be used to identify the distinctive career cultures produced by each of the four organizational career logics I described in part II. Each kind of climbing-frame generates its own kind of moves from job to job.

We can expect careers made on each shape of frame to have a high proportion of particular kinds of work role transition, with certain other kinds also common. The constant search for new experiences that constructional frames require should generate a high proportion of innovation and to a lesser extent iteration moves. Careers on command-centred frames consist in large measure of moves from command to successively more responsible command, which means that a great many of the transitions from post to post will be cosmopolitan, or, less frequently, continuity or expansion. Evolutionary frames involve managers growing with their posts, so that expansion and secondarily continuity should characterize their careers. Finally, we expect turn-around frames to require a high degree of innovation, although there is still the possibility of cosmopolitanism for the 'industry expert'.

When we come to examine the patterns of work role transition in any given organization, we can expect to find the picture rather more complex than the previous paragraph suggests.

First, if the organization is of any size it is likely that there will be parts of it, islands or niches, with different organizational career logics. Some managers might spend part or all of their careers in these niches. The so-called modal organizational career logic is simply the one which predominates in a firm; it does not exclude other possibilities. Some-times, but by no means always, it is possible to have quite a successful career within one of these niches.

Second, not everyone is allowed to move to the higher reaches of a firm's climbing-frame. For many managers, alternative individual logics take over: searching for a different climbing-frame or subsisting on the frame they are on. These individual logics produce their own charac-teristic patterns of work role transition. Searching leaves its mark as innovation or sometimes cosmopolitan moves, while subsisting is likely to generate almost any kind of move except expansion.

In the second part of the chapter I drew on the findings of my own research study to illustrate the theoretical discussion of the first part. I showed how one can identify the shapes of career climbing-frames and looked at some of the research data from the managers' careers which bring out the distinctive features of each business unit's career culture. Finally, using biographical summaries as examples, I showed what climbing each kind of frame can be like in practice and how the kinds of choices individuals can make are still constrained by the organizational logic of the firms in which they work.

9
Career Patterns: Their Effects on Managers

INTRODUCTION

The experience and pattern maps described in part III of the book reveal distinctive patterns of work experience in the biographies of managers building their careers on different kinds of career climbing-frame. There is not a great deal known about how career paths affect managerial behaviour (chapter 2). But if the shape of career climbing-frames predicts the kind of transitions managers go through as they move from job to job, it also has the potential for predicting something of the kind of manager who will emerge as a result. Different organizational career logics can affect managers in two distinct ways.

Firstly, the experience managers gain over the course of their careers must influence the kind of knowledge they acquire. The knowledge can encompass both how to manage and a detailed understanding of how the managers' firms work. Both kinds of knowledge are important, and different climbing-frames will develop them in different relative proportions.

Secondly, the experience is likely to influence the way managers make sense of their business situation. Firms differ in the way that their management teams interpret their business environment and draw inferences about the kinds of strategy that they should adopt. This, in turn, affects the way they go about implementing the strategies (Johnson, 1987; Schwenk, 1988). Different organizational career logics are likely to reinforce different kinds of strategic behaviour.

The knowledge that managers need in order to operate as managers is a complex, controversial subject. Before reviewing each of the organizational career logics, I need to explain the sense in which I shall be using the term 'knowledge' here. I must also show the connection between the account I have just given of the strategy-making process and organizational career processes.

MANAGERIAL KNOWLEDGE AND RATIONALITIES

From a manager's point of view, knowledge is what he or she has to sell on the labour market. Its value may be restricted to a part of one particular company or to the company as a whole; it might be generally marketable within a given industry or it might sell anywhere. It might limit a manager to one particular kind of job but in many different kinds of organization, or it may qualify him or her to manage anything at all. This implies that we can look at the movement of managers across their career climbing-frames as governed by, and governing, the knowledge they acquire as they move from rung to rung.

Managerial knowledge is something of a portmanteau expression. If we are to deduce anything about the impact of different career climbing-frames on managers' knowledge we need to be rather more precise about what it might cover. In chapter 3 I showed that the question of what makes a good manager is far from easily answered. A great many attempts have been made to pin down what managerial knowledge might consist of. Writers and researchers have produced more or less elaborate lists including items like technical, human, conceptual, organizational and institutional skills (for instance Katz, 1974; Shetty and Peery, 1976; Guglielmino and Carroll, 1979; Szilagyi and Schweiger, 1984). Others deal at a more abstract level, for instance drawing a distinction between the timescale over which skills are exercised and the extent to which they are specific to particular situations (Waters, 1980). Yet others (e.g. Welford, 1980) concentrate on the way higher-order skills are better seen as hierarchies of strategies or scripts (Lord and Kernan, 1987), where longer-term strategies consist of scripts for using a particular set of shorter-term strategies.

Two main threads, which could be called *managerial expertise* and *firm-specific knowledge*, run through much of this writing. Very broadly, managerial expertise is knowing how firms work, and firm-specific knowledge is knowing the work of the firm. I shall look at each in turn.

Managerial expertise

Managerial expertise is the expertise that the best salesman, for example, needs in order to become a good sales manager. The literature, both academic and practical, is full of references to it, although writers such as Mintzberg (1973) are far from convinced that it is as widely understood. The movement leading to the development of business education rests at least in part on the assumption that the expertise can be identified and packaged for sale. Technical specialists, for instance, often find themselves facing the 'problem' of becoming promoted to manage other specialists. They worry about how they are to acquire the managerial expertise they need to supplement their professional skills (Medcof, 1985). It is not uncommon for them to become dismayed to find in the end that there is no clear technology of management, in the way that they are used to their own specialism having a technology (Torrington and Weightman, 1982).

Within the (probably countless) lists of what constitutes managerial expertise two distinct kinds of skill can be recognized, which we could call technical and social process skills.

Technical skills   There is a wide array of techniques available using the logic of the mathematician, microeconomist, accountant or strategist to help managers structure and simplify complex business problems. The kind of techniques I have in mind here include linear programming, modelling, simulation, materials requirements planning, discounted cash flow methods, market research, financial portfolio analysis, learning curves, Boston Grid and so on. These tools transform reality into a series of simple statements about profitability, market posture, optimality of arrangements of real or financial assets and so forth. They do it with such power that an understanding of them seems to be a *sine qua non* for anyone trying to succeed in a modern business organization. These skills can be taught on, for instance, business courses. The skill with which they are applied is not so easily learned, however, because it means learning how to analyse complex, unstructured situations and choosing the most appropriate technique.

Social process skills   Writers such as Mintzberg (1973), Stewart (1976, 1982), Kotter (1982) and Boyatzis (1982) describe managing in process terms, looking at the social dynamics of the managerial role or the competencies needed to carry out the social processes of managing. 'Social process skills' is my label for the package of skills which enable managers to make sense of and manage these social processes. The extent to which people can acquire the skills is far from clear. Areas of disagreement include whether leaders are born or made, at which stage in life they acquire the ability to lead and whether being socially skilled is as important as being socially connected.

Firm-specific knowledge

Firm-specific knowledge is to do with the work of the firm. It comes in many forms, ranging from a detailed knowledge of the firm's products and technologies to a broad understanding of how the organization is managed and fits into its industry(ies).

The more detailed the knowledge of products and processes, the less it has to do with the process of managing. In a production manager's job such detail might include knowledge of the products and how they are made, how the production plant works and the workforce. In a marketing job it might cover knowing the company's customers and products, and how to sell the products. In a finance job it might include an understanding of how the firm's accounts are drawn up, how its management control systems work, tax law, or how to go about raising external finance.

Some of this knowledge may be more generalizable than the rest. For instance, research managers in a chemical firm know about the chemistry of the products their company sells and also about which products their company sells. Both are to do with the basic activities of the firm, but the former is more generalizable than the latter because much of it may have been learned independently of the particular firm, perhaps at university.

There are broadly two views about the relevance to managing of detailed knowledge like this, involving a hard and a soft line. The hard line is that this kind of knowledge is completely irrelevant to the business of managing. The soft line is that it is only one kind of knowledge that a manager needs. Knowing detail may help managers, but they will also need to know about how the firm is managed, for instance, how the firm is coordinated and controlled, whom to go to to get things done and whom to avoid, who the customers, suppliers and other important external agents are, whom the firm deals with, who its competitors are and what they are like. Internally, they need to know and understand the firm's culture, and externally they need to know and understand the networks of contacts which connect firms and industries. A good engineer or accountant can only become a good engineering or accounting manager if he or she has a grasp of these broader issues.

As we saw in chapter 2, there is a growing view which holds that this knowledge of the firm is vital to the successful manager. The more that executives depend on it, the less they can be described as 'professional managers', that is, managers who can turn their hands to managing anything because they rely exclusively on their managerial expertise.

So managerial expertise is to do with the way organizations work in general, while firm-specific knowledge is to do with the work of a particular firm. Managerial expertise, which I separated into technical and social process skills, does not necessarily have to be learned on the job, but anyone not versed in it simply cannot make sense of much of what is going on in their firm. Most firm-specific knowledge can only be learned on the job.

If we are trying to understand how management teams operate, we also need to know something about their basic operating assumptions, which I call here 'managerial rationalities' (Whitley, 1987a).

Managerial rationalities

We can picture managerial rationalities as the way managers make sense of their business world. These rationalities render certain actions and possibilities 'sensible' and 'rational' while others are ignored or considered 'unrealistic'. They imply preferences for certain kinds of managerial skills and experiences (Whitley, 1987a) and form an important part of the set of shared beliefs that together make up the organization's overall culture (Schein, 1985).

The managerial rationality of a firm's dominant coalition is likely to have as profound an effect on the way the firm is run as does the managers' expertise and firm-specific knowledge. Indeed, they are closely linked. For instance, imagine a company run by engineers which pursues narrowly technical goals. This may be because the managerial rationality of the top management team holds that this is the way engineering firms should be run. Alternatively, it may be because their knowledge base is centred on engineering, and they have little, if any, managerial expertise between them. It is most likely to be a mixture of both. They have probably not bothered to acquire the necessary managerial expertise because the culture of the firm reinforces the view that they know all they need to know.

Because managerial rationalities are part of the firm's culture they are intimately tied up with organizational career processes (chapter 3). The kind of people who are likely to do well in the firm are the ones who fit the firm's culture and who tend to see the world in the way specified by the firm's dominant rationality. They are involved in producing a firm's distinctive career culture, and in so doing they are affected by it. We cannot say that a particular managerial rationality is 'caused' by a particular career system, or the other way round. When we come to examine each career logic, though, we can see how each reinforces the other.

We can now return to the four organizational career logics to see what impacts each might have on managerial knowledge and rationalities. I shall review each logic in turn.

CAREER CLIMBING-FRAMES AND THE MANAGERS THEY DEVELOP

Evolutionary logic

We can expect that managers building their careers within an evolutionary logic will be high in firm-specific knowledge. They are the quintessential specialists who have built their careers around their business.

There is a large tacit component to firm-specific knowledge of the kind developed by evolutionary logics. Tacit knowledge is the knowledge which people have but cannot explain to anyone else (Polanyi, 1958), in the way that one knows how to ride a bicycle without being able to say how it is done. The organization feels to the managers like an extension of themselves in the way that a car feels to an experienced driver. This was nicely illustrated by one manager in my study. Some years earlier he had designed a particular kind of heavy engineering equipment for his company and he had had a central role in its subsequent development. A whole business division grew from this, which he headed. His office walls were decked with photographs of the product in the way that many others have pictures of their family. It was obvious that he and the product were as one.

It is easy to see why managers in this kind of environment might be thought of as immobile and narrow. Their knowledge base is so clearly identified with their own business. It may well be that evolutionary managers have a very good grasp of managerial skills (technical and social process) as well, but because the evolutionary logic is one of growing one's own business they have not had the chance to demonstrate the fact by trying the skills out on a new business somewhere else. If they did move to something else it would be quite a wrench to leave what they have built.

Nevertheless we know that such managers can move from one environment to another if a strong enough reason exists. The engineer who rescued ISE's troubled division (chapter 8) is a case in point. Because of the way in which evolutionary managers have been involved in 'building a business' they may well be seen as 'good managers' who are worth trying to lure away to another environment, despite the clear organizational specificity of their expertise. Indeed this reflects what we might well expect of evolutionary firms' managerial rationalities.

Firms like these have not grown to a pattern. They have gone into a series of new ventures in unfamiliar environments, and that is how their successful managers have built their careers. If people have visibly succeeded in the firm by building new businesses, then others will be encouraged to emulate them. It is easy to see a career system like this nurturing a managerial rationality which supports a 'prospecting' business strategy (Miles and Snow, 1978), in which the response to business difficulties is to find something new to do. And of course the more successful prospecting the firm does, the greater the number of managers who benefit from the evolutionary career logic that flows from it. So we can expect an evolutionary career logic to nurture a prospecting rationality and vice versa.

Command-centred logics probably come a close second to evolutionary logics in the way they build firm-specific knowledge into a manager. Prestex managers (chapter 8), for instance, would tell me that they could walk through their plants and, without looking, know what percentage of equipment was down because of broken yarn. Whether or not that was true is almost beside the point, although it is unlikely that anyone would idly boast about a skill so easily checked. The point is that there was a widely shared belief not only that plant managers had this task expertise but that they needed it in order to be able to run their plants at peak efficiency.

Similarly, command-centred managers' knowledge of how their firms work is only limited by the extent to which their moves from command to command have taken them around the firm. Whereas evolutionary managers spend a good part of their careers in one part of the firm, command-centred managers move from part to part, so that their knowledge of any one command is likely to be less detailed. On the other hand, they will be building up a generalized picture of what the commands are like and of the structure in which they are embedded. Their organizational knowledge, in other words, will be less specific to individual commands but more to do with the hierarchy the commands fall within.

It can also be that the contacts they build up as part of their cosmopolitanism extend to other firms in the industry. This is common in businesses such as advertising, product development and design which consist of many small firms between which people are constantly on the move. It was also a strong feature of the early careers of the Prestex managers in my study, in some cases persisting throughout their careers. For instance, the international mobility of the manager whose experience map is shown in figure 7.7(d) had come about because he had developed a reputation in the textile business as some-one who was available for overseas work. Still only in his late forties, he had worked in fourteen textile-manufacturing posts for ten different companies in six different countries.

Alternatively, if a manager's commands have been within some kind of professional area of activity, for instance, finance or research, they might connect him or her with professional networks across most sectors of the economy or perhaps even internationally.

Managers are likely to emerge from a lengthy period of building within a command-centred logic with a model of managing strongly coloured by generalizations they have drawn from several, similar commands. Their skills as managers are likely to be a function of the length of time they have spent in their chosen activity overall, rather than of how long they have spent in any one command along the way.

This is certainly what McEnrue (1988) found with a group of restaurant managers she studied.

Paradoxically, although command-centred managers have been more mobile than evolutionary managers, we might expect them to be less transferable out of their industry or firm. Their mobility has probably created a reputation for them as, for instance, a good plant, finance or sales-force manager rather than someone generally good at 'running things' or building a business. The extreme examples of this are the professionals, whose knowledge is highly specific to their particular occupation. For instance, although a mining engineer may be able to find jobs all over the world, he or she will find it hard to get a job outside the extractive industry for which he or she is trained.

Command-centred cultures, then, build expertise in the firm's area of operations but without much moving into anything new because of its history of patterned growth. The managerial rationality most likely to be reinforced in this kind of organization is one which supports a 'defender' strategy (Miles and Snow, 1978). 'Defenders' are companies which are experts in their fields, which concentrate on getting better at what they do rather than searching for new opportunities outside their area of expertise. These are all likely outcomes of a career system in which people advance by demonstrating that they are good at running the basic operations of the business. In Prestex, for instance, the top production executives were widely admired by their subordinates for being the best plant managers in the division.

So if the career system seems to reward this kind of expertise, it is easy to see how it might nurture an inward-turning managerial rationality of the defender type. This, in turn, reinforces the command-centred career logic by making it less likely that the company will change structure or direction. A change of structure carries with it the risk that the commands will disappear, and everyone who has invested a large part of their lives in building their careers by moving between commands will see the value of their investment vanish.

Constructional logic

The managerial expertise most likely to be developed on constructional climbing-frames is to do with social process skills, to the extent that they help managers become effective quickly in unfamiliar settings and to work within complex webs of organizational pathways. It certainly seems likely that a background of frequent moves should make it easier for someone to adapt more quickly to new jobs (Louis, 1980b; Nicholson, 1984), although for geographical moves at least it is not easy to prove it (Pinder and Schroeder, 1987). One often comes across managers in such firms who are clearly on a fast track but none of whose colleagues can tell one quite why, other than that they are socially very skilled. They have gained the reputation amongst their seniors for effectiveness, although it can be very hard to find solid achievements to explain the reputation.

It is possible that constructional climbing-frame managers may acquire some managerial expertise in the form of technical skills, although it is quite likely that the techniques involved will be unique to, or adapted by, the firms they work for. The highly differentiated structure of constructional-logic firms often means that they have their own ways of doing things. For instance, it is quite common for corporations like this to have their own unique management control systems, ways of assessing new projects, and human resource management systems. These can make it hard for people trained elsewhere in the technical skills of management, such as business graduates, to fit in without going through the same induction process followed by managers without business school training. So the technical skills developed on constructional climbing-frames may often be better described as firm-specific knowledge.

The managerial expertise that we can expect to be developed on a constructional climbing-frame, then, is more likely to be related to social process than technical skills. Because these social skills are about coping with mobility, we can expect constructional frames to breed managers who think of themselves as all-purpose generalists, professional managers who can turn their hands to anything. This self-image is unlikely to be shaken by seeing the consequences of their actions, because of the way they are insulated from these consequences by their mobility. As Weick (1979: 84−5) points out:

> it could be argued that people who move around a lot are less likely to see the world as full of causal circuits. The reason for this is that people who are mobile may not stay in a situation long enough to discover the consequences of their actions. The consequences do not come back and affect transients, because transients have moved to a new setting. Transients are left with the impression that what they did had an effect. What they fail to see is that if they had stayed, the effect in turn would have influenced them.

This view of constructional-logic managers as all-purpose generalists is likely to be reinforced by the kind of firm-specific knowledge that we can expect them to acquire.

Unless managers building within a constructional logic have followed a command-centred interlude (chapter 8) it is hard to see how they can acquire much detailed firm-specific knowledge of products, technologies and processes. Because they are constantly moving from job to different job they gain an overview of many different activities but master none. Even if they do spend some time with one activity it is quite likely that when they reach a senior level and find that activity within their portfolio again, what remains of their detailed knowledge will be obsolete. Furthermore, unless the firm they are building their career within is small, they have no hope of doing every significant job in it. Although the constructional logic is supposed to be about building 'complete' managers who know in detail how the company works, the reality must be that managers from large firms can only be partially complete.

However, while they might not learn much about the detail of what their firm does, they are likely to pick up a good deal about how it, and quite possibly its industry(ies), are managed. Their movement up, around and across the firm will help them to learn how it fits together and to build internal networks of contacts. They may also acquire industry contacts, although their professional networks (networks crossing industries) are likely to be less well-maintained because of the way they keep changing professions.

The political component of the constructional logic is often very apparent in these careers. Norchem, for instance, has a key production coordination department which lies at the heart of the division's operations. Anyone working in it gains a valuable overview of the division's activities, but — perhaps equally important — they also get high visibility to the rest of the division (Forbes, 1987). Special assignments reporting to senior management, often a key feature of the careers of high-flyers in constructional career logics, have much the same value.

There is nothing necessarily wrong with the political side of either overview-gaining or visibility. In order to be effective managers have to get to know their colleagues in the management team (Penrose, 1980), which may be large. Senior managers need to identify their potential successors. Similarly, the bright young people have to learn their way around, how to operate within the organization's culture, and what makes it 'tick'. One of the splendid recurring themes in the BBC television series *Yes [Prime] Minister*, which is almost a distance learning course in building a constructional career, concerns Bernard, the minister's private secretary, the perpetual novice learning the UK Civil Service's oral tradition.

It is very hard to be explicit about the nature and value of such organizational knowledge. There is a large tacit component to it concerning norms and values, so that it might take such forms as

- knowledge of how the organization fits together;
- knowledge of the various subcultures of the firm so that the managers know instinctively how to present themselves and their ideas to gain acceptability;

- shared experience they can refer back to to gain credibility with their colleagues and subordinates ('as an accountant/production man/researcher/salesman I ...').

But because it is tacit it is hard to explain its importance to anyone else. If that is so, we can expect it to be undervalued when people are assessing what it is that they need in their top managers. It is not easy to admit that someone might make a good choice for a senior job just because they 'know their way around' in some general, inexplicit sense. It is much more ideologically acceptable to concentrate on their managerial expertise, even though it may not always be entirely clear what this expertise is, how it has been developed by the managers' experience with the company or how the expertise will help them to become effective in the new post. This, in turn, will reinforce the view that managers who have built their careers on constructional climbing-frames make good, all-purpose professional managers.

One should be careful about making too ready a prediction about the kind of managerial rationality nurtured by a constructional career system. It is tempting, nevertheless, to speculate that it is supportive of the 'analyser' strategy (Miles and Snow, 1978). The non-recursive, highly differentiated structures which provide the basic frame for the constructional career mean that managers rarely get to see a business venture in the round. These firms are often also beset by multiple levels of committees which have to look at every new business idea, and there can be a long and painful process that has to be gone through for any changes to be authorized. By the time the change has happened, the manager who started it can easily be in another job, well away from the action. Growing a business, in fact, can easily be seen as a career dead-end in this kind of culture, which does not encourage people to start new business ventures. This suggests that the strategies such firms may follow involve the careful analysis and risk avoidance of the analyser. It could also be that the bureaucratic pathologies become completely paralysing, in which case the culture will encourage the firm to be more of a 'reactor' (Miles and Snow, 1978).

Turnaround logic

It is hard to see how turnaround managers' firm-specific knowledge can be anything other than low, if only because they rarely work for one firm for long enough to build much. It is possible that they have some industry knowledge in the form of access to networks, of contacts across firms and industries, and in other vital sectors such as financial services. Indeed it might well have been their contacts with the financial world which led to their being appointed in the first place if the firm's problems emerged as a financial crisis (cf. Boswell, 1983: 157). But however well they may be connected with the business world, we are still left with the puzzle of the skills they use to manage their firms. As with constructional career logics, we find ourselves having to concentrate on their managerial expertise to make up for their lack of firm-specific knowledge.

There are differences between constructional and turnaround careers which call for caution in looking for too close a parallel between the managerial expertise developed by each logic. I suggested that constructional managers might be high on the skills of social process and that there might not necessarily be a great call for the technical skills of management. For turnaround managers the opposite might often be the case.

The technical skills of management are called for in a way that they are not in constructional careers. Turning around businesses is a different job from fitting into a complex organization and is much more likely to need the kind of expertise that is taught, for instance, in business schools. In my study I found managers whose management skills had clearly been sharpened by the turnaround role and managers who had been selected for the job because they were known to be skilled technicians in that sense. It is hard to see anyone being effective in the role unless they are, for instance, able to speak the language of bankers and accountants, of marketing specialists and, perhaps, business strategists.

There are undoubtedly turnaround situations where the social skills of the charismatic leader are just what is needed to take a defeated group of people and get them moving again. These skills were clearly possessed in abundance by the manager who had rescued the division of ISE which had nearly brought the Group down. Robert Townsend describes his time at Avis in these terms (Townsend, 1978), as does Lee Iacocca at Chrysler (Iacocca and Novak, 1986). But managers such as these also talk about the need for hard decisions, and perhaps the polar opposite of the charismatic leader is the caricature 'hatchet man' who solves crises by ruthless cutting of businesses and people. There are many cases of turnaround managers celebrated for their abrasive and dictatorial styles, whose model of encouraging their staff is to operate by fear. This is often done by operating in a distant mode, working from a remote office through a small, trusted staff the manager has brought with him from outside.

Once again it seems as if we have a career culture which develops people who see themselves as all-purpose generalists. Whatever the pre-crisis career culture, the new career success model which the turnaround manager holds up to the rest of the firm is all about mobility, apparently demonstrating by example that managing is managing wherever it is done. Firm-specific knowledge will very likely become devalued amongst the company's ambitious managers at the expense of the managerial expertise their new top management clearly seems to have.

The question of the effect of turnaround career logics on managerial rationalities is more complex, if only because the frames span companies and what can happen in crises is so unpredictable. Perhaps the best way of looking at the effects is to think in terms of an 'unfreezing' of cherished attitudes. This unfreezing process can be helped by the way the old regime will have been discredited. In such situations, most things come up for criticism whether they deserve it or not (Gephart, 1978; Handy, 1985: 19). Quite where the unfreezing takes the firm is impossible to predict without knowing the specifics of the situation, in particular the beliefs of the turnaround manager himself. This, in turn, will probably depend on the turnaround manager's own career background.

One well-known behaviour pattern is for incoming managers to set about duplicating the environment they are familiar with. They might bring in their 'strategic replacements' (Gouldner, 1954), but equally they might introduce organizational control devices with which they are familiar from past jobs. Nicholson (1984: 176) refers to this process in a kind of role transition he calls 'determination', which is when individuals are hardly affected by the new role although it is very different for them:

> there is evidence from less systematic investigations that determination is a significant outcome of transition, notably in the succession of political leaders to new offices (Burns, 1978) and the career progression of entrepreneurs (Steiner and Miner, 1977). In both cases the occupants imprint the stamp of their identity and unique skills upon the role and its surrounding milieu.

SUMMARY

In this chapter I concluded the process I began in chapter 8 of drawing together the two themes of the book, by exploring the ways in which the themes might inform the question of the link between managerial careers and behaviour.

I looked at two aspects of managing: the managerial knowledge developed by each career climbing-frame, and the managerial rationalities each frame will nurture. I distinguished between two aspects of managerial knowledge, managerial expertise (how firms work) and firm-specific knowledge (the work of the firm). I divided managerial expertise, in turn, into the technical skills of managing and social

Table 9.1 *Organizational logics and managerial cultures*

| Organizational logic | Firm-specific knowledge | Managerial expertise | | Managerial rationality[b] |
		Technical	Social process	
Evolutionary	Own business unit	?	?	Prospector
Command-centred	Own specialism	?	?	Defender
Constructional	Own organization	?	Yes	Analyser[a]
Turnaround	Inter-firm networks	Yes	?	Unfreezing

[a] After Miles and Snow (1978).
[b] Or possibly reactor.

process skills. Firm-specific knowledge covers anything from knowledge of the basic work of the organization to knowledge of how the firm is put together and of its environment.

I next reviewed each of the four organizational career logics. Table 9.1 summarizes my conclusions.

Table 9.1 draws out the way different career logics can produce different kinds of manager, from command-centred managers 'stuck' within their specialism, through the possibly mobile evolutionary business builders, to the apparently mobile constructional and turnaround managers. It also shows that there are good reasons for expecting different career climbing-frames to foster distinctly different organizational cultures. There are many ways in which organizational cultures become self-sustaining, and this analysis helps us to understand the part career processes can play.

10
Conclusion

INTRODUCTION

The aim of this book was to present new ways of looking at managerial careers. To recapitulate very briefly: first, I explored the organizational logics underlying managerial careers. I showed how firms' structures and growth histories define the structure of career opportunities available to their managers and lead to predictable, distinctive career cultures. In metaphorical terms, firms can be thought of as climbing-frames or jungle gyms over which managers move to make their careers. The shape of the frame determines in large part the shapes of the careers. Managers' routes over the climbing-frames can vary, depending on their preferences and their success within the system. Second, I described a technique for analysing managers' careers in terms of their work experience which allows us to map their paths across and between their climbing-frames. Third, I showed how the mapping technique identifies distinctive career cultures in large corporations, and speculated on the effect of the cultures on the kind of managers and managerial rationalities they might develop and sustain.

In this chapter I shall look at some further implications of these ideas, both for those with an interest in theory and research on managerial careers and for practitioners. By 'practitioner' I mean both those responsible for managing other people's careers, either as line managers or as human resource specialists, and anyone concerned with their own career.

IMPLICATIONS FOR RESEARCH ON MANAGERIAL CAREERS

The career logics model: contributions to theory

This study helps us to understand the systemic nature of managerial careers. The career logics model provides a new perspective on managerial careers because of the way in which it integrates structure and process at both organizational and individual levels of analysis. The individual level of analysis produces explanations known to the actors (managers) themselves, although the explanations may be expressed differently by an observer. The organizational level generates explanations, to do with circumstances which act on the individuals, which may or may not be well understood by the individuals affected by the circumstances (Giddens, 1984: xix).

Rather than looking on a career as the outcome of individual choices, of randomly triggered vacancies for which individuals compete, or as the pay-off from a particular social or educational background, the career logics model begins to tie together some of these phenomena into coherent patterns. It puts forward reasons for expecting distinctive career cultures within firms which can be explained in terms of both the structure of the company and the way in which it has developed. Using only three characteristics of a firm, the recursiveness of its structure, the extent to which it has grown to a pattern and the extent to which it has experienced central continuity, I showed how four distinct ideal-type organizational career logics could be expected. As we saw in chapter 8, each logic is associated with its own patterns of experience-building and experience-shedding which can be mapped comparatively easily.

If the career logics model points to distinctive ways in which managerial structures are renewed in firms, it also allows for variation about organizations' modal career patterns. Some of this variance arises because firms, especially large ones, may have more than one organizational career logic at work. Some of it comes from the way people either make their own choices on the basis of what I called their individual career logics or have choices forced on them which prevent them from continuing to move over the firm's career climbing-frame. In addition, some of the variance is simply because the climbing-frame model is essentially probabilistic. An organizational career logic describes the logic underlying career moves, not what happens in every case.

The model encourages us to delve below superficial statistics which tell us nothing about managers' actual work experience. It predicts the kind of work experience managers have in different organizational career logics (chapter 8), which allows us to draw inferences about the kinds of managers they might turn out to be and about the kind of managerial rationality that is nurtured in the firm (chapter 9).

This means that career processes can be brought into the wider enquiry about how large corporations are managed. As Whitley (1987a) argues, careers reveal a great deal about managerial rationalities because they are open to observation within the firm as well as to outsiders. All kinds of culturally dependent preferences are exposed: for particular kinds of people, for particular ways of looking at the firm's business world, for particular ideas about what constitute 'proper' managerial activities and for particular views about what the firm ought to be doing.

There is a growing awareness that these rationalities play a central role in governing the strategic behaviour of corporations (Johnson, 1987; Schwenk, 1988). They have been given a variety of labels, among them 'strategic frames', 'interpretive schemes', 'paradigms', 'recipes' and 'logics of action' (Karpik, 1978; Hodgkinson, Gunz and Johnson, 1988). The idea common to these concepts is the set of shared beliefs which causes management teams to place particular interpretations on their business situation, draw particular inferences about the kinds of strategy they should adopt and go about implementing the strategies in particular ways.

If we were to summarize strategy implementation as resulting in a set of business outcomes – for instance growth, contraction, diversification – and a set of structural arrangements, then we can see how the career logics model fits into the picture. The model explains how business outcomes and organizational structures shape the careers of firms' managers. It describes these shapes in terms of the work experience the managers get, from which it is possible to draw inferences about the kind of managers they might be and the kind of managerial rationalities that the career logic nurtures. The model exposes an important feedback loop in organizations, helping to explain how they 'learn' and how their cultures are sustained.

In addition, the model shows how career processes are not some kind of exogenous variable which can be manipulated at will by, for instance, management development managers or particular elite power groups. That is not to say that these people cannot have any influence, but simply that what they do is constrained by and constrains many other organizational-level processes.

The career logics model, then, can provide valuable insights into the connection between careers and the management of our large corporations. But as I have described it here, it is only a first step along the way with a great deal of potential for further development.

The career logics model: potential for development

There are many ways in which the ideas I have described in this book might be taken forward. I shall list some of the more obvious.

The discussion of organizational career logics centred on an account of four climbing-frames, based on my observations in a small number of manufacturing corporations. I showed how these four logics could be derived from an analysis of organizations' structures and modes of growth. It was necessary to do this in order to establish that there were theoretical reasons for expecting four distinct logics. It was not simply that they were the ones I found in the corporations. But it would be surprising if it did not prove possible to extend the framework in at least three directions.

Firstly, there may be other kinds of career logic waiting to be 'discovered' in other industial and national environments. We know, for instance, that careers in large Japanese, German and French corporations differ in many important respects (see, for example, Granick, 1972; Bauer and Cohen, 1981; Cohen and Bauer, 1985; Haller et al., 1985; Trevor, Schendel and Wilpert, 1986). A major area for development is to find out whether it is possible to identify different organizational career logics in these very different cultures. Such work should provide a valuable new line of attack for cross-cultural studies of the management of large corporations and also shed light on the structure of careers in multinational companies.

Secondly, the concept of career logics spanning organizations and even industries has the potential to yield further understanding of the inter-organizational networks which seem to be so important to the way the corporate sector is managed (chapter 2). By suggesting a structural basis from which to make sense of inter-firm movements (cf. Pfeffer and Leblebici, 1973), the career logics framework encourages us to look beyond the traditional areas of concern amongst researchers in this area. These have tended to concentrate on kinship and social connections between the business elite. There is every reason to expect that the way industries are structured and inter-linked will be just as important.

Thirdly, we know that there can be significant differences in the way firms are managed within any given industrial environment (Porter, 1980). It may well help understanding of these differences if the organizational career logics as I have specified them here are subjected to finer-grained analysis. Different variants of each logic may help explain some of these intra-industry differences.

My description of the organizational career logics was based on three organizational dimensions. There is bound to be a great deal more to be learnt about the influences shaping managerial careers by extending this work. To date, organizational demography has tended to use fairly simple structural models of organizations as a basis for modelling the flow of people through firms. Such properties as recursiveness and the extent to which corporate growth is patterned could well be used to enrich these models, to give a deeper understanding of how managerial labour markets are segmented.

A major area of enquiry which the career logics framework opens up concerns the impact of managerial careers on behaviour. A first step in this direction is being taken by a number of researchers, who are using techniques of cognitive psychology to study the way individual managers perceive their business environment (Hodgkinson, Gunz and Johnson, 1988). These perceptions are likely to be shaped by a number of influences, amongst which career background figures largely. By linking organizational structure and business outcome to work experience, the organizational climbing-frame concept provides a theoretical framework for designing studies to explore this issue. Chapter 9 forms a research agenda by offering what is, in effect, a range of propositions for investigation. Further, the techniques for mapping and analysing work experience that I described in part III provide the necessary methodological tools.

The next step along this particular route involves studying what managers actually do, to see whether it bears any relation to what the cognitive mapping techniques have revealed of how they see their business world. Once again the career logics framework suggests lines of attack, because of the way it is possible to draw inferences about managerial rationalities from the career logics to be found in different kinds of firm.

One particular area of managerial behaviour which is illuminated by the career logics framework concerns the management of change, of strategy implementation. The extent to which managers espouse particular courses of action depends, among other things, on how they will benefit from the change. Each of the organizational career logics reinforces a particular kind of business strategy (chapter 9), suggesting reasons which might explain why it can be so hard to change strategic direction. Managers in command-centred logics, for instance, will resist change which devalues their expertise, and those in constructional logics may avoid the kind of new venture management that diversification programmes might need because they sense that it will lead to a career dead-end. But the framework also suggests circumstances in which change might come about very quickly. For example crises can lead to the imposition of a different kind of top management on the firm from outside, which can change perceptions drastically about what managers should do to get ahead.

Even the structural differences which give rise to different career logics can be expected to influence the way change can be managed. For instance the distinction between constructional and command-centred logics rests on the further distinction between non-recursive and recursive structures. This draws one's attention to what might be thought of as the 'plasticity' of an organization's structure. Command-centred logics tend to be associated with structures in which each similar post corresponds to some factory, plant, branch or geographical territory which needs managing. Of course factories can be combined for administrative purposes and areas split up, but there is something real and identifiable about them which is lacking in many non-recursive structures where it seems that people are endlessly tinkering about, trying to find new ways of handling the difficult problem of integrating their disparate tasks. If the tasks were not as disparate, the structure probably would not have been as non-recursive. This suggests that the posts in command-centred organizations have an enduring quality which is lacking in the complexity and fluidity of constructional organizations, and that when a command-centred firm grows or shrinks it has to do this to quite a significant degree in packets: by opening or closing factories, for instance. A constructional-logic firm, by contrast, should be able to change much more incrementally simply by reorganizing some of its posts.

These are just some of the potentially fruitful areas of investigation to which we are led by looking at how the business and structural consequences of managerial actions feed back into career opportunities, which in turn influence managerial actions. The areas of development I have listed so far have built on the theoretical contribution of the career logics model. The approaches to mapping and analysing career patterns which I discussed in part III open up new approaches to the study of managers' backgrounds.

Much previous work on managers' careers has been hampered by the kind of methodological difficulties which I discussed in chapters 2 and 6. The experience mapping technique and the analytical techniques which flow from it can be adapted in many ways to help overcome these difficulties. After refinement, they could well find application as human resource planning tools. Questionnaire instruments can be developed from them which could be used on large-scale surveys to build a better picture of the general population of managers and how it may divide into sub-populations. More sophisticated pattern-recognition techniques could enhance the analysis of the maps and allow more dimensions to be added, for instance level of seniority and different kinds of employer change, perhaps leading to the identification of different classes of career pattern. A key part of such developments must be to understand managers' subjective experience of their careers, for which the individual career logics of building, searching and subsisting provide a framework. The analyses could be yet further enriched by supplementing them with data on the consequences of the managers' actions. One could think of this as a form of business history, but applied to individuals rather than firms, which is likely to yield different and complementary information to that produced by experience mapping.

These are only some of the directions in which the ideas I have described in this book might be taken. They add up to a sizeable research agenda. In a sense the book will have met its purpose if only some of them are taken up.

Finally, I shall consider some of the implications of the career logics framework for career practitioners.

IMPLICATIONS FOR CAREER PRACTITIONERS: LIMITS TO TAKING CHARGE

At the beginning of this chapter I distinguished between two kinds of career practitioner: those responsible for managing other people's careers either as line managers or as human resource specialists, and anyone concerned with their own career.

Mountains of advice have been produced for both groups, often very good advice aimed at encouraging people to take charge. Career managers are warned of the hazards of letting things drift. Examples of the problems this can cause include 'age bulges' and other demographic imbalances, blocked promotion ladders and a lack of successors available for top management. Individuals are encouraged to plan their own career strategies in the light of their own desires and ambitions, rather than letting 'the system' push them into corners which they might later regret occupying.

All of this advice is good and necessary: the dangers are obvious enough. But the climbing-frame metaphor that I have explored in this book points to limits to which one can take charge. Careers, I have argued, are not under the sole control of individuals. The way a company is organized and managed limits the kinds of careers its managers can have, regardless of what they actually want. This means that it may not be enough for firms who have ideas about the way they want to develop their managers to have well-designed career development systems. They may have to adopt much broader structural or strategic solutions as well.

In the final part of this chapter I shall look at a number of situations in which the climbing-frame perspective has something to say, from the point of view first of the career manager and then of the individual.

Implications for the career manager

The concept of the organizational climbing-frame helps us see why managers might have the kinds of careers they do in a given corporation. It helps us to predict which other kinds of firm might share that kind of pattern and to understand why it can be so hard to change the pattern. Schein has defined an essential and central function of leadership as the manipulation of organizational culture (Schein, 1985), and I have tried to show in this book how intimately organizational and career cultures are interlinked. The implication is that career systems –

management development systems − are not just the province of the specialist human resource executive. They are, as many major corporations readily recognize, a central function of top management.

I shall illustrate this by looking at three common problems: developing 'intrapreneurs' in large firms, 'professionalizing' the management of evolutionary firms, and bridging the operational−general management gulf in command-centred structures.

Intrapreneurs in the large firm   Large firms with constructional climbing-frames often find themselves trying to develop new businesses in order to diversify. This, in turn, means that they have to develop executives with the entrepreneurial abilities and commitment to developing their own business within the firm. These figures have sometimes been called 'intrapreneurs'.

But as we saw in chapters 4 and 9, all the career signals in constructional cultures are to do with continually getting new experience and with not getting trapped into a specialist niche. The danger is that intrapreneurs may look on their new business ventures as something of an intellectual exercise, a stage along the way rather than an end in itself. Means may become more important than ends: it could be more important to them to be seen to be going about things in the correct way than to produce results. In this way they are able to distance themselves from failure should the venture turn out badly. Examples of this were apparent in one of the four companies I studied (Cemco), parts of which had clear constructional cultures. The new ventures which the corporation urgently needed to escape from its doomed basic technology were put under the charge of young managers, who were given the chance of making their mark by building them into successful businesses. But the young managers were usually keeping more than half an eye on the next post and worrying about getting trapped in their own little business. They were clear in their own minds that they would never reach the corporate board without a corporate career. So the diversification programme suffered.

The climbing-frame model suggests a way out. Such a firm is trying to abandon its previous mode of growth to a familiar pattern. We have seen (chapter 4) that a firm growing to an unfamiliar pattern tends to have an evolutionary career logic because of the way that the new offshoots have their own, local managerial labour markets. This, of course, is exactly what happens when a managerial buyout takes place: the managers running the offshoot cut themselves off from the parent firm's career structure and identify with making the new business a success.

The intrapreneurship question therefore becomes: can the large firm segment its managerial labour market without creating a buyout? Clearly, structural solutions play a central role, so that a separate business unit can be identified for its managers to build. But there is a gulf between just setting up a new structure and gaining broad recognition that anyone joining it is committing themselves to staying within it. Somehow the firm must create the expectation that making a career within a business unit will not cut high-flying executives off from reaching the main board.

This is not easy, but it can be done. For instance, a major international oil company reorganized itself into separate, comparatively self-contained 'business streams' within which managers were expected to make their careers. The point is that unless the problem is tackled structurally like this, so that the goal of growing a business unit becomes more attractive to executives than that of growing their career by moving across the wider climbing-frame of the total organization, the firm will probably not grow the intrapreneurs it needs.

Professionalizing the management of evolutionary firms A common worry in evolutionary firms concerns the professionalism of their senior managers. Such firms are grown by managers developing their own business units with which the managers identify closely. But it is not always evident that they have the kind of managerial expertise to help them run their units as well as they could, or the corporate perspective to see how their units fit into the company as a whole. Further, just as it is hard to find successors for entrepreneurs who have grown large companies, firms which have grown in an unpatterned way face difficult problems of ensuring smooth management succession in each of their business units. As each business moves to maturity a different kind of manager from the founder is often needed with greater managerial expertise (Porter, 1980: 252–3), and this kind of manager tends not to be developed in an evolutionary culture. Similarly, when a top business unit manager, who has no obvious successor within his or her business unit, leaves the company it may be hard to find a replacement. The knowledge of managers from other units may be too specific to the units they come from.

To most firms in this position the obvious solution is to institute a policy of group-wide career development for a selected elite of high-flyers, overriding the logic of the evolutionary climbing-frame. But there is a danger in this. The point of the evolutionary career logic – allowing managers to identify closely with their own businesses which, because of the way the group has grown, are very different from the others – is lost. The group ends up with a cadre of highly 'professional' managers who lack the understanding of and personal commitment to their businesses. As we have seen (chapter 2) there is a growing belief that such managers do not run their companies as well as executives with expert knowledge of their organization and industry, although it has to be admitted that this view is not well supported by hard evidence.

The new elite career patterns may even feed back into the company's strategy. As top careers lose their evolutionary pattern, so the firm loses its ability to grow new, unfamiliar businesses successfully.

Climbing-frames, then, may be altered by determined attempts to change career paths. This could be entirely desirable, but it is vital to forecast as accurately as possible the potential consequences of changing career patterns for the firm's strategy in order to avoid unpleasant surprises. An evolutionary firm may still be able to professionalize its executives while keeping its evolutionary culture by concentrating on development strategies which keep the focus on managers and their jobs. Well-established examples include action learning, personal development programmes and management education programmes tailor-made for the company.

Bridging the operational—general management gulf in command-centred structures   A common problem faced by firms with command-centred climbing-frames concerns the gulf between operational and general management. The structural feature that makes them command-centred is the large number of similar commands they comprise, for instance factories, distribution depots, retail outlets and bank branches. A typical career may involve executives in many years of moving between commands, essentially in specialist jobs, so that the transition between operational and general management is a major problem for them. So the board of such companies can consist of a group of specialists with very little in common and none of the skills or perspective of the true general manager. How is such a firm to manage the careers of its executives?

Not surprisingly, such companies are often tempted to try to develop elite cadres of generalists. But the apparently obvious solution, giving operational managers experience of different business functions, may not be a practical proposition. Firms like these are usually organized in functional hierarchies such as production, sales or finance, within one of which command-centred careers are made. In such a culture which places a great premium on professional expertise it can be hard for anyone to move into a new hierarchy halfway up, having to report to and take charge of people clearly more skilled than they are.

It can be even more difficult when some functions are more prestigious than others. Many firms have their dominant group: accountants in some, engineers in others, production managers in yet others. In these kinds of organization, promotion away from the dominant function is easily seen as demotion, while people brought in from functions lower in the pecking order tend to be regarded as 'passengers'.

It may be possible to change the shape of the climbing-frame to reduce the gap at the top of the functional hierarchies. For instance managers can sometimes be given experience of 'mini'-general management jobs much earlier in their careers by reorganizing the company so that each individual command has a broader range of business functions within it, in other words by decentralizing control of the hierarchies. As we saw in chapter 4, Chandler argues that this was one of the benefits corporations gained from adopting divisionalized structures (Chandler, 1962). Even if it is not possible to decentralize completely, companies sometimes find that they can group together a number of functions in this way, for instance by giving production plant managers responsibility for support activities such as engineering maintenance.

This, of course, changes the shape of the frame for the managers who might otherwise be building their careers within the command-centred hierarchies which have been subsumed by the decentralized structure. That may be too high a cost to bear, unless it is possible to allow them to choose between joining the general management stream or becoming specialist resources for the overall organization. Decentralized structures face the problem of duplicating resources and maintaining standards, so they often need central professional support services.

This kind of approach may be difficult to implement when several powerful hierarchies compete to be seen as the natural source of unit management, such as often happens in public administration or health care systems. These organizations are often tempted to look outside for executives with the broad experience that their own managers lack.

The most likely source of such 'broader' managers is either a constructional or a turnaround climbing-frame. As we saw in chapter 9, both frames provide highly mobile careers for their most successful executives. Mobility has a number of effects including that of separating managers from the long-run effects of their actions. It is all the more likely that people who have built their careers on these frames will come to believe in the concept of management as a profession.

It would be wrong to sound too nihilistic about the dangers of professionalism. It is unquestionably the case that managers need to know about many of the kind of things I listed in chapter 9 under the headings of technical and social process skills. But the history of the professions suggests that professionalism has its own dynamic (see Saks, 1983, for a recent summary of perspectives on the issue). Unchecked, it can take over the control of labour markets so that jobs become closed to the 'unqualified', regardless of the real value of the skills and expertise of the members of the profession. Expertise may have more to do with closing the doors to outsiders than with what actually goes on in the job. It could easily be used, for instance, as a means of defending a labour market position or justifying inequalities. Each 'measure' of expertise becomes value-laden and part of a political game, with jobs and power going to the winners.

Managing is particularly vulnerable to this negative side of professionalism because there is so little agreement on what skills managers really need. There is at least a case for wondering whether the skills of managing would have to have been invented even if they do not really exist (chapter 3), simply to legitimate the position of the mobile manager. It is hard to know how real the risk is, but it is clearly the danger of the 'gospel of pseudo-professionalism' against which Hayes and Abernathy (1980) are warning us (chapter 2).

So although managers from evolutionary or turnaround climbing-frames may look ideally qualified to handle the problems of command-centred organizations with several powerful hierarchies, they often turn out to be bad choices. Organizations like these have particularly difficult problems of authority and control between the hierarchies, and someone coming from a more conventional kind of business can find it very difficult indeed to become effective. Managers from con-structional climbing-frames can find themselves completely lost without the backup of the many complex interlinkages and support systems they are used to. Turnaround managers may simply discover that they lack the personal authority that they would normally expect in a company facing severe difficulties. Both kinds of manager typically lack the professional credibility with each of the hierarchies they are supposed to be managing, because they are not from any of those professions.

Here, as with the previous two examples, the climbing-frame perspective points out the limits to managerial action more than it suggests specific solutions. The general point behind each of the examples I have chosen is that simply tinkering with job descriptions or career plans is unlikely to be enough. It could even, as we saw in the case of professionalizing evolutionary managers, produce unwanted results. In each case the problems can be traced back through the organizational career logic to the firm's structure or growth history. The climbing-frame model of managerial careers implies that problems like these need organizational solutions, even though the solutions may not always be easy to find.

Implications for the individual

In chapter 5 I discussed some of the ways in which people's orientation to their careers may vary. The detail of these theories and their critiques does not matter here. What does matter is that people differ, and they change as they get older, so different people can be attracted to different kinds of climbing-frame. Some may like the specialization of the command-centred career and the way it allows them to measure their personal growth as their commands grow in significance. Others may prefer the variety of the constructional career and the constant challenge of quite unfamiliar situations. Yet others may welcome the chance the evolutionary career gives them of building something of their own.

But once having started on one kind of climbing-frame it can be hard to change to another, although some frames are more compatible than others. It is probably harder for someone to leave a command-centred frame than a constructional or evolutionary frame because of its professional specialization (chapter 9). People are often aware that they are in some kind of career 'rut' and that it has something to do with the opportunities they have, say as an engineer in a firm dominated by accountants. But it is not easy to hold a clear picture in one's mind about all the factors that have gone into shaping one's career (chapter 6). It is even more difficult if the effect of corporate structures and growth patterns on career paths are not understood, and it becomes just too easy to repeat mistakes. Indeed career counselling sessions are often designed to help people map where they have been in a way which helps them decide what they would like to do next.

Recruitment literature is not usually much help, as Petras and Petras (1986) point out in a useful book for young Americans starting out on corporate careers. The literature often refers vaguely to early careers being spent in 'functional management' followed by 'general management' for the most able, which is not so much misleading as not particularly meaningful. As Kotter (1982) points out, general management can mean many different things. A senior functional management job in – say – a giant oil company can be much more general than a so-called GM's job in a smaller firm.

The recruitment literature may give examples of what has happened to successful young people who have moved from exciting job to yet more exciting job, which might give hints about the shape of the firm's climbing-frame. But their experience is probably not at all typical of what happens to most recruits. And what appeals to a youngster is not necessarily still so appealing to someone with children at school, a partner with a career of his or her own and all the many other reasons people accumulate for dreading the moment when they are offered promotion which involves moving house.

The climbing-frame perspective provides a way of looking at careers which helps people make sense of what is happening to them and what their future is likely to be in their current firm or with a prospective employer. The more clearly executives understand the logics which lay behind the moves which led them to their present job and which constrain their future moves, the better their chances of making well-informed choices about how to plan the rest of their career.

SUMMARY

This chapter continued the process I started in chapter 9, of considering the implications of the frameworks I presented in this book for viewing managerial careers. First, I discussed their implications for research on managerial careers and the understanding of how managerial cultures are developed and sustained. Next, I discussed their potential for development.

The second part of the chapter was given over to considering the implications of the framework for career practitioners. The idea which lies behind this book is that organizational careers are made within organizations, which on the face of it is a tautology. Too often the significance of this idea is missed. The shape of the organization, and the way it grows and changes, define the structure of career opportunities presented to a firm's managers which constrain the kinds of experience they can look forward to. So although there is a great deal of virtue in advice to practitioners which encourages them to take charge of career processes, the implications of this study are that there are limits to how much can be taken charge of and that it is important to recognize the limits.

Understanding the shapes of career climbing-frames, then, helps executives to

- make sense of the shapes of careers in firms, of the possible career patterns each firm might or might not have,
- make educated guesses about the kind of skills that the management of a particular company might have, given that they are likely to have had careers of a particular type,
- pick an appropriate management development model for the firm and avoid models which do not solve the basic problem it faces,
- avoid recruiting executives with apparently appropriate qualifications but who may come from incompatible backgrounds, and
- increase their chances of choosing an employer likely to give them the kind of career they personally will find most satisfying.

Appendices

A   Derivation of the Five Transition Classes

In this appendix I give more detail on the three-step derivation of the five transition classes I introduced in chapter 7: continuity, cosmopolitanism, innovation, iteration and expansion.

STEP 1: CLASSIFYING LOCATION TRANSITIONS AND ACTIVITY TRANSITIONS SEPARATELY

We have no way of measuring the 'size' of an activity or a location: the scales, technically, are nominal rather than ratio. So for simplicity I shall ignore the absolute number of activities or locations added or dropped as a manager changes posts. This limits the number of kinds of transition to eleven if we look at activities or locations separately, where the last seven are simply different combinations of the first four. One can always relax the condition ignoring absolute numbers of activities or locations added or dropped later when examining individual cases, by distinguishing between the degree of importance of the activities or locations being added or dropped.

The first four transition types can be described as follows (figure A.1).

A   *Stasis:* no change, in principle indistinguishable from the situation in which the manager stays in the same post.
B   *Novelty:* the new post involves novel activities or locations.
C   *Reversion:* the manager returns to previous activities or locations.
D   *Rationalization:* some of the manager's current activities or locations are lost.

Each of these transition types can occur by themselves. Stasis (A) is the mark of the specialist, the textile manager in figure 7.2. Because

Appendices

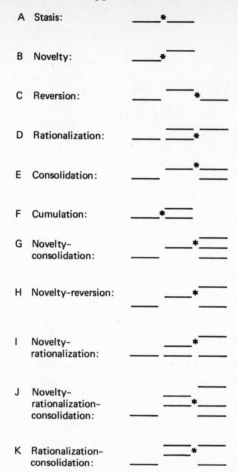

Figure A.1   Full list of transition types. The asterisk indicates the transition to which the label refers

stasis involves no significant change to the breadth of the manager's responsibilities it is indistinguishable, from the point of view of the mapping technique, from the situation in which the manager has not changed posts at all.

Novelty (B) is the opposite of stasis, and involves a discontinuity in a manager's career of the kind which characterizes the generalist. An example of such a transition was experienced by a Norchem manager, who started his career in computing and management services and was moved after a few years to the entirely unfamiliar world of engineering maintenance.

Reversion (C) and rationalization (D) both involve losing some or all of the manager's current responsibilities without acquiring anything novel. Reversion represents a return to a past activity or location, while rationalization is a kind of thinning-out process in which some, but not all, of the manager's responsibilities are lost. Both these patterns might, for instance, be found in the career of someone who is reaching their career plateau and beginning to be shuffled around by their employer to make room for the careers of their more successful juniors.

If we combine rationalization with stasis we get consolidation (E), which involves picking up earlier activities or locations in addition to those the manager currently has. It turns out to be a comparatively common move later on in a career as managers take over responsibility for a number of areas they have worked in earlier. For instance one of the directors of Norchem had worked in many parts of the division, but in his promotion to the board he was given responsibility, in a consolidating move, for a great many activities and locations, including most of the posts he had worked in previously.

If novelty occurs in combination with other transition types it simply indicates novelty without the overtones of complete discontinuity. For instance cumulation (F, involving both stasis and novelty) is what one would expect to find in the career of a rising manager for whom each successive post has broader responsibilities than the previous one.

The rest of the transition types are more complex blends of the first six. Some of the eleven involve novelty (B, F, G, H, I, J), and some the retention of existing activities or locations (A, D, E, F, G, I, J, K). Some imply a discontinuity to new things (B), to earlier experience (C) or to both (H).

We have now reached the point where we can classify work role transitions along two dimensions. For instance, the first job change of the cosmopolitan manager shown in figure 7.4 can be classified as follows: the activity change is an example of stasis, while the location change is one of novelty.

It would be convenient to combine these two dimensions into a single classification scheme, partly to make it easier to look at careers of managers from an organization in aggregate, and partly in recognition of the point that the two dimensions are not fully independent (chapter 6). This is the second step in developing the classification scheme.

STEP 2: A UNIFIED CLASSIFICATION SCHEME

The classification scheme I have just described tells only half of the story. It can be used to distinguish between transitions from the point

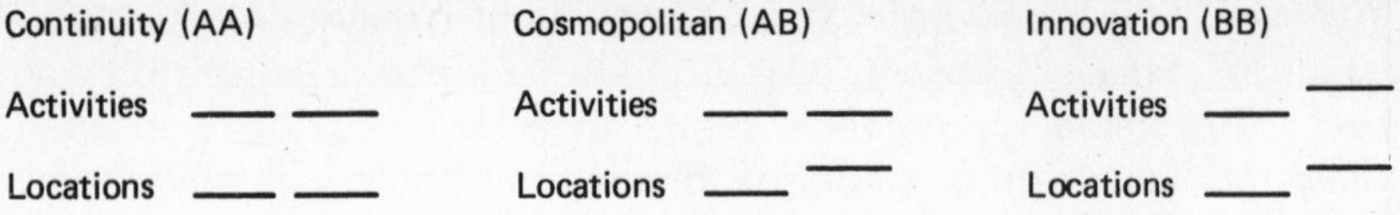

Continuity (AA)	Cosmopolitan (AB)	Innovation (BB)
Activities ＿＿ ＿＿	Activities ＿＿ ＿＿	Activities ＿＿ ‾‾
Locations ＿＿ ＿＿	Locations ＿＿ ‾‾	Locations ＿＿ ‾‾

Figure A.2 Selected combinations of stasis and novelty in activities and locations (codes A and B refer to figure A.1)

of view of changing activities, such as when the Norchem computer scientist became a maintenance engineer, or changing locations, for instance when he moved from the computer department at Norchem's head office to one of the division's factory sites. But it does not give us the picture from both points of view simultaneously, which we need to get a full description of a transition. If we describe transitions as the ordered pairs (activity transition type, location transition type) we get the unified classification we need (figure A.2).

For instance the Norchem ex-computer scientist's move to maintenance engineering would have been drawn as in figure A.2, as a 'BB' innovation transition (novelty in both activities and locations). A cosmopolitan such as a design engineer who moves from one design office to another could be shown as in figure A.2, as an 'AB' transition (stasis in activities, novelty in locations). Finally, the only 'move' the textile manager in figure 7.2 made was of the continuity kind shown in figure A.2, an 'AA' transition (stasis in both activities and locations).

Table A.1 presents the pairs of transition types in an alternative format. Cells 1, 2 and 4 correspond to figures A.2, but cell 3 is the type which, as we saw in chapter 6, does not sound too probable, involving a complete change in activity but no change in location.

For each transition in a manager's career, then, we need to look at

Table A.1 Matrix representation of figure A.2

Locations

		A	B
Activities	A	1 Continuity	2 Cosmopolitan
	B	3 Innovation	4 Innovation

Table A.2   Cross-tabulation of activity transition types against location transition types from empirical study (numbers of transitions; transition types A−K are described in figure A.1)

Activity transitions	Location transitions												
	A	B	C	D	E	F	G	H	I	J	K	NS[a]	Total
A	116	139	11	10	6	36	5	14	5	0	0	0	342
B	6	142	1	10	0	13	5	0	5	0	0	0	182
C	2	37	13	2	2	0	1	6	2	0	0	0	65
D	4	29	3	4	1	2	1	0	4	1	0	0	49
E	2	13	2	1	6	4	2	2	1	1	2	0	36
F	8	28	2	1	0	38	4	0	6	0	0	0	87
G	1	2	0	0	2	3	0	1	0	1	0	0	10
H	0	7	0	0	0	1	0	2	0	0	0	0	10
I	2	9	0	0	0	1	0	0	2	0	0	0	14
J	0	1	0	0	0	0	0	1	0	2	0	0	4
K	0	2	0	0	0	0	0	0	1	0	0	0	3
NS[a]	4	7	0	0	0	0	0	0	1	0	0	8	20
Total	145	416	32	28	17	98	18	26	27	5	2	8	822

[a] NS, not stated (insufficient information to assign the transition to a particular category).

both aspects of the move: changes in locations and in activities. But this presents the same kind of practical problem that beset Smith and White (1987) with their two-dimensional classification of career experience. There are 121 possible combinations of the eleven different types of location and activity change. By way of illustration of the practical consequences, table A.2 shows the results of coding the careers of all the managers in my study. The 115 managers had experienced a total of 822 transitions, of which all but twenty could be coded according to the scheme in figure A.1.

It is evident from table A.2 that there are some kinds of transition which are a good deal more common than others. For instance, the three transition types in cells 1, 2 and 4 of table A.1 account for something like half of the 802 codeable transitions. On the other hand, 78 per cent of the cells in the table have fewer than five transitions in them. Clearly some further grouping of the transition types is called for to simplify things to a manageable level, and this is the third step in developing the classification scheme.

STEP 3: A FIVE-WAY CLASSIFICATION OF WORK ROLE TRANSITIONS

Despite the fact that the first step in developing this classification scheme involved the apparently drastic simplification of ignoring the actual number of locations and activities added or dropped as managers move from one post to the next, the second step yielded too many categories for comfort. It consisted of an 11 × 11 table with 121 different categories, many of which − at least amongst the managers I interviewed − turned out to be very rare. The final step in developing the scheme, then, involves collapsing the 121 categories into a more manageable number.

There are many ways in which this could be done, and the method I describe here was developed from an analysis of the data shown in table A.2, bearing in mind the need to ensure that the final categories made sense in terms of the career logics framework. First, the eleven kinds of location transition and eleven kinds of activity transition were re-grouped to give five of each. Second, the 5 × 5 table which resulted was examined to see how the twenty-five categories might be grouped further.

As table A.2 shows, two transition types (stasis − A − and novelty − B) were both common and distinctive in the careers of the managers I interviewed, as was the combination of stasis and novelty I called cumulation (F, which is the transition pattern of the pyramid-climber shown in figure 7.5).

The remaining eight transition types were not so common, and they involved complex patterns of acquiring new locations or activities and dropping old ones. Their chief distinguishing mark was whether or not the managers had moved into anything which was new to them, for instance a marketing manager taking over a new product group, a production manager adding a new plant to his portfolio or a personnel

Table A.3   Transition types regrouped

New label	Comprising (figure A.1)	Description
Stasis	A	As before
Novelty	B	As before
Cumulation	F	As before
Modified stasis	C, D, E, K	Combinations of past experience, but with nothing novel
Modified cumulation	G, H, I, J	Combinations of past experience, but also with new experience of some kind

Table A.4 Definitions of continuity, cosmopolitanism, innovation, iteration and expansion

			Locations		
Activities	A	B	F	L	M
A	s	c	e	i	e
B	(1)	g	e	i(2)	e
F	e	c	e	e	e
L	i	c	e	i	e
M	e	c	e	e	e

A, stasis; B, novelty; F, cumulation; L, modified stasis (C+D+E+K); M, modified cumulation (G+H+I+J); s, continuity; c, cosmopolitanism; e, expansion; i, iteration; g, innovation.

(1), (2) are borderline cases for classification; for (1), see the discussion in chapter 6 of the extent to which activities and locations form orthogonal dimensions. Together, these transition types accounted for only 2 per cent of the total number of transitions.

manager trying his hand at management training for the first time. If the transition did involve something novel to the manager I called it 'modified cumulation', to indicate that growth had been involved. If there was nothing new in the post he had moved to I called it 'modified stasis', implying that it was a reformulation in some way of things he had done before. The difference between modified cumulation and modified stasis, in other words, is simply that modified cumulation is modified stasis with an aspect of novelty to it.

Table A.3 summarizes the position we have reached. Instead of eleven different ways of describing how the locations of one post compare with its predecessors and eleven for activities, we now have five. If we combine five location transition types with five activity transition types we get twenty-five combinations, from which the definitions of the five classes of transition (continuity, cosmopolitanism, innovation, iteration and expansion) can be derived as in table A.4.

B   The Research Study

In chapter 8 I draw on a number of findings from my study of the careers of 115 managers from four large industrial corporations. In this appendix I give some more information about the managers as background to the discussion in the chapter. Further details about the study are given by Gunz and Whitley (1985) and Gunz (1986).

BASIC STATISTICS ON CAREERS

The managers were selected from a variety of levels and business functions in each of the four corporations (Gunz and Whitley, 1985). I met managers who had had very successful careers and managers who had been less successful, and examples of careers from at least several of the possible pathways in each firm. The basic statistics on their careers reveal differences between the companies which reflect other features of their structures, modes of growth and career logics (chapter 8).

Prestex managers have had significantly longer careers overall than the other three, which were more closely grouped together (table B.1). Career length correlates closely with age ($r = 0.933$) and I use it here because it forms the time-base for the career maps. There are two reasons for the longer Prestex careers, relating (a) to their education and (b) to the firm's history of growth.

1   Prestex managers have spent less time than the others in full-time education. A high proportion of Norchem, ISE and Cemco managers are university graduates, ranging from 67 per cent in the case of ISE to 85 per cent in the case of Norchem. Only 11 per cent of the Prestex managers are graduates because a very high proportion had left elementary school at fourteen. But this difference, which is

Table B.1 *Career lengths (years) of managers in sample, by organization (number of managers)*

Career length (years)	Norchem	Prestex	ISE	Cemco	Whole sample
0–9	1	1	0	3	5
10–19	14	2	9	15	40
20–29	9	10	15	11	45
30–39	3	11	6	1	21
40–49	0	4	0	0	4
Total	27	28	30	30	115
Mean	19.0	30.3	23.6	18.4	22.8
Standard deviation	8.0	8.5	6.8	7.4	8.9
Median	16.0	30.2	23.3	16.1	23.0

For the four subsamples, $F = 15.1$ with three and 111 degrees of freedom ($p < 0.01$).

significant (chi square of graduates versus non-graduates by company is 35.6 with three degrees of freedom; $p < 0.005$), reflects a different pattern of education, not on the whole a lack of it: 68 per cent of Prestex managers have a professional qualification of some kind, usually in textile technology. This was almost invariably the result of many years' study at night school, often when their families were young.

2 While Prestex has been affected by the history of decline and plant closures in the textile industry, the other three firms have experienced growth for many years, although not latterly. We can therefore expect Prestex to have an older management structure in consequence.

The number of employers the managers have worked for varies from firm to firm: there is a significant difference between the number of managers in each firm who have worked for one, two and more than two employers (see table B.2; chi square is 14.1 with six degrees of freedom; $p < 0.05$). 'Involuntary' employer changes, when managers' employers are acquired by another firm, are not counted here. Overall almost half of the sample have worked for only one employer, a quarter for two, and 14 per cent for three, while the remaining 15 per cent have worked for anything up to ten employers. Norchem and ISE managers have changed firms least, while there are more mobile managers in Prestex and to a lesser extent Cemco.

Further, the time the managers have spent working for employers other than their present ones varies considerably (table B.3). By 'current

Table B.2 Numbers of employers that managers have worked for (excluding involuntary changes of employer) (number of managers)

Number of employers	Norchem	Prestex	ISE	Cemco	Total
1	17	9	18	7	51
2	5	8	6	11	30
3	5	3	2	7	17
4	0	3	2	3	8
5	0	3	2	0	5
7	0	1	0	2	3
10	0	1	0	0	1
Total	27	30	28	30	115
Mean	1.6	2.8	1.8	2.5	2.2
Standard deviation	0.8	2.1	1.2	1.5	1.6
Median	1.3	2.1	1.3	2.2	1.7

employer' I mean the organization in its current legal form or one of its precursors. Overall, 63 per cent of the managers have spent at least 80 per cent of their careers within the organizations in the study.

The most striking difference table B.3 shows is between Norchem and ISE on the one hand and Prestex and Cemco on the other. Norchem and ISE managers have spent much less time working for anyone else; in the cases of Norchem and Prestex, time spent working for other divisions is not counted as current employer. Prestex managers who did not start with Prestex or its precursors almost invariably spent their earlier careers working for other textile firms so that they could be said to have had industry, rather than company, careers, while Cemco managers have had a much wider scatter of experiences. Norchem managers have, on the whole, been occupied with building

Table B.3 Career time spent within current employer or its precursors (number of managers)

Years spent working outside current employer	Norchem	Prestex	ISE	Cemco	Total
0	17	10	17	7	51
0.1–5.0	5	4	7	10	26
5.1–10.0	5	4	1	5	15
Over 10	0	10	5	8	23

Comparing Norchem and ISE on the one hand with Prestex and Cemco on the other, chi square is 13.6 with three degrees of freedom ($p < 0.005$).

Table B.4   Number of posts occupied by managers during their careers (number of managers)

Number of posts	Norchem	Prestex	ISE	Cemco	Total
2–5	6	2	4	7	19
6–7	6	7	12	8	33
8–9	6	11	6	7	30
10–11	6	3	7	5	21
12–16	3	5	1	3	12
Total	27	28	30	30	115
Mean	8.3	8.6	7.9	7.8	8.2
Range: max.	16	16	13	15	16
min.	4	2	4	3	2
Standard deviation	3.1	3.0	2.3	2.8	2.8
Median	8.0	8.2	7.3	7.5	7.8

careers within its complex constructional logic, and ISE managers likewise within that firm's evolutionary logic.

Finally, the number of posts the managers have held varies between two and sixteen without very noticeable differences between companies (table B.4). Obviously length of career has something to do with this since the longer the career, the more posts they could have held given that the average tenure of a post was just over three years. Even so, some managers have moved more regularly than others, and once again the findings are consistent with what else we know of the firms: the difference in mean tenure of post between the firms is significant at the 1 per cent level ($F = 5.99$ with three and 111 degrees of freedom). Norchem's constructional logic and Cemco's mixed logic caused their managers to experience the shortest average tenures (2.4 and 2.5 years respectively), fitting the picture of a group of people busily putting together their experiences as fast as they could. ISE managers' longer average tenure (3.2 years) is what we would expect from the continuity resulting from an evolutionary logic, although this statistic has to be treated with caution since the result of this logic is that the boundaries between one post and the next can be rather fuzzy (chapter 4). Prestex managers have experienced the longest average tenure (4.2 years, reducing to 3.7 if one outlying case is removed), which is most likely to be a reflection of the lack of long-term growth in the firm and its flat hierarchical structure.

CODING THE MANAGERS' CAREERS

In this section I shall outline briefly how I coded the managers' careers. It was evident from the interviews that the process of telling one's life story to a stranger is often far from a matter of imparting facts objectively and dispassionately. Sometimes I was being told a success story, sometimes the converse, sometimes the narrative centred on what it had felt like to be subjected to turbulence and change in the firm and what part the speaker had played in this, and so on. The stories varied from comparatively neutral descriptions of a series of moves from post to post and what each entailed to dramatic accounts of the events which lay behind the moves. I was being allowed access to privileged information which was being presented in a highly subjective way. So any attempt to code and abstract from it is bound to leave out much of the reality of what had happened during the managers' careers.

I coded the careers for the locations and activities the managers had experienced by going through the interview notes, step by step, and examining what they had told me about each post for clues about when a particular activity could be said to have started and another to have come to an end, and when they had moved from one location to another. I evolved a number of rules to handle some of the inevitable ambiguities. The main ones were as follows.

1 I defined a 'post' as a period of time during which the manager's job did not change notably, using his or her definition of whether change had or had not taken place. Clearly there are occasions when there is some uncertainty over whether a post has become a new one, and this was especially noticeable in ISE because of the way the evolutionary logic blurred bureaucratic role definitions.
2 Initial training periods, during which young managers moved between a number of short assignments, were counted as one post.
3 Periods of full-time education or national service were ignored if they were entirely unconnected with anything the manager did before or later.
4 When there was a choice over the extent to which a post should be divided into separate activities or locations I went for more detail, since the aim was to look for the extent to which experiences either did or did not repeat themselves during the course of a career. This tends, when looking at the later stages of senior managers' careers, to over-emphasize the importance of activities which they had also experienced earlier at the expense of those which they had not and about which I knew less, if only because they had talked about them less. It could, of course, reflect their behaviour in their jobs, given the common tendency to respond to the uncertainties of high office by focusing unduly on what they once knew about.

References

ABELL, D. F. 1980: *Defining the Business*; Hemel Hempstead: Prentice-Hall.

ACTON SOCIETY TRUST 1956: *Management Succession: The Recruitment, Selection, Training and Promotion of Managers*; London: The Acton Society Trust.

ALBAN-METCALFE, B. and NICHOLSON, N. 1984: *The Career Development of British Managers*; British Institute of Management Foundation, Management Survey Report.

ALLEN, M. P. 1978: Continuity and change within the core corporate elite; *The Sociological Quarterly*, 19, Autumn, 510–21.

ALLEN, M. P. and PANIAN, S. K. 1982: Power, performance and succession in the large corporation; *Administrative Science Quarterly*, 27, 538–47.

ANDERSON, J. C., MILKOVICH, G. T. and TSUI, A. 1981: A model of intra-organizational mobility; *Academy of Management Review*, 6 (4), 529–38.

ARON, R. 1970: *Main Currents in Sociological Thought (2)*; Harmondsworth: Penguin.

ARTHUR, M. B. and LAWRENCE, B. S. 1984: Perspectives on environment and career: an introduction; *Journal of Occupational Behaviour*, 5, 1–8.

ASTLEY, W. G. 1985: The two ecologies: population and community perspectives on organizational evolution; *Administrative Science Quarterly*, 30, 224–41.

ASTLEY, W. G. and VAN DE VEN, A. H. 1983: Central perspectives and debates in organization theory; *Administrative Science Quarterly*, 28, 245–73.

BAILYN, L. and LYNCH, J. T. 1983: Engineering as a life-long career: its meaning, its satisfactions, its difficulties; *Journal of Occupational Behaviour*, 4, 263–83.

BALTES, P. B. and NESSELROADE, J. R. 1984: Paradigm lost and paradigm regained: critique of Dannefer's portrayal of life-span developmental psychology; *American Sociological Review*, 49 (6), December, 841–47.

BARON, J. N., DAVIS-BLAKE A. and BIELBY, W. T. 1986: The structure of opportunity: how promotion ladders vary within and among organizations; *Administrative Science Quarterly*, 31, 248–73.

BARTOLOME, F. and EVANS, P. A. L. 1980: Must success cost so much?; *Harvard Business Review*, March–April, 137–48.

BARTOLOME, F. and LAURENT, A. 1987: The Janus head: learning from the superior and subordinate faces of the manager's job; *INSEAD Working Paper Series* No. 87/12, Fontainebleau.

BASS, B. M. 1976: Life goals and career success of European and American managers; *Rivista Int. di Scienze Economiche e Commericiali*, 23 (2), February, 154−68.

BAUER, M. and COHEN, E. 1981: *Qui Gouverne les Groupes Industriel?*; Paris: Seuil.

BAZERMAN, M. H. and SCHOORMAN, F. D. 1983: A limited rationality model of interlocking directorates; *Academy of Management Review*, 8 (2), 206−17.

BEATTY, R. P. and ZAJAC, E. J. 1987: CEO change and firm performance in large corporations: succession effects and manager effects; *Strategic Management Journal*, 8, 305−17.

BEER, S. 1979: *The Heart of Enterprise*; New York: Wiley.

BERLE, A. A. 1960: *Power Without Property: A New Development in American Political Economy*; London: Sidgwick and Jackson.

BHASKAR, R. 1979: *The Possibility of Naturalism: A Philosophical Critique of the Contemporary Human Sciences*; Brighton: Harvester.

BOEHM, V. R. 1981: Scientific parallelism in personnel mobility research: a preview of two approaches; *Academy of Management Review*, 6 (4), 527−8.

BOSWELL, J. S. 1983: *Business Policies in the Making: Three Steel Companies Compared*; London: George Allen & Unwin.

BOUCHET, J. L. 1976: *Diversification: Composition of the Top Management Team and Performance of the Firm*; EGOS Conference on the Sociology of the Business Enterprise, Oxford, 15−18 December.

BOWER, J. L. 1970: *Managing the Resource Allocation Process*; Cambridge, Mass.: Harvard University Press.

BOYATZIS, R. E. 1982: *The Competent Manager: A Model For Effective Performance*; New York: Wiley.

BROWN, R. G. S. 1970: *The Administrative Process in Britain*; London: Methuen.

BURGOYNE, J. and STUART, R. 1976: The nature, use and acquisition of managerial skills and other attributes; *Personnel Review*, 5 (4), Autumn, 19−29.

BURNHAM, J. 1940: *The Managerial Revolution*; New York: Day.

BURNS, J. M. 1978: *Leadership*; New York: Harper & Row.

BURNS, T. and STALKER, G. 1966: *The Management of Innovation*; London: Tavistock.

CAMPBELL, J. P., DUNNETTE, M. D., LAWLER, E. E. and WEICK, K. E. 1970: *Managerial Behaviour, Performance and Effectiveness*; New York: McGraw-Hill.

CARNAZZA, J. P., KORMAN, A. K., FERENCE, T. P. and STONER, J. A. 1981: Plateaued and non-plateaued managers: Factors in job performance; *Journal of Management*, 7 (2), 7−25.

CARROLL, G. R. and MAYER, K. U. 1986: Job-shift patterns in the Federal Republic of Germany: the effects of social class, industrial sector and organizational size; *American Sociological Review*, 51, June, 323−41.

CHANDLER, A. D. 1962: *Strategy and Structure: Chapters in the History of the Industrial Enterprise*; Cambridge, Mass.: MIT Press.

CHANDLER, A. D. and DAEMS, H. 1980: *Managerial Hierarchies: Comparative Perspectives on the Rise of the Modern Industrial Enterprise*; Cambridge, Mass.: Harvard University Press.

CHANNON, D. F. 1973: *The Strategy and Structure of British Enterprise*; London: Macmillan.

CHAPMAN, R. A. 1970: *The Higher Civil Service in Britain*; London: Constable.

CLARK, D. G. 1966: *The Industrial Manager: His Background and Career Pattern*; London: Business Publications.

CLEE, G. H. 1970: The new manager: a man for all organisations; in R. Mann (ed.), *The Arts of Top Management*; London: McGraw-Hill.

CLEMENTS, R. V. 1958: *Managers: A Study of their Careers in Industry*; London: George Allen & Unwin.

COHEN, E. and BAUER, M. 1985: *Les Grandes Manoevres Industrielles*; Paris: Pierre Belfond.

COPEMAN, G. H. 1955: *Leaders of British Industry*; London: Gee and Co.

CYERT, R. M. and MARCH, J. 1963: *A Behavioural Theory of the Firm*; Englewood Cliffs, N.J.: Prentice-Hall.

DALTON, D. R. and KESNER, I. F. 1983: Inside/outside succession and organization size: the pragmatics of executive replacement; *Academy of Management Journal*, 26, 736–42.

DALTON, D. R. and KESNER, I. F. 1985: Organizational performance as an antecedent of inside/outside Chief Executive succession: an empirical assessment; *Academy of Management Journal*, 28 (4), 749–62.

DALTON, G. W., Thompson, P. H. and Price, R. L. 1977: Four stages of professional careers – a new look at performance by professionals; *Organizational Dynamics*, Summer, 19–42.

DALTON, G. W. and THOMPSON, P. H. 1986: *Novations: Strategies for Career Management;* Glenview, Ill.: Scott, Foresman.

DANNEFER, D. 1984a: Adult development and social theory: a paradigmatic reappraisal; *American Sociological Review*, 49, 100–16.

DANNEFER, D. 1984b: The role of the social in life-span developmental psychology, past and future: rejoinder to Baltes and Nesselroade; *American Sociological Review*, 49 (6), December, 847–50.

DEARBORN, D. C. and SIMON, H. A. 1958: Selective perceptions: a note on the departmental identification of executives; *Sociometry*, 21, 140–44.

DERR, C. B. 1986: *Managing the New Careerists*; San Francisco, Calif.: Jossey-Bass.

DERR, C. B. and LAURENT, A. 1987: The internal and external careers: a theoretical and cross-cultural perspective; *INSEAD Working Paper Series*, No. 87/24, Fontainebleau.

DOMMERMUTH, W. P. 1966: On the odds of becoming company president; *Harvard Business Review*, May/June, 65–72.

DRIVER, M. J. 1979: Career concepts and career management in organizations; in C. L. Cooper (ed.), *Behavioural Problems in Organizations*; Englewood Cliffs, N.J.: Prentice-Hall, 79–139.

DRIVER, M. J. 1980: Career concepts and organizational change; in C. B. Derr (ed.), *Work, Family and Career*; New York: Praeger, 34–41.

DRIVER, M. J. 1982: Career concepts: a new approach to career research; in R. Katz (ed.), *Career Issues in Human Resource Management*; Englewood

Cliffs, N.J.: Prentice-Hall, 23−32.

DYL, E. A. 1985: Reinganum on management succession; *Administrative Science Quarterly*, 30, September, 373−4.

EDSTROM, A. and GALBRAITH, J. 1977: Transfers of managers as a coordination and control strategy in multi-national organizations; *Administrative Science Quarterly*, 22, June, 248−63.

EVANS, M. G. 1984: Reducing control loss in organizations: the implications of dual hierarchies, mentoring and strengthening vertical dyadic linkages; *Management Science*, 30 (2), February, 156−68.

EVANS, M. and GILBERT, E. 1984: Plateaued managers: their need gratifications and their effort performance expectations; *Journal of Management Studies*, 21 (1), 99−108.

EVANS, P. 1986: New directions in career management; *Personnel Management*, December, 26−9.

FARRELL, M. P. and ROSENBERG, S. D. 1981: *Men at Midlife*; Boston, Mass.: Auburn House.

FEATHERMAN, D. L. and LERNER, R. M. 1985: Ontogenesis and sociogenesis: problematics for theory and research about development and socialization across the lifespan; *American Sociological Review*, 50, October, 659−76.

FERENCE, T. P., STONER, J. A. F. and WARREN, E. K. 1977: Managing the career plateau; *Academy of Management Review*, 602−12.

FIDLER, J. 1981: *The British Business Elite*; London: Routledge and Kegan Paul.

FORBES, J. B. 1987: Early intraorganizational mobility: patterns and influences; *Academy of Management Journal*, 30 (1), 110−25.

FRANKO, L. G. 1976: *The European Multinationals*; London: Harper and Row.

GABARRO, J. J. 1985: When a new manager takes charge; *Harvard Business Review*, 63 (3), May/June, 110−23.

GALBRAITH, J. R. and NATHANSON, D. A. 1978: *Strategy Implementation: The Role of Structure and Process*; St. Paul, Minn.: West.

GENTRY, D. L. and HAILEY, W. A. 1980: The CEO: beginnings and backgrounds; *Business*, September−October, 15−19.

GEPHART, R. P. JR. 1978: Status degradation and organisational succession: an ethnomethodological approach; *Administrative Science Quarterly*, 23, December, 553−81.

GIDDENS, A. 1981: Agency, institution and time-space analysis; in K. Knorr-Cetina and A. V. Cicourel (eds), *Advances in Social Theory and Methodology: Towards an Integration of Micro- and Macro-Sociologies*; London: Routledge and Kegan Paul.

GIDDENS, A. 1984: *The Constitution of Society· Outline of the Theory of Structuration*; Cambridge: Polity Press.

GILLEN, D. J. and CARROLL, S. J. 1985: Relationship of managerial ability to unit effectiveness in more organic versus more mechanistic departments; *Journal of Management Studies*, 22 (6), November, 668−75.

GOLDBERG, A. I. and SHENHAV, Y. A. 1984: R&D career paths: their relation to work goals and productivity; *IEEE Transactions on Engineering Management*, EM−31 (3), August, 111−17.

GOULD, S. 1979: Characteristics of career planners in upwardly mobile occupations; *Academy of Management Journal*, 22 (3), 539−50.

GOULDNER, A. W. 1954: *Patterns of Industrial Bureaucracy*; New York: The Free Press.

GOULDNER, A. W. 1957: Cosmopolitans and locals: toward an analysis of latent social roles I; *Administrative Science Quarterly*, December, 281–306.

GOULDNER, A. W. 1958: Cosmopolitans and locals: toward an analysis of latent social roles II; *Administrative Science Quarterly*, March, 444–80.

GOWLER, D. and LEGGE, K. in press: Careers, reputations and the rhetoric of bureaucratic control; in M. B. Arthur, D. T. Hall and B. S. Lawrence (eds), *Handbook of Career Theory*, Cambridge: Cambridge University Press.

GRANDJEAN, B. D. 1981: History and career in a bureaucratic labor market; *American Journal of Sociology*, 86 (5), 1057–92.

GRANICK, D. 1972: *Managerial Comparisons of Four Developed Countries: France, Britain, United States and Russia*; Cambridge, Mass.: MIT Press.

GRANROSE, C. S. and PORTWOOD, J. D. 1987: Matching individual career plans and organizational career management; *Academy of Management Journal*, 30 (4), 699–720.

GRUSKY, O. 1961: Corporate size, bureaucratisation and managerial succession; *American Journal of Sociology*, November, 261–9.

GUERRIER, Y. and PHILPOT, N. 1978: *The British Manager: Careers and Mobility*; London: British Institute of Management.

GUGLIELMINO, P. J. and CARROLL, A. B. 1979: The hierarchy of management skills: future development for mid-level managers; *Management Decision*, 17 (4), 341–5.

GUNZ, H. P. 1978: Dual ladders in research: a paradoxical organisational fix; *R&D Management*, 9 (1), 29–32.

GUNZ, H. P. 1986: *The Structure of Managerial Careers: Organisational and Individual Logics*; University of Manchester: Unpublished PhD thesis.

GUNZ, H. P. and WHITLEY, R. D. 1985: Managerial cultures and industrial strategies in British firms; *Organization Studies*, 6 (3), 247–73.

GUPTA, A. K. 1986: Matching managers to strategies: point and counterpoint; *Human Resource Management*, 25 (2), 215–34.

HALL, D. T. 1979: Mid-career change: there's less there than meets the eye; Presented to Annual Meeting of Academy of Management, Atlanta, Ga.

HALL, D. T. 1987: Careers and socialization; *Journal of Management*, 13 (2), 301–21.

HALL, D. T. and ISABELLA, L. A. 1985: Downward movement and career development; *Organizational Dynamics*, Summer, 5–23.

HALL, D. T. and NOUGAIM, K. 1968: An examination of Maslow's hierarchy in an organizational setting; *Organizational Behaviour and Human Performance*, 3 (1), 12–35.

HALL, M. 1968: The death of the career company; *Management Today*, September, 58–61.

HALLER, M., KONIG, W., KRAUSE, P. and KURZ, K. 1985: Patterns of career mobility and structural positions in advanced capitalist societies: a comparison of men in Austria, France & US; *American Sociological Review*, 50, October, 579–603.

HAMBRICK, D. C. and MASON, P. A. 1984: Upper echelons: the organization as a reflection of its top managers; *Academy of Management Review*, 9 (2), 193–206.

HANDY, C. B. 1985: *Understanding Organisations*; Harmondsworth: Penguin, 3rd edition.

HARRIGAN, K. R. 1983: *Strategies for Vertical Integration*; Lexington, Mass.: Lexington Books.

HAYES, R. and ABERNATHY, W. 1980: Managing our way to economic decline; *Harvard Business Review*, July–August, 67–77.

HEARN, J. 1977: Towards a concept of non-career; *Sociological Review*, 25 (2), May, 273–88.

HELMICH, D. L. 1974: Organizational growth and succession patterns; *Academy of Management Journal*, 17, 771–5.

HELMICH, D. L. 1975a: Succession: a longitudinal look; *Journal of Business Research*, 3 (4), October, 355–64.

HELMICH, D. L. 1975b: Corporate succession: an examination; *Academy of Management Journal*, 18 (3), 429–41.

HELMICH, D. L. and BROWN, W. B. 1972: Successor type and organizational change in the corporate enterprise; *Administrative Science Quarterly*, 17, 371–81.

HICKSON, D. J., HININGS, C. R., LEE, C. A., SCHNECK, R. E. and PENNINGS, J. 1971: A strategic contingencies' theory of intraorganizational power; *Administrative Science Quarterly*, 16, 216–29.

HODGKINSON, G. P., GUNZ, H. P. and JOHNSON, G. N. 1988: Understanding competitive strategy from a management cognition perspective; a critical evaluation and some research hypotheses; *Manchester Business School Working Paper Series No. 168*.

HOLLAND, J. L. 1973: *Making Vocational Choices: A Theory of Careers*; Englewood Cliffs, N.J.: Prentice-Hall.

HUDSON, L. 1966: *Contrary Imaginations*; Harmondsworth: Penguin.

HUGHES, E. C. 1937: Institutional office and the person; *American Journal of Sociology*, 43, November, 404–13.

HUGHES, E. C. 1958: *Men and Their Work*; Glencoe, Ill.: The Free Press.

HUTTON, S. P. and GERSTL, J. 1963: Career patterns of mechanical engineers; *Professional Engineer*, 8, 85–9.

IACOCCA, L. and NOVAK, W. 1986: *Iacocca: An Autobiography*; New York: Bantam.

JACOBS, D. 1981: Toward a theory of mobility and behavior in organizations: relationships between individual performance and organizational success; *American Journal of Sociology*, 87 (3), November, 684–707.

JENNINGS, E. E. 1971: *The Mobile Manager: a Study of the New Generation of Top Executives*; New York: McGraw-Hill.

JOHNSON, G. N. 1987: *Strategic Change and the Managerial Process*; Oxford: Basil Blackwell.

KANTER, R. M. 1977: *Men and Women of the Corporation*; New York: Basic Books.

KARPIK, L. 1978: Organizations, institutions and history; in L. Karpik (ed.), *Organization and Environment: Theory, Issues and Reality*, London: Sage.

KATZ, R. L. 1971: Skills of an effective administrator; in E. C. Bursk and T. B. Blodgett (eds), *Developing Executive Leaders*, Cambridge, Mass.: Harvard University Press, pp. 55–64.

KATZ, R. L. 1974: Skills of the effective administrator; *Harvard Business*

Review, 52 (1), 90–102.

Kay, N. M. 1982: *The Evolving Firm: Strategy and Structure in Industrial Organization*; London: Macmillan.

Keen, P. G. W. 1977: Cognitive style and career specialization; in J. Van Maanen (ed.), *Organizational Careers: Some New Perspectives*; New York: Wiley.

Kerin, R. A. 1981: Where they come from: CEOs in 1952 and 1980; *Business Horizons*, Nov–Dec, 66–9.

Kets de Vries, M. F. R. 1978: The midcareer conundrum; *Organizational Dynamics*, Autumn, 45–62.

Knorr-Cetina, K. and Cicourel, A. V. (eds) 1981: *Advances in Social Theory and Methodology: Towards an Integration of Micro- and Macro-Sociologies*; London: Routledge and Kegan Paul.

Koestler, A. 1967: *The Ghost in the Machine*; London: Hutchinson.

Kohn, M. L. and Schooler, C. 1982: Job conditions and personality: a longitudinal assessment of their reciprocal effects; *American Journal of Sociology*, 87 (6), 1257–86.

Kolb, D. A. and Plovnick, M. S. 1977: The experiential learning theory of career development; in J. Van Maanen (ed.), *Organizational Careers: Some New Perspectives*; New York: Wiley.

Kotter, J. P. 1982: *The General Managers*; New York: The Free Press.

Kram, K. E. 1983: Phases of the Mentor Relationship; *Academy of Management Journal*, 26 (4), 608–25.

Kram, K. E. and Isabella, L. A. 1985: Mentoring alternatives: the role of peer relationships in career development; *Academy of Management Journal*, 28 (1), 110–32.

Latack, J. C. 1984: Career transitions within organizations: an exploratory study of work, nonwork, and coping strategies; *Organizational Behaviour and Human Performance*, 34, 296–322.

Latack, J. C. and Dozier, J. B. 1986: After the ax falls: job loss as a career transition; *Academy of Management Review*, 11 (2), 375–92.

Laurent, A. 1986: The cross-cultural puzzle of international human resource management; *Human Resource Management*, 25 (1), 91–102.

Lawrence, B. S. 1984: Age grading: the implicit organizational timetable; *Journal of Occupational Behaviour*, 5, 23–35.

Lawrence, P. R. 1981: Organization and environment perspective: the Harvard Organization and Environment Research Program; in A. H. Van de Ven and W. F. Joyce (eds), *Perspectives on Organizational Design, and Behaviour*, New York: Wiley.

Lawrence, P. R. and Lorsch, J. W. 1967: *Organization and Environment: Managing Differentiation and Integration*; Boston: Harvard University Press.

Lee, G. L. 1981: *Who Gets to the Top? A Sociological Study of Business Executives*; Aldershot: Gower.

Lee, R. 1985a: The theory and practice of promotion processes: Part One; *Leadership and Organization Development Journal*, 6 (2), 3–21.

Lee, R. 1985b: The theory and practice of promotion processes: Part Two; *Leadership and Organization Development Journal*, 6 (4), 17–21.

Leggatt, T. 1978: Managers in industry: their background and education; *Sociological Review*, 26, 807–25.

LEVINSON, D. J., DARROW, C., KLEIN, E., LEVINSON, M. and McKEE, B. 1978: *The Seasons of a Man's Life*; New York: Knopf.

LEVINSON, H. 1980: Criteria for choosing chief executives; *Harvard Business Review*, July–August, 113–20.

LEVINSON, H. 1983: A second career: the possible dream; *Harvard Business Review*, May–June, 122–7.

LIPSET, S. M. and MALM, F. T. 1955: First jobs and career patterns; *The American Journal of Economics and Sociology*, 14, 247–61.

LOASBY, B. J. 1976: *Choice, Complexity and Ignorance: An Enquiry Into Economic Theory and the Practice of Decision-Making*; Cambridge: Cambridge University Press.

LOCKYER, K. G. and JONES, S. 1980: The function factor; *Management Today*, September, 53–64.

LONDON, M. 1983: Towards a theory of career motivation; *Academy of Management Review*, 8 (4), 620–30.

LONDON, M. and STUMPF, S. A. 1984: How managers make promotion decisions; *Journal of Management Development*, 3 (1), 56–65.

LORD, R. G. and KERNAN, M. C. 1987: Scripts as determinants of purposeful behaviour in organizations; *Academy of Management Review*, 12 (2), 265–77.

LOUIS, M. R. 1980a: Career transitions: varieties and commonalities; *Academy of Management Review*, 5 (3), 329–40.

LOUIS, M. R. 1980b: Surprise and sense making: what newcomers experience in entering unfamiliar organizational settings; *Administrative Science Quarterly*, 25, June, 226–51.

LUBATKIN, M. 1983: Mergers and the performance of the acquiring firm; *Academy of Management Review*, 8 (2), 218–25.

LUTHANS, F., ROSENKRANTZ, S. A. and HENNESSEY, H. W. 1985: What do successful managers really do? An observation study of managerial activities; *The Journal of Applied Behavioural Science*, 21 (3), 255–70.

MAHONEY, T. 1967: Managerial Perceptions of organisational effectiveness; *Management Science*, 14 (2), October, B76–91.

MAHONEY, T. A. and MILKOVICH, G. T. 1973: An investigation of the internal labour market concept; *Proceedings, Academy of Management*, Minneapolis, Minn., 33–9.

MAINIERO, L. A. 1986: Early career factors that differentiate technical management careers from technical professional careers; *Journal of Management*, 12 (4), 561–75.

MANT, A. 1983: *Leaders We Deserve*; Oxford: Martin Robertson.

MARCH, J. G. and SIMON, H. A. 1958: *Organizations*; New York: Wiley.

MARTIN, N. and STRAUSS, A. 1956: Patterns of mobility within industrial organisations; *Journal of Business*, 29 (2), 101–10.

MATURANA, H. R. and VARELA, F. J. 1980: *Autopoiesis and Cognition*; Dordrecht: D. Reidel.

McCAIN, B. E., O'REILLY, C. and PFEFFER, J. 1983: The effects of departmental demography on turnover: the case of a university; *Academy of Management Journal*, 26 (4), 626–41.

McENRUE, M. P. 1988: Length of experience and the performance of managers in the establishment phase of their careers; *Academy of Management Journal*,

31 (1), 175–85.

MEDCOF, J. W. 1985: Training technologists to become managers; *Research Management*, January–February, 18–21.

MELROSE-WOODMAN, J. 1978: *Profile of the British Manager*; British Institute of Management Foundation, Management Survey Report 38.

MERTON, R. K. 1968: *Social Theory and Social Structure*; New York: The Free Press.

MIHAL, W. L., SORCE, P. A. and COMTE, T. E. 1984: A process model of individual career decision making; *Academy of Management Review*, 9 (1), 95–103.

MILES, R. E. and SNOW, C. C. 1978: *Organization Strategy, Structure and Process*; New York: McGraw-Hill.

MILKOVICH, G. T., ANDERSON, J. C. and GREENHALGH, F. L. 1976: Organisational careers – environment, organizational and individual determinants; in L. Dyer (ed.), *Careers in Organizations*, Ithaca, N.Y.: NY State School of Industrial Relations, Cornell University.

MILLER, D. and FRIESEN, P. H. 1984: *Organizations: a Quantum View*; Englewood Cliffs, N.J.: Prentice-Hall.

MILLS, C. W. 1959: *The Sociological Imagination*; London: Oxford University Press.

MINTZBERG, H. 1973: *The Nature of Managerial Work*; New York: Harper and Row.

MORGAN, G. 1986: *Images of Organization*; Beverly Hills, Calif.: Sage.

MULLER, H. 1970: *The Search for the Qualities Essential to Advancement in a Large Industrial Group*; The Hague.

NEAR, J. P. 1984: Reactions to the career plateau; *Business Horizons*, July–August, 75–9.

NICHOLSON, N. 1984: A theory of work role transitions; *Administrative Science Quarterly*, 29 (2), 172–91.

NISBETT, R. E. and WILSON, T. De C. 1977: Telling more than we can know: verbal reports on mental processes; *Psychological Review*, 84 (3), May, 231–59.

NORBURN, D. 1987: Corporate leaders in Britain and America: a cross-national analysis; *Journal of International Business Studies*, Fall, 15–32.

OFFE, C. 1976: *Industry and Inequality*; London: Edward Arnold.

ONDRACK, D. 1985: International transfers of managers in North American and European MNEs; *Journal of International Business Studies*, Fall, 1–19.

OSBORN, R. N., JAUCH, L. R., MARTIN, T. N. and GLUECK, W. F. 1981: The event of CEO succession, performance and environmental conditions; *Academy of Management Review*, 24 (1), 183–91.

PAHL, J. M. and PAHL, R. E. 1971: *Managers and their Wives: A Study of Career and Family Relationships in the Middle Class*; Harmondsworth: Penguin.

PALMER, D. 1983: Broken ties: interlocking directorates and intercorporate coordination; *Administrative Science Quarterly*, 28, 40–55.

PENNINGS, J. M. 1980: *Interlocking Directorates*; San Francisco, Calif.: Jossey-Bass.

PENROSE, E. T. 1980: *The Theory of the Growth of the Firm*; Oxford: Basil Blackwell, 2nd edn.

PERHAM, J. 1985: How executives get on boards; *Dun's Business Month*, April, 52–4.

PERROW, C. 1963: Goals and power structure: a historical case study; in E. Friedson (ed.), *The Hospital in Modern Society*, Chicago: Free Press, 112–46.

PETRAS, R. and PETRAS, K. 1986: *Inside Track: How to Get Into and Succeed in America's Prestige Companies*; New York: Vintage.

PFEFFER, J. 1985: Organizational demography: implications for management; *California Management Review*, 28 (1), Fall, 67–81.

PFEFFER, J. and LEBLEBICI, H. 1973: Executive recruitment and the development of interfirm organizations; *Administrative Science Quarterly*, 18, 449–61.

PFEFFER, J. and SALANCIK, G. R. 1978: *The External Control of Organizations: A Resource Dependence Perspective*; New York: Harper and Row.

PINDER, C. C. and SCHROEDER, K. G. 1987: Time to proficiency following job transfers; *Academy of Management Journal*, 30 (2), 336–53.

PITTS, R. A. 1977: Strategies and structures for diversification; *Academy of Management Journal*, 20, 197–208.

POLANYI, M. 1958: *Personal Knowledge*; London: Routledge and Kegan Paul.

POLLARD, S. 1965: *The Genesis of Modern Management: A Study of the Industrial Revolution in Great Britain*; London: Edward Arnold.

POOLE, M., MANSFIELD, R., BLYTON, P. and FROST, P. 1981: *Managers in Focus: The British Manager in the Early 1980s*; Aldershot: Gower.

PORTER, M.E. 1980: *Competitive Strategy: Techniques for Analyzing Industries and Competitors*; New York: The Free Press.

POSTON, T. and STEWART, I. 1978: *Catastrophe Theory and its Applications*; London: Pitman.

QUINN, J. B. 1980: *Strategies for Change and Logical Incrementalism*; Hemel Hempstead: Irwin.

RAPOPORT, R. N. 1970: *Mid-Career Development – Perspectives on a Developmental Community for Senior Administrators*; London: Tavistock.

REINGANUM, M. R. 1985a: The effect of executive succession on stockholder wealth; *Administrative Science Quarterly*, 30, March, 46–60.

REINGANUM, M. R. 1985b: The effect of executive succession on stockholder wealth: a reply; *Administrative Science Quarterly*, 30, September, 375–6.

RHODES, S. R. and DOERING, M. 1983: An integrated model of career change; *Academy of Management Review*, 8 (4), 631–9.

RIDLEY, F. F. (ed.) 1968: *Specialists and Generalists*; London: George Allen & Unwin.

ROCHE, G. R. 1975: Compensation and the mobile executive; *Harvard Business Review*, 53 (6), November, 53–62.

ROSENBAUM, J. E. 1979: Tournament mobility: career patterns in a corporation; *Administrative Science Quarterly*, 24, 220–41.

ROSENBAUM, J. E. 1984: *Career Mobility in a Corporate Hierarchy*; London: Academic Press.

ROSENFELD, R. A. 1980: Race and sex differences in career dynamics; *American Sociological Review*, 45, August, 583–609.

ROTH, J. A. 1963: *Timetables: Structuring the Passage of Time in Hospital Treatment and Other Careers*; New York: Bobbs-Merrill.

ROY, W. G. 1983: The unfolding of the interlocking directorate structure of the United States; *American Sociological Review*, 48, April, 248–57.

SAKS, M. 1983: Removing the blinkers? A critique of recent contributions to the sociology of the professions; *Sociological Review*, 31 (1), February, 1–21.

SAYLES, L. R. 1964: *Managerial Behaviour: Administration in Complex Organizations*; New York: McGraw-Hill.

SAYLES, L. R. 1976: Matrix management: the structure with a future; *Organizational Dynamics*, Autumn, 2–17.

SCHEIN, E. H. 1971: The individual, the organization and the career: a conceptual scheme; *Journal of Applied Behavioural Science*, 7, 401–26.

SCHEIN, E. H. 1977: Career anchors and career paths: a panel study of management school graduates; in J. Van Maanen (ed.), *Organizational Careers: Some New Perspectives*; New York: Wiley.

SCHEIN, E. H. 1978: *Career Dynamics: Matching Individual and Organizational Needs*; Reading, Pa.: Addison-Wesley.

SCHEIN, E. H. 1985: *Organizational Culture and Leadership*; San Francisco, Calif.: Jossey-Bass.

SCHEIN, E. H. 1986: Culture as an environmental context for careers; *Journal of Occupational Behaviour*, 5, 71–81.

SCHOLL, R. W. 1983: Career lines and employment stability; *Academy of Management Journal*, 26 (1), 86–103.

SCHUMPETER, J. A. 1947: The creative response in economic history; *Journal of Economic History*, 7, November, 149–59.

SCHWARTZ, K. B. and MENON, K. 1985: Executive succession in failing firms; *Academy of Management Journal*, September, 680–6.

SCHWENK, C.R. 1988: The cognitive perspective on strategic decision making; *Journal of Management Studies*, 25 (1), January, 41–55.

SCOTT, J. and GRIFF, C. 1984: *Directors of Industry: The British Corporate Network 1904–76*; Cambridge: Polity Press.

SHAPIRO, E., HASELTINE, F. and ROWE, M. 1978: Moving up: role models, mentors and the 'patron system'; *Sloan Management Review*, 19, 51–8.

SHETTY, Y. K. and PEERY, N. S. Jr. 1976: Are top executives transferable across companies?; *Business Horizons*, 19 (3), 23–8.

SLOCUM, J. W., CRON, W. L., HANSEN, R. W. and RAWLINGS, S. 1985: Business strategy and the management of plateaued employees; *Academy of Management Journal*, 28 (1), 133–54.

SMITH, D. R. 1983: Mobility in professional occupational-internal labor markets: stratification, segmentation and vacancy chains; *American Sociological Review*, 48, June, 289–305.

SMITH, M. and WHITE, M. C. 1987: Strategy, CEO specialization, and succession; *Administrative Science Quarterly*, 32, 263–80.

SOFER, C. 1970: *Men in Mid-Career*; Cambridge: Cambridge University Press.

STARBUCK, W. H. 1983: Organizations as action generators; *American Sociological Review*, 48, February, 91–102.

STEINER, G. A. and MINER, J. B. 1977: *Management Policy and Strategy*; New York: Macmillan.

STEWART, A., PRANDY, K. and BLACKBURN, R. M. 1980: *Social Stratification and Occupations*; London: Macmillan.

STEWART, A. and STEWART, V. 1976: *Tomorrow's Men Today: the Identification and Development of Managerial Potential*; London: IPM; and Falmer: Institute of Manpower Studies, University of Sussex.

STEWART, R. 1976: *Contrasts in Management: A Study of Different Types of Managers' Jobs: Their Demands and Choices*; London: McGraw-Hill.

STEWART, R. 1982: *Choices for the Manager: a Guide to Managerial Work and Behaviour*; London: McGraw-Hill.

STEWMAN, S. and KONDA, S. 1983: Careers and organizational labor markets: demographic models of organizational behaviour; *American Journal of Sociology*, 88 (4), 637–85.

STINCHCOMBE, A. L. 1965: Social structure and organizations; in J. G. March (ed.): *Handbook of Organizations*; Skokie, Ill.: Rand McNally, 142–93.

STINCHCOMBE, A. L. 1983: *Economic Sociology*; London: Academic Press.

STOKMAN, F. N., ZIEGLER, R. and SCOTT, J. (eds) 1985: *Networks of Corporate Power: A Comparative Analysis of Ten Countries*; Cambridge: Polity Press.

STUMPF, S. A. and LONDON, M. 1981: Management promotions: individual and organizational factors influencing the decision process; *Academy of Management Review*, 6 (4), 539–49.

SUPER, D. E. 1984: Career and life development; in D. Brown et al. (eds), *Career Choice and Development*; San Francisco, Calif.: Jossey-Bass, 192–234.

SWINYARD, A. W. and BOND, F. A. 1980: Who gets promoted?; *Harvard Business Review*, September–October, 6–18.

SZILAGYI, A. D. Jr and SCHWEIGER, D. M. 1984: Matching managers to strategies: a review and suggested framework; *Academy of Management Review*, 9 (4), 626–37.

THOMAS, A. B. 1981: The career graph: a tool for mid-career development; *Personnel Review*, 10 (3), 18–22.

THOMAS, L. E. and ROBBINS, P. I. 1979: Personality and work environment congruence of mid-life career changes; *Journal of Occupational Psychology*, 52, 177–83.

THOMPSON, J. D. 1967: *Organizations in Action*; New York: McGraw-Hill.

THOMPSON, P. H., KIRKHAM, K. and DIXON, J. 1985: Warning: the fast track may be hazardous to organizational health; *Organizational Dynamics*, Spring, 21–33.

TOLBERT, C. M. II 1982: Industrial segmentation and men's career mobility; *American Sociological Review*, 47, August, 457–77.

TORRINGTON, D. and WEIGHTMAN, J. 1982: Technical atrophy in middle management; *Journal of General Management*, 7 (4), Summer, 5–17.

TOWNSEND, R. 1978: *Up the Organization*; New York: Fawcett.

TREVOR, M., SCHENDEL, J. and WILPERT, B. 1986: *The Japanese Management Development System: Generalists and Specialists in Japanese Companies Abroad*; London: Frances Pinter.

TRIFTS, J. W. and WINKLER, D. T. 1987: The value of corporate leadership: the case of CEO successions; *University of South Carolina: Working Papers in Banking, Finance, Insurance, and Real Estate*, DOR C–87–06.

TSUI, A. S. 1984: A role set analysis of managerial reputation; *Organizational Behavior and Human Performance*, 34, 64–96.

TUCKEL, P. and SIEGEL, K. 1983: The myth of the migrant manager; *Business Horizons*, January–February, 64–70.

USEEM, M. 1984: *The Inner Circle*; New York: Oxford University Press.

USEEM, M. and McCORMACK, A. 1981: The dominant segment of the British business elite; *Sociology*, 15 (3), 381–406.

USEEM, M. and KARABEL, J. 1986: Pathways to top corporate management; *American Sociological Review*, 51, April, 184–200.

VAN MAANEN, J. (ed.) 1977: *Organizational Careers: Some New Perspectives*; New York: Wiley.

VARDI, Y. 1980: Organizational career mobility: an integrative model; *Academy of Management Review*, 5 (3), 341–55.

VARDI, I. S. and HAMMER, T. H. 1977: Intra-organisational mobility and career perception among rank and file employees; *Academy of Management Journal*, 20, December, 622–34.

VEIGA, J. F. 1981: Do managers on the move get anywhere?; *Harvard Business Review*, 59 (2), 20–42.

VEIGA, J. F. 1983: Mobility influences during managerial career stages; *Academy of Management Journal*, 26 (1), 64–85.

VIRANY, B. and TUSHMAN, M. L. 1986: Top management teams and corporate success in an emerging industry; *Journal of Business Venturing*, 1, 261–74.

VON BERTALANFFY, L. 1968: *General System Theory*; New York: George Braziller.

WAGNER, W. G., PFEFFER, J. and O'REILLY, C. A. 1984: Organizational demography and turnover in top-management groups; *Administrative Science Quarterly*, 29, 74–92.

WAKABAYASHI, M. and GRAEN, G. B. 1984: The Japanese career progress study: a 7–year follow-up; *Journal of Applied Psychology*, 69 (4), 603–14.

WALKER, J. W. 1976: Let's get realistic about career paths; *Human Resource Management*, Autumn, 2–7.

WALSH, J. P. 1988: Top management turnover following mergers and acquisitions; *Strategic Management Journal*, 9, 173–83.

WATERS, J. A. 1980: Managerial skill development; *Academy of Management Review*, 5 (3), 449–53.

WATSON, W. 1964: Social mobility and social class in industrial communities; in M. Gluckman (ed.), *Closed Systems and Open Minds*, Edinburgh: Oliver and Boyd.

WATTS, A. G. 1981: Career patterns; in A. G. Watts, D. E. Super and J. M. Kidol (eds), *Career Development in Britain*; CRAC/Cambridge, Hobsons Press, 213–45.

WEICK, K. E. 1979: *The Social Psychology of Organizing*; Reading, Pa.: Addison-Wesley.

WEISS, J. W. 1981: The historical and political perspective on organizations of Lucien Karpik; in M. Zey-Ferrell and M. Aiken (eds), *Complex Organizations: Critical Perspectives*, Glenview, Ill: Scott, Foresman.

WELFORD, A. T. 1980: On the nature of higher-order skills; *Journal of Occupational Psychology*, 53, 107–10.

WHITE, H. C. 1970: *Chains of Opportunity*; Cambridge, Mass.: Harvard University Press.

WHITLEY, R. D. 1980: The impact of changing industrial structure on business elites, managerial careers and the roles of business schools; *International Studies of Management and Organization*, 10 (1–2), Spring–Summer,

110–36.

WHITLEY, R. D. 1987a: Taking firms seriously as economic actors: towards a sociology of firm behaviour; *Organization Studies*, 8 (2), 125–47.

WHITLEY, R. D. 1987b: On the nature of managerial task and skills: their distinguishing characteristics and organisation; *Manchester Business School Working Paper Series, No. 153*.

WHITLEY, R. D., THOMAS, A. B. and MARCEAU, J. 1981: *Masters of Business?*; London: Tavistock.

WILENSKY, H. L. 1960: Work, careers, and social integration; *International Social Science Journal*, 12 (4), 543–60.

WILLIAMS, K., WILLIAMS, J. and THOMAS, D. 1983: *Why Are the British Bad At Manufacturing?*; London: Routledge and Kegan Paul.

WILLMOTT, H. 1987: Studying managerial work: a critique and a proposal; *Journal of Management Studies*, 24 (3), May, 250–70.

WITKIN, H. A., DYK, R., PATTERSON, J., GOODENOUGH, D. and KARP, S. 1962: *Psychological Differentiation*; New York: Wiley.

WOODWARD, J. 1965: *Industrial Organization: Theory and Practice*; London: Oxford University Press.

ZEY, M. G. 1984: *The Mentor Connection*; Homewood, Ill.: Dow-Jones-Irwin.

ZIMAN, J. 1987: *Knowing Everything About Nothing: Specialization and Change in Research Careers*; Cambridge: Cambridge University Press.

Index